SYDNEY LOCAL NATIVE
150 in-depth native plant profiles for gardeners
Pittwater edition

Hazel Malloy

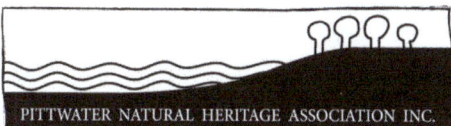

PITTWATER NATURAL HERITAGE ASSOCIATION INC.
Protecting Pittwater's Environment

Published in Australia in 2023 by
Hazel Malloy
Scotland Island, New South Wales

sydneylocalnative@gmail.com
PO Box 361, Church Point NSW 2105 Australia

A catalogue record for this book is available from the National Library of Australia

Catalogued in the National Library of Australia as
SYDNEY LOCAL NATIVE: 150 in-depth native plant profiles for gardeners.

ISBN 978-0-646-88109-6

This book was created using free open-sourced software in Linux Ubuntu (Focal Fossa), a free open-sourced operating system. Text written in LibreOffice Writer. Cover designed in Scribus. Photos edited in The Gimp.

Printed in Melbourne, Australia by Ingram Content Group

Cover photos are by Susan Hazel Malloy except as noted below.

The plants on the cover and title page include:
Acacia decurrens (Black Wattle)
Brachyscome graminea (Grass Daisy)
Elaeocarpus reticulatus (Blueberry Ash). Photo by Lew Walker.
Ozothamnus diosmifolius (Rice Flower)
Commelina cyanea (Scurvy Weed)
Xanthorrhoea arborea (Broad-leaf Grass Tree)

Contents

Geological map of the Northern Beaches

Sydney's Northern Beaches clay-based soils are generally derived from the Narrabeen Group of Triassic-age sedimentary rock, shown in **teal** on the map. A large part of the Barrenjoey peninsula falls into this category. These soils are often referred to by gardeners as shales.

On top of the Narrabeen strata lies a capping of Hawkesbury Sandstone, a later Triassic layer, shown in **pale green** on the map.

Before the area was cleared for residences, sites with both the shale and the sandstone type of soils around Pittwater supported **Pittwater Spotted Gum Forest** – an endangered ecological community. Together with a similar ecological community in Gosford on the north side of the Hawkesbury River, this ecological community has been given the official name of Pittwater-Wagstaffe Spotted Gum Forest (PWSGF). For more details, see the sections in the back of the book relating to PWSGF.

Many of these PSGF or PWSGF species are excellent garden subjects, and they make up more than a third of the species featured in this book. They tend to be very hardy and are sure to thrive on Pittwater sandstone or shale-based soils. They would also thrive on clay soil in Sydney's Inner West and Cumberland Plain, and most of them are native there too, as well as farther north up the coast in NSW and Queensland where there are similar Spotted Gum Forest ecological communities.

Also see the detailed maps and species lists in the free online booklet *Pittwater Gardening Guide*. The url is in the section titled "Useful free online resources". It is now somewhat out of date but still very useful.

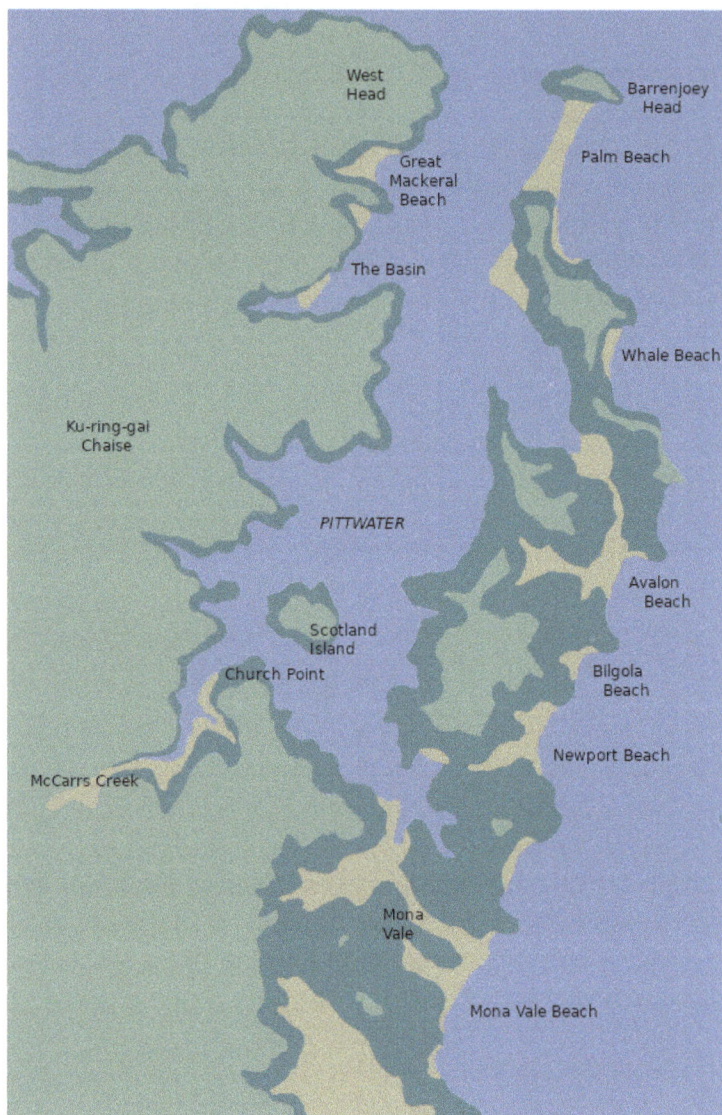

Acknowledgments

Thank you to my dear husband Kevin for putting up with my sometimes distracted obsession with writing this book, once the idea had taken hold of me. I also thank him for encouraging me in my efforts to plant local Sydney natives on our block.

Thank you to the many photographers who have kindly allowed me to use their photographs of the plants, birds and butterflies featured in this book. A book like this would be a much more costly endeavour without such collaberation.

A special thanks goes to Gillian Gutridge, whose blog not only provides a photographic record of plants she has seen on local Northern Beaches bushwalks, but also lists which plants can be seen on which trails. See her blog *Native Plants of the Northern Beaches, Sydney,* at https://nbplantareas.com/.

Thank you to my dear friend CB Floyd, who tirelessly proofread several different versions, and went beyond that to fulfill the role of editor impressively. She many times saved me from making terrible gaffes.

Thank you to my new friend Marita Macrae, who wrote a section on how to plant and provided much helpful advice. Thank you to Pittwater Natural History Association, the organisation Marita runs. The members kindly reviewed and commented on the text, and agreed to allow me to attach their logo to the book.

Any mistakes are my own.

Introduction

This book profiles 150 of the many plants native to the Sydney region that are superb additions to gardens anywhere in Sydney. In addition to the 150, there are another five profiles of non-locally native species. The non-local species are exceptions to the rule which I explain in the section "Why plant locally native?". Purists will want to avoid these when planning their "Sydney native" gardens.

I have written the book from the perspective of the beautiful Pittwater area in Sydney's Northern Beaches, with a little local geology and tips on where to buy the plants locally, and where they can be seen on local bushwalks. I haven't included much such information for other areas of Sydney, mostly for lack of time. Perhaps I will add it in a later edition, or perhaps someone from those regions will offer to collaberate with me. But even as it is, the book would be useful for gardeners across Sydney and in many other areas along the east coast with similar climate.

Many of the plants profiled are natives of Scotland Island, where I live, or failing that, components of **Pittwater-Wagstaffe Spotted Gum Forest (PWSGF)**[†]. PWSGF is the type of ecological community that naturally grows on Scotland Island and other areas around Pittwater where the soil (or subsoil) is derived from the Narrabeen Group of sedimentary rocks, and there is protection from direct ocean winds[*].

[†]   See "History of surveys" section for more information on PWSGF.

[*]   See geological map in front showing the extent of Narrabeen Group bedrock. Map source: redrawn based on the Sydney 1 to 100,000 Geological Map, New South Wales Government, 2017. https://gmaps.geoscience.nsw.gov.au/100K/Sydney/

A little more than a third of the plants profiled in this book are components of PWSGF, although studies have disagreed in some cases. A list of these species can be found in the Index section, along with several other useful lists. A partial list from the study on which the PWSGF official description was based can be found after the Index under "Dry PWSGF and Moist PWSGF". Also see the species lists in the free online booklet *Pittwater Gardening Guide*. The url is in the section titled "Useful free online resources". It is now somewhat out of date but still useful.

More than eighty percent of the species profiled in this book prefer clay-based soil or at least tolerate it. A list of these "clay lovers" can be found in the "Index by growth type and other categories" section. Many of the sandstone-loving species are also worth trying on clay soils if you can site them on a slope, or build up a mound to give them better drainage.

With a few exceptions as noted, the species can all thrive and even flower in Pittwater gardens without supplemental water – at least in La Niña years – but many will look better if watered during dry periods. If your garden is outside the Pittwater area, you may need to provide supplemental water if your rainfall is less than what Pittwater receives[Ψ].

I have noted some species that are especially attractive to birds and butterflies. But probably the easiest way to create a haven for wildlife is to include a wide variety of local native plant species, and a variety of forms, such as shrubs, vines, groundcovers, grasses, and trees.

This is the book I wished I'd had when I moved to Scotland Island six years ago.

Why plant "locally native" and what does it mean?

There are two location-related terms that gardeners frequently confuse: "native" and "endemic". *Native* means the plant species is naturally found occuring in the area; "indigenous" means basically the same as native. The species may have dispersed there from somewhere else at some time in the past, but if so, human activity was not involved. *Endemic* means that the plant is native and also not found anywhere else outside of the area. A species that is native to an area is not necessarily endemic to that location. The word "local" by itself doesn't specify whether the plant is native or endemic, but simply helps to get across what area is being discussed.

If a plant has spread outside the area where it is native by means of human activity, and has become self-perpetuating there, it is said to be "naturalised" in the new area. Many weeds fall into this category.

There are no plants profiled in this book that are endemic to Scotland Island or any other location in the Pittwater area. All of these plants are also found in numerous locations throughout the Sydney basin. What is unique to Pittwater, or to any other location, is the assemblage of those species. By assemblage, I mean the way the species occur in combinations, such as the Pittwater Spotted Gum Forest (PWSGF) plant community mentioned in the Introduction. Though Spotted Gum occurs elsewhere in Sydney and also in forest in Victoria and Queensland, PWSGF only occurs in the Pittwater area. For more information on PWSGF, see the sections towards the end of the book with "PWSGF" in their names.

With five exceptions, the 156 species profiled in this book are all natives of the Sydney region.

Ψ   Average annual rainfall in Newport is 1425 mm since 2010, according to the Willy Weather website, as accessed 16/7/2023. https://rainfall.willyweather.com.au/nsw/sydney/pittwater--newport-wharf.html

I have included the five exceptions in order to provide an opportunity to present a simple rule, which is: ***plant locally native species***. From the gardener's point of view, this makes obvious sense because local native species are known to thrive in that particular area.

From an ecological point of view, this is also obviously a good idea since the local wildlife are adapted to utilise the local native species.

But there is another reason, which is that when planted outside of their place of origin, sometimes plant species become invasive and escape into surrounding bushland (i.e. they become naturalised). Even worse, they can then hybridise with locally native species, which dilutes their gene pool or even drives them to extinction if the locally native species is already endangered.

Such is the case with the very fast-growing Cootamundra Wattle (*Acacia baileyana)*, which is native and endemic in a small area of southern inland NSW but widely planted and naturalised in other Australian states. In Sydney it hybridises with other wattles, including the endangered Sydney native Downy Wattle (*Acacia pubescens)*.

Another example of an Australian native that has spread elsewhere is Fishbone Fern (*Nephrolepis cordifolia)*. It is native to northeastern Australia and the foothills of the Himalayas, but very well known as an unwelcome naturalised weed in tropical and warm temperate areas around the world, including the Sydney area and Pittwater. It is tenacious due to its underground bulbs, which store water and can resprout. It took me many months to eradicate it from my garden on Scotland Island.

The non-local natives that I have chosen to profile in this book as exceptions to the "plant local" rule are the following:

- the spectacular native *Rhododendron viriosum*, which is endemic to a few mountaintops in Queensland

- the very useful Midgim Berry (*Austromyrtus dulcis)*, native to NSW and Queensland some 600 km north of Sydney, which is nearly perfect for for a low-maintenance path edging plus a delicious and refreshing snack

- the beautiful endangered species *Zieria prostrata*, which is restricted (i.e. endemic) to four NSW headlands

- the charming and well-behaved groundcover *Hibbertia procumbens*, which is endangered and endemic to a small area of the Central Coast

- the astonishing *Leptospermum macrocarpum*, which is native to Sydney only if you consider the Blue Mountains to be part of it. Ecologically speaking it does make sense to speak of the "Sydney Basin", which includes the eastern side of the Blue Mountains.

These five species are unlikely to escape from Sydney gardens into surrounding Sydney bushland, and have all been in cultivation for a long time, so that their characteristics are well known. But there is a risk, and so purists may choose not to plant them. If you choose to plant them, be conscious of your garden's conditions and if they seem to be doing a little too well so that they might become self-perpetuating (naturalised), maybe stick to the true locals.

How to use this book

It is important when you are plant shopping to stay focused and not let the sales staff at the nursery sell you plants that are wrong for your conditions; such plants will rarely survive or prosper. No nursery will have all the plants in this book all of the time, but unfortunately they will always have plenty of completely inappropriate species all of the time, and many of those are very lovely indeed. You need to be prepared when you shop, so that you don't give in to such temptation.

If you have the time, read each **profile** and jot down which species appeal to you that match your garden's conditions. Take the list when you go plant shopping at your local native plant nursery (see section titled "Local native plant nurseries" for a list of recommended nurseries). Include your second and third choices in addition to your first choices as no nursery will have them all.

If you are in a hurry, flip to the back where there are **indexes by plant growth form** (shrubs, trees, etc.), and make your plant shopping list by checking the individual profiles to find plants that match your garden's conditions.

If you are in even more of a hurry, flip to the section of **comparison tables** which show the most important features of the species for each plant growh form (tolerance for sun, drought, shade, soil etc.) Photocopy the table(s) and mark the plants that could possibly work for your site, and take that with you to your local native plant nursery (see list in the back of nurseries in the Northern Beaches area).

When you get to the nursery, if a plant you see is not on your list, don't buy it.

How to plant

It is generally best to buy plants in what is known as forestry tubestock pots, or just plain tubestock, as they settle in faster than larger plants. Generally these pots are 50 x 50 x 120 mm. Some online nurseries sell plants in smaller pot sizes because they are cheaper to ship and faster to grow, but the plants in those don't survive as well.

Most native nurseries are happy to provide detailed instructions for planting native plants from tubestock pots. Another way to learn good planting technique (and much more besides) is attending a session or two with your local bush regeneration group.

Below are some basic instructions, kindly provided by Marita Macrae, President of Pittwater Natural Heritage Association.

1. Water the plants the day before. It can be hard to get plants out of containers when they have just been watered, and the weight of the excess water can break fragile roots.

2. Scrape aside leaf litter or mulch and save for reapplying afterwards.

3. Dig hole in mineral soil (i.e. the soil under the leaf litter) 2 or 3 times wider and about 10 cm deeper than the container the plant is in. Keep grass and leaves out of hole, and pile finer soil for back-filling.

4. Check depth. Will the plant be in the centre of a depression or basin when planted? The basin is necessary in order to hold

water long enough for it to soak in. Make sure the plant's rootball will not stick up out of the basin, or else it will dry out too fast.

5. Remove plant from container. Keep it upright while squeezing the sides. A sharp tap with a trowel or small rock on the rim of the pot will loosen the roots from the sides, keeping the root ball intact.

6. Tip the pot upside down, holding the soil and plant between your fingers so it can't fall out. Tap again if the roots haven't let go of the pot yet.

7. Keep root ball intact as you place plant in the hole.

8. Backfill with finer soil, NOT grass or large lumps of soil. Is the plant in the centre of a depression?

9. Firm down soil around roots, gently (do not step on it). Is it still in a depression?

10. If using a tree guard, insert stakes through slots of cardboard tree guard. Position guard over tree, ensure all the foliage is inside the guard. Hammer down stakes so guard is touching the ground around the tree. For plastic tree guard, use 3 stakes. Aim to have plant in centre of a triangle. Place one stake about 15 cm from the plant and another 15 cm away from plant, slip guard over plant and both stakes, then use third stake to complete the triangle, adjusting position so that guard is tight between the stakes.

11. Water slowly to fill the depression and let it soak in, then water again – about ¼ bucket of water.

12. Reapply the leaf litter you saved, or mulch. Keep mulch or leaf litter away from the stem of the plant, as it can cause rot.

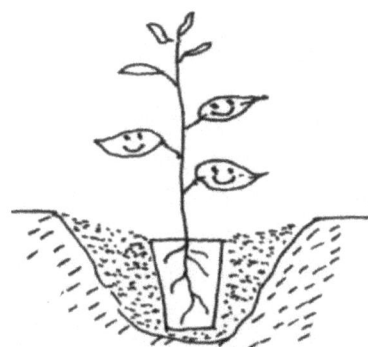

After planting, you will need to continue watering for the first couple of years or while the plant is small, whenever the weather doesn't provide good rains. For the first few weeks, water every third day, then after that you may be able to switch to weekly. When in doubt, feel the soil down a finger joint's depth under the surface. If the soil is very dry (e.g., during a severe drought), you may need to water every day; otherwise other, better-established plants may steal the water away.

Don't make the basin too big if rain is likely, or the plant may get drowned (water-logged). You may need to go out and check after the first few rains to make sure that water is not sitting in the basins for more than an hour after the rain ends.

Most of the plants profiled in this book do not tolerate water-logging. If water does not drain quickly from your garden, see the Index for a list of plants that tolerate water-logging.

About weeds

It is generally best to eliminate weeds before attempting to plant a native garden. If you have a lot of weed seeds in the soil, you may have a biggish job ahead of you. Unfortunately, that is outside the scope of this book. A good source of advice would be your local bush regeneration group.

Tips for choosing plants

Sun or shade

Where your block is will play a big part in whether or not you can grow a particular species. For example, if your block is on a south-facing slope, it may be shaded during winter, but get plenty of sun in spring and summer, so you can grow summer-flowering species. Spring and winter-flowering species may not be able to get enough light on south-facing blocks in order to flower well. Conversely, if your garden faces north, you may not have enough shade to grow most ferns.

Note that "full sun" generally means more than four hours of direct sun per day, all year. A few minutes of passing sun at high noon is not going to be enough for plants requiring full sun. "Light shade" generally means that the sun is lightly filtered by the branches of tall trees but not otherwise blocked. "Part shade" means that the sun is blocked by buildings or heavy vegetation for part of the day, but there are a few hours of direct sun. "Dappled" means that the sun is heavily filtered by tree branches but not otherwise blocked. "Heavy shade" means that the site receives no direct sun, or hardly any.

Soil – clay or sand

Sandy soil is defined as soil containing 80 to 100% sand. Clay soil is defined as soil containing 50 to 100% clay. Loam soal is defined as containing approximately equal quantities of sand, clay and silt. If you don't know whether your soil is clay, sandy, or loamy, there is an easy, simple, and fun test you can do at home with a glass jar, a marker and some water[Σ]. You can repeat this test with soil taken from different depths and from different areas of your garden. Experienced gardeners can also use the squeeze test: you take a damp handful and squeeze it in your hand. If it retains the shape, it is clayey, and if the soil tends to fall through your fingers, it is sandy.

It can be difficult to determine what kind of soil you have if you are in a drought phase. Even very sandy soil with virtually no clay can transform from soft and pourable like beach sand into a very hard substance that gives a good imitation of sun-baked adobe (or concrete) after a few weeks of drought and heat. In order to be able to scoop or dig easily in such soil, you may need to moisten it first. If in doubt, do the glass jar test.

The soil of much of Scotland Island and many other areas of the Northern Beaches is clay-based, often with a thin sandy topsoil over the top of that. If your garden is in the Northern Beaches, understanding how that came to be may help you choose appropriate plants for your garden. Look at the geological map at the front of the book when reading this section.

Σ   See https://deepgreenpermaculture.com/2020/07/23/three-simple-soil-tests-to-determine-what-type-of-soil-you-have/

The most common soil[Ω] in the Pittwater and Northern Beaches area is derived from sedimentary rock of the extensive and immensely thick (800 m) sedimentary layer known collectively as the Narrabeen Group. The Narrabeen Group covers a swathe of the Central Coast, with different layers exposed in different locations.[Φ] The particular layer that is exposed at the surface in Pittwater Spotted Gum Forest areas, called the **Newport Formation**, is a 49 m layer among the youngest (top) layers of the Narrabeen Group, consisting of very finely layered sandstone interleaved with siltstone and shale (laminite); sandstone; and red claystone.[Ψ] Over time, exposed areas of the Newport Formation have weathered to a rusty, stony, clay-rich, sandy soil. Above the Newport Formation sits a thick capping of the geologically younger formation known as **Hawkesbury Sandstone**, which makes up roughly the top third of the rock profile you can see on the western side of Pittwater Bay. (There isn't an obvious boundary between the two, as both are largely sandstone.) Soils formed from weathering of the upper layers of Hawkesbury Sandstone are very porous, light-coloured and infertile, and often have outcroppings of sandstone rock at the surface of the soil.

If you look from Scotland Island to the plateau on the Ku-ring-gai side of Pittwater Bay – e.g., from the ferry – you see that the island is some 80 m shorter in profile than the plateau. The island and the western foreshores of Pittwater Bay, as well as large parts of the Northern Beaches peninsula, have lost most of the thick Hawkesbury cap they must have once had 18,000 years ago before the end of the ice ages, when what is now an island was then a hilltop in a valley. The island's soil today derives predominantly from the clay-rich Newport Formation, which underlies much of the island, mingling together with the sandy soils that have eroded downwards from the remains of the Hawkesbury cap. Consequently, some areas on the the island have topsoil that is predominantly clay-based, and some areas are more sandy.

The clay content can vary within the same block, depending on how much of the eroded sand from the top of the island has accumulated in a particular spot. And even within areas still well-covered by Hawkesbury Sandstone – where you might think that all the soil is sandy – there can be local patches or lenses of clay soil, as can be seen in many places along the dirt road at the top of Scotland Island.

Independently of the kind of topsoil you have, your subsoil may be clay or clay-based. You may need to dig down a shovel length or two to see the subsoil. All but the smallest groundcover plants will need to get their roots into the subsoil if they are to thrive. And if you are planting where there is little topsoil – perhaps due to erosion – you may be planting directly into the subsoil.

The difference from the plants' point of view is that clay is **richer in minerals**, and is better at **retaining moisture** compared to sandy soil. Many of the wildflowers found in Ku-ring-gai Chase National Park, such as the Waratah, have evolved on the infertile, fast-draining sandy soil derived from Hawkesbury Sandstone. They fail miserably on the island, because they are intolerant of clay soil. You can try to combat this by planting on a slope, or in raised beds, or adding various soil amendments.

Ω   For a gentle introduction to soil formation, see the relevant section of the Physical Geology book in the free LibreTexts project. https://geo.libretexts.org/Bookshelves/Geology/Book%3A_Physical_Geology_(Earle)/05%3A_Weathering_and_Soil/5.04%3A_Weathering_and_the_Formation_of_Soil

Φ   John Martyn, *Towards a Richer Understanding of Local Geology*, STEP INC, https://www.step.org.au/index.php/item/176-towards-a-richer-understanding-of-local-geology, downloaded 18 Dec., 2022

Ψ   Australian Stratigraphics Units Database https://asud.ga.gov.au/search-stratigraphic-units/results/13874

Or you can plant species that thrive in clay-based soil. More than 80% of the plants in this book either prefer clay or have no preference one way or the other, except as noted.

Water – too much, too little or just right

You also need to add water into your calculations. Many of the plants in this book prefer some degree of shade, and can also thrive in full sun (i.e. 4 hours or more of direct sun per day), **but only if they are given supplemental water.** So if supplemental watering is not an option for you, or you just want to stay on the safe side, you had better choose plants that prefer the light and water levels your garden has naturally.

What kind of soil you have (or have built up) can give you some wiggle room regarding water needs: gardens on soil that is clay-based and/or has aged compost added to it and also mulched can get by on less water than gardens on unamended, sandier soil. But if you choose plants that match your actual conditions, you needn't fuss with amendments. Mulch is usually a good idea, though, as long as you keep the mulch away from the plants' stems (to prevent rot).

On blocks that are sloping, water does not sit on plant roots for too long when there are major rain events. In contrast, flat sites with clay-based soils will quickly become waterlogged, and then the roots can't conduct gas exchange, one of their necessary functions.[†] Sloping gardens generally have well-drained soil even if the soil is clay-based.

Most of the plants in this book will not tolerate waterlogging, and should not be planted in areas that remain soggy for more than a day or so after a hard rain. The profiles note which species are particularly sensitive. A few species have no problem with waterlogging, such as *Acacia longissima,* and this is noted in the profiles. There is also a list of them in the Index section. You can plant these ones in sites that stay soggy for days, and they will thrive.

Gullies can carry torrents of runoff after hard rains, but the surrounding soil may or may not become waterlogged, depending on how quickly the water escapes. You probably know a lot about waterlogging if you are in one of the two big gullies on the south side of Scotland Island. There are also six other smaller gullies on the island, divided by a number of ridges.

Don't confuse gully torrents, which are natural, with road runoff, which is manmade. Road runoff in a big rain event can flow right down the center of a ridge due to the fact that people tend to place roads and trails along ridges – for example, Fitzpatrick Trail on Scotland Island. Yet the soil along the sides of Fitzpatrick Trail (where I live) tends to be very dry much of the time, as it is a ridge, not a gully.

Moisture will be retained in (true) gully areas far longer than the surrounding areas. Ridges will conversely be drier than the average (even if they have road runoff in big rain events).

Even on blocks with gully torrents, the top layers of soil may eventually dry out between rain events in the summer, but the dry periods will be shorter than for the dry ridges. Most of the plants profiled in this book as "gully plants", such as *Callicoma serratifolia,* will be fine with the moisture they get naturally from rain plus the extra moisture they absorb from alongside the gully channel, as long as you plant them near enough. Plants that dislike waterlogging, such as *Dodonaea triquetra,* should not be planted too near a gully channel, even if the ground is sloping.

---

†   https://www.soilquality.org.au/factsheets/waterlogging

The terrain of a gully, depending on its orientation to the sun, may additionally provide shading from the hot afternoon sun in the summer.

In order to have a garden that looks good all year round, you may need to restrict the growth of shade-loving plants such as ferns or violets that "volunteer" thanks to the extra moisture of spring or autumn. Otherwise, when summer comes round, you will be faced with the choice of seeing them shrivel to a crisp, or having to water them. This is especially important in positions where there is no overhead shade in summer, which is easily determined simply by looking up.

This book will help you select plants that will thrive with the soil, amount of water, and the light levels they will encounter naturally in your garden, making your job of caring for them much easier.

About where the plants are "native to"

This information can help you choose species for your garden that will be easy for you to grow.

You should determine what moisture-related zone your garden is in. For example, the south and east sides of Scotland Island generally fall into Bell & Stables' **Moist PWSGF** zone, and the north and west sides of the island – especially the ridges – fall into Bell & Stables' **Dry PWSGF** zone. See "History of surveys" section for more about the Bell & Stables 2012 study. For the lists themselves, see "Dry PWSGF and Moist PWSGF" section.

I've tried to give four or five pieces of location-related information about each species:

- Whether it is native to Sydney region.

- Whether it is native to Scotland Island.

- Whether it is typical of PWSGF, and if so, whether it is on the species lists for Dry PWSGF, Moist PWSGF, or both.

- If it isn't typical of PWSGF, whether it occurs natively in areas other than Scotland Island where PWSGF occurs (or used to) occur.

- If it doesn't occur in other PWSGF areas, whether it occurs natively in KCNP (Ku-ring-gai Chase National Park) or other Northern Beaches areas of native vegetation.

- If it doesn't occur in or near the Northern Beaches, where the nearest place is where it does occur naturally.

Not surprisingly, different researchers have come up with different lists of PSGF or PWSGF, depending on where they pick their sample sites and perhaps other factors. For each species, I have also checked against the list of PSGF species from the large 2016 NSW Office of Environment and Heritage study of Sydney Flora. Although this was a Sydney-only study, they did include some sites from Wagstaffe, as Bell and Stables had also done. They also included Scotland Island among the 22 sites sampled. I give details when the 2016 OEH result differs from Bell & Stables. See "History of surveys" section for where you can download the 2016 OEH study's data.

Species that occur in KCNP but are not typical of PWSGF are generally either widespread species that are easy to grow, or they fall into the category of Hawkesbury Sandstone flora. The sandstone species will likely be more difficult for gardeners with clay-based soil, and should be planted on a slope in these gardens to help ensure better drainage.

To get location data for species that are not native to Scotland Island or part of PWSGF, I used the online search facility of The Australasian Virtual Herbarium. See section titled "Useful free online resources" for the url.

Species profiles

Acacia binervia

Common name(s): Coast Myall

Max. height, usually: 16 m, but some forms are shrubs to 2 m high.

Max. width, usually: 3 m

Form: Shrub to small tree.

Soil: Most free-draining soils; tolerates drought and salt spray.

Light: Full sun to light shade.

Flower season: Pale yellow (occasionally bright yellow or white) spikes in spring, Aug to Oct.

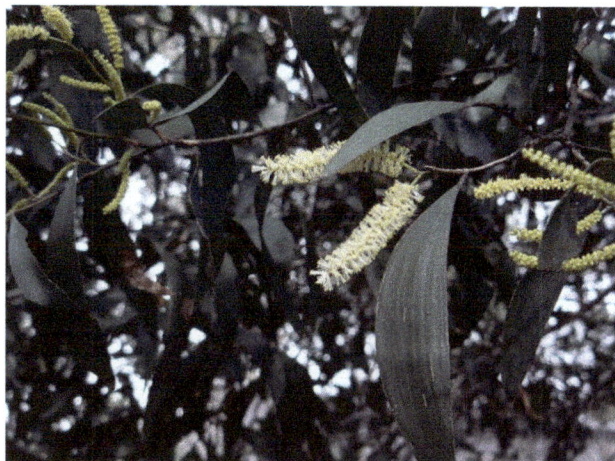

Photos (above and below): http://lepidoptera.butterflyhouse.com.au/plants/mimo/acacia-binervia.html

Best features: Fast growing and relatively long lived (around 25 years); very showy flowers; blue-green to silvery foliage.

Propagation: Seed.

Native to: Sydney and also Scotland Island*. Not typical of PWSGF. Nearest wild-collected record was at Palm Beach in 1987.

Distribution: Dry sclerophyll forest or heath on rocky slopes, often near streams; NSW south from Hunter Valley; Vic.

Other notes: Good screener or a specimen plant.

When not in flower, closely resembles Turpentine (*Syncarpia glomulifera*), with a tall straight trunk and dark, fissured, fibrous bark. Phyllodes (the "leaves") are 3-veined.

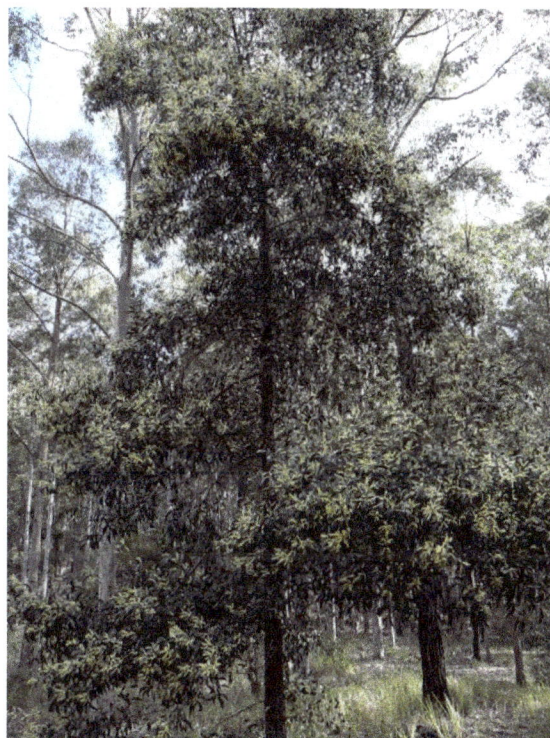

Not currently available at local native plant nurseries, but may be available in commercial nurseries, marketed as "Silver Spray". A cascading cultivar is available from some commercial nurseries as "Sterling Silver" (aka "Stirling Silver").

---

* Recorded by Brad Jones as occurring in Elizabeth Park as of 2010.

Acacia decurrens

Common name(s): Black Wattle, Early Black Wattle, Early Green Wattle, Sydney Green Wattle

Max. height, usually: 12 m

Max. width, usually: 6 m

Form: Green-barked tall shrub to tree; leaves bipinnate (feathery), with fine leaflets widely spaced, like a comb.

Soil: Not fussy; prefers moist, well-drained clay-based soil; tolerates drought.

Light: Sun or shade.

Flower season: Bright yellow puffs starting in July or Aug.

Photo: Dan Clarke https://resources.austplants.com.au/plant-database/

Best features: Hardy and grows quickly; showy when in flower. Fragrant flowers. Interesting sculptured green bark. Shiny, bright green feathery leaves create soft shade.

Propagation: Seed, which is ripe Nov to Jan.

Native to: Sydney and also Scotland Island[*]. Not typical of PWSGF. Nearest wild-collected record was from dry sclerophyll forest near Woy Woy in 1971.

Distribution: Endemic to NSW, but widely cultivated and naturalised (or even weedy) elsewhere. Dry sclerophyll forest, woodland or heath, often on river banks and on rises.

Other notes: Unripe seed said to be eaten by cockatoos.

Good screen when young and can be hedged.

May be short-lived due to borer attack. May be used as a "nurse" tree; quickly establishes shade which then allows growth of more long-lived trees.

Sculptured green bark. Photo: H Malloy

Similar to *A. dealbata*, which was formerly considered a subspecies of *A. decurrens*. *A. dealbata* is a longer-lived species, growing to 30 m (i.e., the height of a Spotted Gum).

---

[*]   There is now at least one individual I know of in Elizabeth Park, which apparently grew following the 2019 hazard reduction burn. Recorded as native to Scotland Island by Craig Burton in his 1978 unpublished survey. Not recorded in surveys since then.

Acacia falcata

Common name(s): Sickle Wattle, Sally Wattle

Max. height, usually: 5 m

Max. width, usually: 1.5 m

Form: Spindly and flexuous silvery shrub or small tree, somewhat weeping.

Soil: Well-drained; drought-tolerant.

Light: Full sun to light shade.

Flower season: White flowers May to Aug.

Best features: Fast-growing; winter flowering; attractive "leaves"; very tough plant.

Photo: Neil Murphy, Eatons Hill, Qld

Propagation: Seed, which matures from Sept to Dec.

Native to: Sydney and also Scotland Island. Not typical of PWSGF, but recorded as native near various PSGF sites such as Morning Bay, Paradise Beach and Avalon.

Distribution: Sclerophyll forest, mainly coastal; NSW, Qld.

Other notes: Good for hot dry sites and for stabilising hillsides. No maintenance required. May be short-lived as a garden specimen, typically 5 to 10 years.

Photo: Carol and Trevor Deane. http://butterfliesdorrigo.weebly.com/imperial-hairstreak-jalmenus-evagoras.html

Looks great in a group: there is a nice grove of them in Elizabeth Park on Scotland Island.

Seed relished by King Parrots and Eastern Rosellas.

A food plant for a half dozen butterfly species including the Imperial Hairstreak.[*] This species is one of many butterflies whose caterpillars are attended by ants. The ants protect them from birds and parasitic wasps, and in return, the caterpillars provide the ants with a honey-dew-like substance from special organs.[†]

Photo: Kym Farnik. https://www.flickr.com/photos/cypheroz/11081304724/in/photolist-hTdzQ1-a8zhNM-a8CadA-a8zhGZ https://creativecommons.org/licenses/by-nc-nd/2.0/

---

[*] http://lepidoptera.butterflyhouse.com.au/plants/mimo/acacia-falcata.html
[†] http://butterfliesdorrigo.weebly.com/imperial-hairstreak-jalmenus-evagoras.html

Acacia fimbriata

Common name(s): Fringed Wattle, Brisbane Golden Wattle

Max. height, usually: 7 m

Max. width, usually: 6 m

Form: Shrub to small tree with graceful slightly pendant branches.

Soil: Prefers well-drained moist sandy loam; tolerates most soils, including clay soil; tolerates drought.

Light: Semi-shaded to full sun; protected from wind.

Flower season: Profuse yellow scented flowers Aug to Sept.

Best features: Fast growing with dense foliage; good screen. Spectacular when in flower.

Propagation: Seed; cuttings.

Native to: Sydney and also Scotland Island.[*] Not typical of PWSGF. Recorded in KCNP.

Distribution: From Sydney to southern Qld, occurring on the coast and in the adjoining tablelands. It grows in open eucalypt forests on hillsides, preferring well drained, moist sandy loams in semi-shaded to full sun protected positions.

Other notes: Like many wattles, useful life is 8-12 years. Cut back new growth by a third after flowering to make it denser and increase flowers. Can be grown as hedge.

King Parrots and Eastern Rosellas love the developing seeds.

Available in dwarf forms, e.g., "Crimson Blush".

Photo: H Malloy

Male King Parrot feeding on *Bursaria spinosa* seeds. Photo: https://avithera.blogspot.com/2017/04/australian-king-parrot.html

---

[*] Not recorded in vegetation studies of the island, but there are three individuals that I know of in Elizabeth Park, including two young ones that grew following the 2019 hazard reduction burn.

Acacia floribunda

Common name(s): Sally Wattle, White Sally, Sallow Wattle, Gossamer Wattle

Max. height, usually: 6-8 m

Max. width, usually: 3-4 m

Form: Small tree with pendulous branches.

Soil: Moderately well-drained; drought-tolerant.

Light: Full sun to light shade or afternoon shade.

Flower season: Pale yellow or cream flowers in cylindrical spikes June to Sep.

Best features: Fast-growing when given sufficient water; showy when in flower; pendulous branches are attractive.

Propagation: Seed.

Native to: Sydney but not Scotland Island. Not typical of PWSGF*. Nearest wild-collected record is KCNP.

Distribution: Vic, NSW & Qld; mainly in coastal sclerophyll communities, often in sandy alluvial soil and along watercourses.

Other notes: Widely cultivated. Good screen or hedge plant. Said to grow well in gullies, as well as drier locations.

Like many other wattles, may be short-lived due to attack by borer beetles.

Easily confused with *A. longissima*, which has longer and narrower phyllodes with one main vein, and flowers in summer; in contrast to *A. floribunda* which flowers in winter or spring, and has phyllodes 2-10 mm wide with up to 4 main veins.

A dwarf cultivar (1 m x 1 m) is available commercially as "Little Flori".

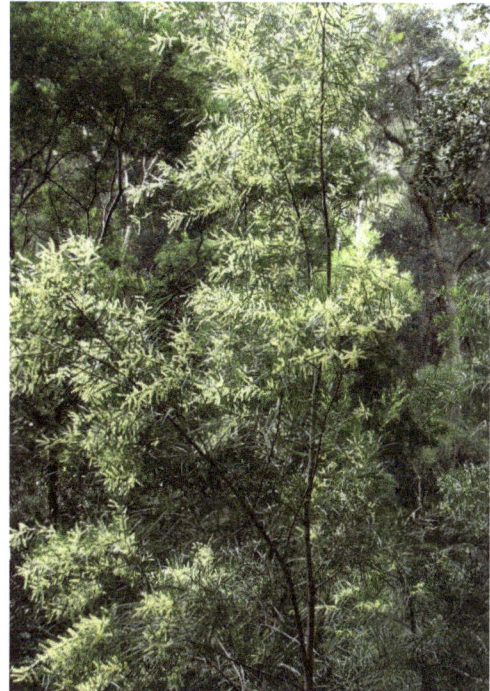

Cream-flowering form. Photo: Dan Clarke
https://resources.austplants.com.au/plant-database/

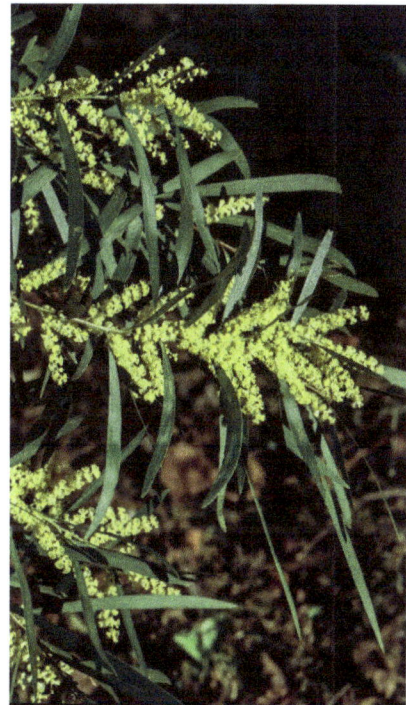

Yellow-flowering form. Photo: Alan Fairley
https://resources.austplants.com.au/plant-database/

---

* It was included in the NSW Threatened Species Scientific Committee's 1998 description of Pittwater Spotted Gum Forest. Subsequently, it was removed from the re-defined Pittwater and Wagstaffe Spotted Gum Forest, 2013.

Acacia implexa

Common name(s): Hickory Wattle, Lightwood, Screw Pod Wattle

Max. height, usually: 12 m

Max. width, usually: 2 m

Form: Small to medium-sized narrow upright tree with open crown, sometimes multi-stemmed; often makes suckers from roots.

Soil: Clay, loam or sand; drought-tolerant; can be planted along watercourses; somewhat salt tolerant.

Light: Prefers full sun; tolerates light shade.

Flower season: White or cream puff balls in summer (Dec to Apr) with some flowers at other times; strongly perfumed, but flowers not showy.

Photo: Donald Hobern, Pittwater Online News

Best features: Very hardy; fast growing; flowers in summer; interesting twisted seed pods.

Propagation: Seed; use caution because dust from the pods can irritate nose and throat.

Native to: Sydney and Scotland Island. Typical of Dry PWSGF.

Distribution: Widespread in a variety of communities; Vic, NSW, Qld.

Other notes: Suitable for bank planting and erosion control due to its suckering habit.

Suitable for planting on hot, dry, north- or west-facing slopes to provide shade for more delicate plants. Attractive willow-like foliage.

Similar to the much bigger *A. melanoxylon,* which flowers in winter.

Seed pods curved, coiled and twisted.

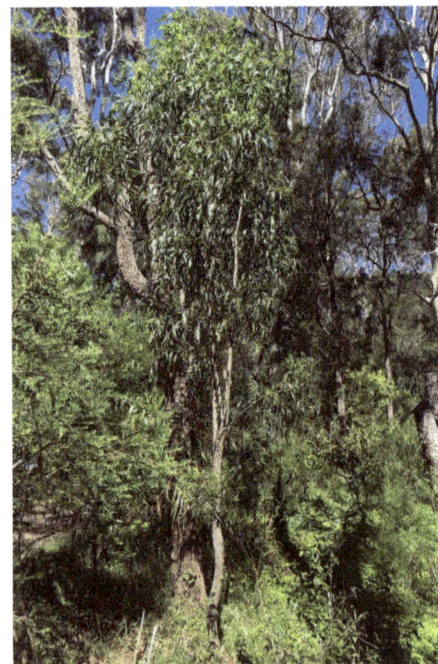
Along Fitzpatrick Trail. Photo: H Malloy

Ripening seeds are said to be relished by rosellas and other parrots.

Often self-seeds when there is a mature tree nearby.

Acacia linifolia

Common name(s): Flax Wattle, White Wattle

Max. height, usually: 3 m

Max. width, usually: 3 m

Form: Tall shrub or sparsely branched small tree.

Soil: Well-drained clay, loam, sandy loam, or clay loam; drought-tolerant.

Light: Prefers light to half shade; tolerates full sun if kept moist.

Flower season: Anise-scented pale yellow, cream or white flowers Jan to Aug. Sometimes after flowering in summer, it has a second, smaller flowering in winter.

Photo: H Malloy

Best features: Fast growing; graceful, slightly weeping habit; profuse fragrant flowers in summer – when few other plants are in flower; attractive bottle-brush appearance of "leaves".

Propagation: Seeds.

Native to: Sydney but not Scotland Island. Not typical of PWSGF. Recorded in KCNP.

Distribution: Dry sclerophyll forest, woodland and heath in sandy, often skeletal soils on sandstone, also clayey soils on shale in NSW, especially Sydney region.

Other notes: Looks better with supplemental water in summer, especially the first few summers. Very hardy after establishment.

As is true for many other wattles, the "leaves" are not botanically speaking the equivalent of the typical leaves of most plants. Instead, the leaf-like things (called phyllodes) are evolutionarily derived from the leaf stems (called petioles). Wattle species with phyllodes generally switch from producing typical leaves to phyllodes in an early stage when they are still seedlings. They sometimes revert to producing typical leaves when damaged. Phyllodes, with their thick leathery surfaces, are an advantage in times of drought.

Acacia longifolia subsp. longifolia[*]

Common name(s): Long-leaf Wattle, Golden Wattle, Sallow Wattle, Sydney Golden Wattle

Max. height, usually: 7 m

Max. width, usually: 4 m

Form: Large bushy shrub.

Soil: Clay, loam, or sand; prefers well-drained sandy soil. Drought-tolerant. Dislikes waterlogging.

Light: Full sun to light shade.

Flower season: Bright yellow to pale yellow cylindrical flower spikes in June to Oct.

Best features: Fast-growing, hardy; stunning when in flower.

Photo: Gillian Gutridge, *Native Plants of the Northern Beaches, Sydney.*
https://nbplantareas.com/

Propagation: Seed[Ψ]

Native to: Sydney and Scotland Island. Not a component of PWSGF. Nearest wild-collected record KCNP.

Distribution: In sclerophyll communities – heathlands to woodlands to tall forests; NSW, Vic, and widely naturalised (or even weedy) elsewhere.

Other notes: Good for screening. Can be pruned annually by one third after flowering to maintain it as a bushy shrub, e.g., if screening is desired at a lower level. Hedgeable. However, for low screening or an informal hedge you may want to consider its sister subspecies (profiled on next page) which is naturally low-growing but otherwise very similar.

This is one of the first yellow-flowered wattles of the season to flower in our area, and it is certainly one of the cheeriest ones when it explodes into flower just barely past the winter solstice. You can really hardly have enough of these when they are in flower, though the rest of the year it is on the modest side.

Useful life as an attractive garden subject may be limited to less than 8 years, though pruning should help. In a natural setting, lifespan is said to be around 50 years[†].

Forms hybrids with *A. oxycedrus*, *A. floribunda* and *A. mucronata*, as well as with its sister subspecies (profiled on next page).[†]

---

[*]   The full name is needed to distinguish it from its sister subspecies, which is profiled on the next page.

[Ψ]   Germination is low due to a very long dormancy period (> 10 years) in 90% of seed. Around 10% of fresh seed germinates with no dormancy.

[†]   http://herbiguide.com.au/Descriptions/hg_Sydney_Golden_Wattle.htm

Acacia longifolia subsp. sophorae

Common name(s): Coastal Wattle

Max. height, usually: 3 m

Max. width, usually: 4 m

Form: Prostrate to bushy shrub.

Soil: Not fussy; prefers well-drained sandy soil. Drought-tolerant. Dislikes waterlogging.

Light: Full sun to light shade.

Flower season: Bright yellow to pale yellow cylindrical flower spikes in late winter or early spring.

Best features: Fast-growing, hardy; stunning when in flower.

Propagation: Seed[†].

Native to: Sydney but not Scotland Island. Not a component of PWSGF. Nearest wild-collected record is from near Woy Woy, 1971.

Distribution: Heath and sclerophyll forest, coastal headlands, sand dunes and adjacent alluvial flats; NSW, Qld, Vic, Tas.

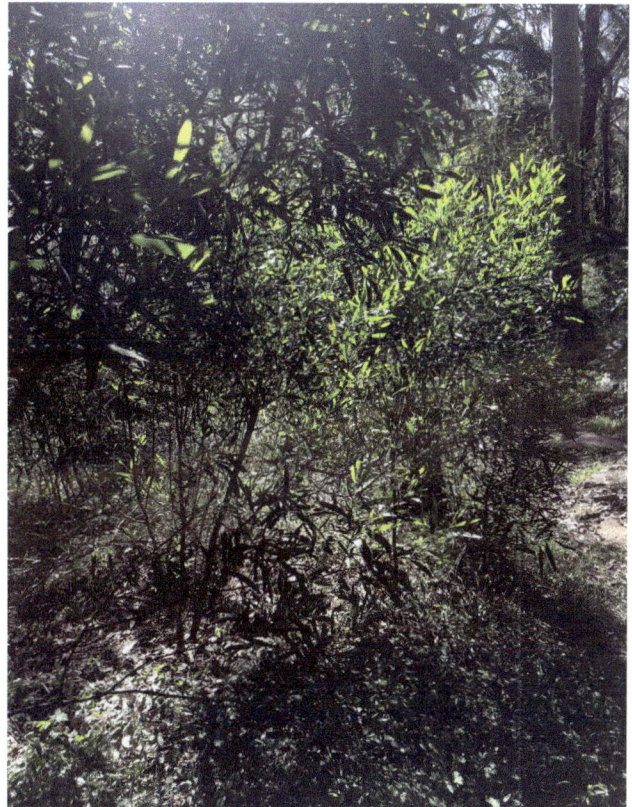

Some four-year old Coastal Wattles planted along Fitzpatrick Trail for screening. Photo: H Malloy

Other notes: Similar to its sister subspecies *longifolia*, except that Coastal Wattle is adapted to the tougher environment of hind-dunes and headlands, having shorter, wider phyllodes, and shorter habit. Its natural distribution is much wider than its sister subspecies, reflecting its hardier nature.

May be a better choice than its sister subspecies if a low-growing screener is desired, since it is naturally lower growing. Prune to keep it even more compact, if desired.

Growing on dunes of nearly pure sand. Photo: M Fagg, Australian National Botanic Gardens http://www.anbg.gov.au/photo

Though adapted to harsh dune conditions, it also does well in the same pampered garden situations where its sister subspecies thrives.

There are naturally occurring intermediates and hybrids between the two subspeces. There is also individual variation in the height of Coastal Wattle plants.

[†]   As is also true for its sister subspecies, germination is low due to a very long dormancy period (> 10 years) in 90% of seed. Around 10% of fresh seed germinates with no dormancy.

Acacia longissima

Common name(s): Narrow-leaf Wattle or Long-leaf Wattle

Max. height, usually: 6 m

Max. width, usually: 2 m

Form: Tall shrub or small upright tree.

Soil: Not fussy; tolerates drought as well as moderate waterlogging.

Light: Full sun to light shade.

Flower season: Small cylindrical somewhat sparse spikes of pale yellow to white flowers mostly Jan to May, with some flowers at other times from Oct to Mar.

Best features: Fast-growing. Hardy in both dry and inundated conditions, meaning that it can be planted in and near gully torrents. Flowers in the heat of summer over a long period.

Propagation: Seed. Fruit is infrequently set and pods are difficult to see as they resemble the leaves.

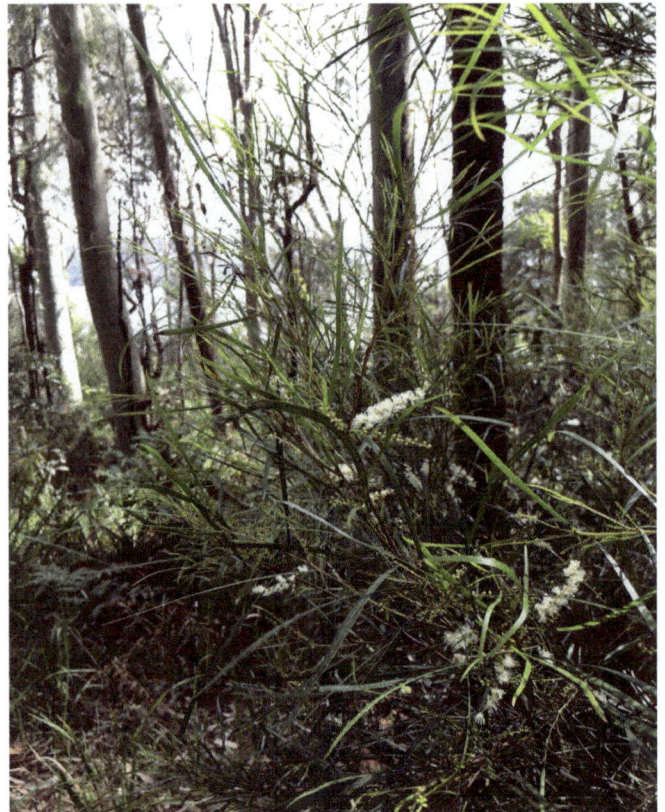

Growing in a grove in Elizabeth Park, Scotland Island. Photo: H Malloy

Native to: Sydney and Scotland Island. Studies differ as to whether it is a component of PWSGF[*].

Distribution: Gullies in wet and dry sclerophyll forest, in sandy to clay soils; NSW, Qld.

Other notes: Though it naturally occurs in gullies or near seepages, it grows very well if planted in drier situations. Apparently the extra moisture of gullies or seepages is only required in the seedling stages. Would be useful planted along gully torrents to take up some of the water and reduce erosion.

Looks best when growing in a cluster or grove of five or more (as in the photo), as the fine-textured foliage can appear sparse otherwise. Good screener when used this way.

Flowers are relatively small for a wattle and not showy, but on the plus side, they appear when little else is in flower. Flowers better with generous watering.

Though it tolerates filtered shade very well, heavier shade may cause it to lean towards the light.

Resembles *A. floribunda* (see profile), which has wider phyllodes and yellow or cream flowers in spring.

---

[*]   Bell & Stables 2012 do not report it. OEH 2016 report it as typical for PSGF.

Acacia ulicifolia

Common name(s): Prickly Moses

Max. height, usually: 2 m

Max. width, usually: 1-2 m

Form: Prickly shrub.

Soil: Prefers sandy well-drained soil. Dislikes clay soils. Will not tolerate waterlogging. Tolerates drought.

Light: Full sun or light shade.

Flower season: White flowers in winter and spring.

Best features: Prickles provide refuge for small birds; winter flowers.

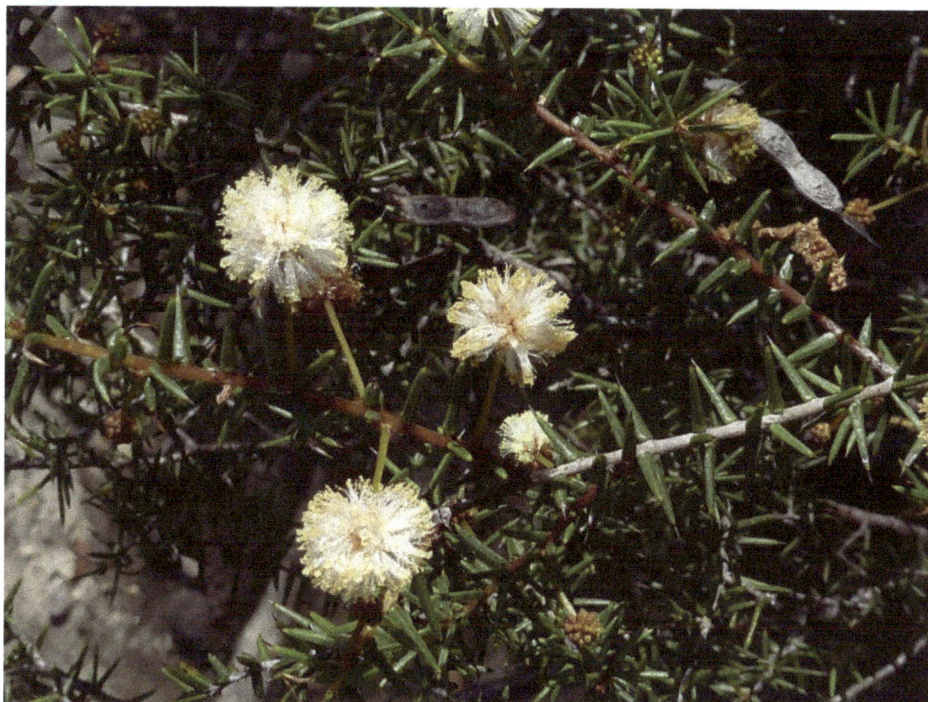

Photo: Dan Clarke https://resources.austplants.com.au/plant-database/

Propagation: Seed, cuttings.

Native to: Sydney and also Scotland Island. Typical of Dry PWSGF.

Distribution: Dry sclerophyll forests and woodlands, as well as heathlands, in NSW, Vic, Qld and Tas, up and down the entire coast of NSW and west to the western slopes, usually on sandy soil and sandstone-influenced areas.

Other notes: Long-lived when happy. Profuse flowers look like twinkling fairy lights.

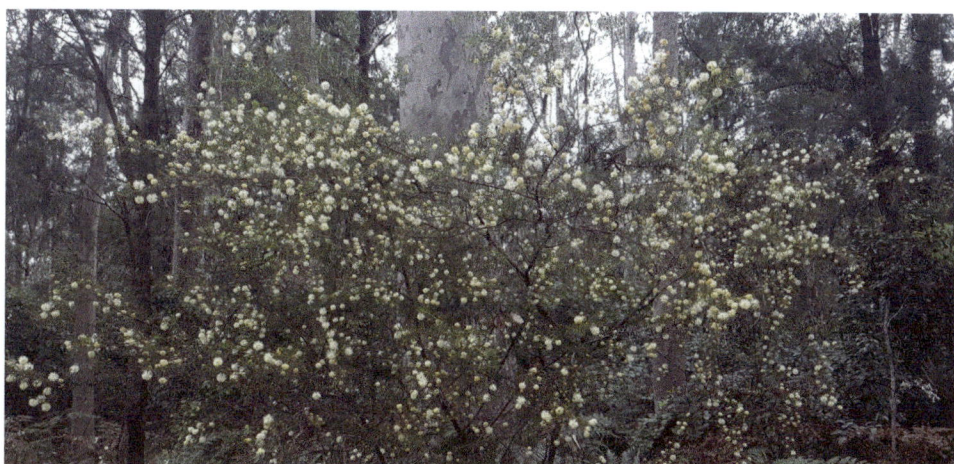

In CB's sandy garden on the east side of Scotland Island. Photo: CB Floyd

Acmena smithii (also known as Syzygium smithii)[Ω]

Common name(s): Common Lilly Pilly

Max. height, usually: 5 m

Max. width, usually: 3 m

Form: Large shrub or small tree.

Soil: Most reasonably drained soils; drought-tolerant.

Light: Full sun to fairly heavy shade.

Flower season: White flowers in summer (Nov to Feb) that are underwhelming on their own, but together make a modest display, followed by underwhelming edible fruits in autumn and winter.

Photos (above and below): Gillian Gutridge, *Native Plants of the Northern Beaches, Sydney.* https://nbplantareas.com/

Best features: Attractive dark, glossy foliage; one of the best plants for screening; very hardy.

Propagation: Seeds, cuttings.

Native to: Sydney and Scotland Island; typical component of moist PWSGF.

Distribution: Widespread in rainforest, from the coast to ranges, often along watercourses; NSW, Qld, Vic.

Other notes: In cultivation for many years. There are many cultivars and hybrids available, generally varying in growth habit. Beware that a bewildering number of related species are also known as "lilly pilly"[Ψ], and some plants sold in commercial nurseries are sold under the wrong name[Σ]. See also the profile for Magenta Lilly Pilly (*Syzygium paniculatum*).

In rainforest it can reach 20 to 30 m, but garden conditions are very different to rainforest, in terms of nearly everything that matters to a plant: light levels, humidity, moisture and soil. In exposed locations or gardens it is a hardy shrub; a good coloniser.

Often used for tall hedging. When grown as a multi-stemmed shrub, the foliage is dense enough for an Australian Boobook (*Ninox boobook)* to take up daytime residence, as one did in ours for a month or two.

[Ω] Wikipedia (accessed 7 Mar 2023) has a summary of how this species came to be known as *Acmena* smithii in NSW and Qld, and (in more recent years) as *Syzygium smithii* elsewhere in Australia.

[Ψ] https://ultimatebackyard.com.au/lilly-pilly-varieties/

[Σ] https://www.burkesbackyard.com.au/fact-sheets/in-the-garden/flowering-plants-shrubs/best-lilly-pilly-varieties/

Adiantum hispidulum

Common name(s): Rough Maidenhair Fern, Five-fingered Jack

Max. height, usually: 70 cm

Max. width, usually: 1 m or more.

Form: Fern spreading by short rhizomes.

Soil: Moist well-drained soil with added organic matter; somewhat drought-tolerant (for a fern). Does not tolerate waterlogging.

Light: Part shade to dappled shade; grows faster when it receives some sun; can even tolerate noontime sun, but then of course it will need more watering in most cases.

Flower season: n/a

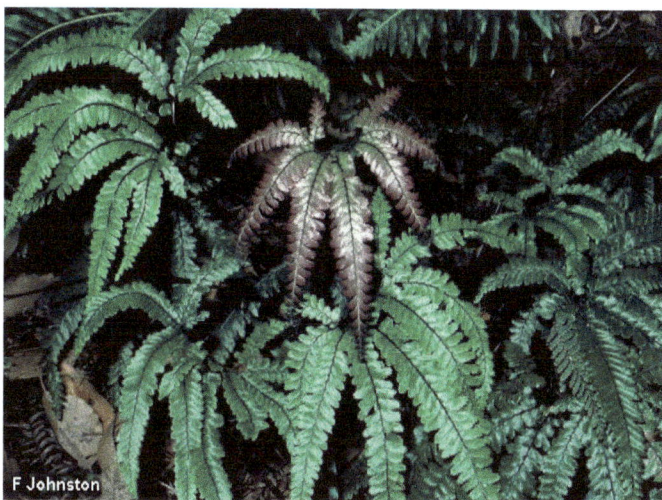

Photo: Fred Johnston, Australian Native Plants Society (Australia). https://anpsa.org.au/native-plant-profiles/

Best features: Attractive palmate (hand-shaped) fronds; pinkish new growth; dark green older leaves; hardy.

Propagation: Spores, division.

Native to: Sydney and Scotland Island; not part of PWSGF.

Distribution: Widespread in rainforest and open forest, often amongst rocks; NSW, Qld, Vic, NT; also Eastern Africa, Madagascar, Malaysia, New Zealand and Pacific Islands.

Other notes: Popular in cultivation and there are some named cultivars. Grows well in containers, even indoors as long as it is not kept too wet. Like most ferns, it responds well to fertilisers. Works well as a rockery plant, as the fronds have a natural pendulous habit.

In good conditions it spreads moderately though slowly, and it is easy to propagate from spores, even if that is not what you had in mind. Not surprisingly given its adaptability, it has naturalised in numerous warm places outside its native range (which was already impressively large), including the southeastern United States and Hawaii.

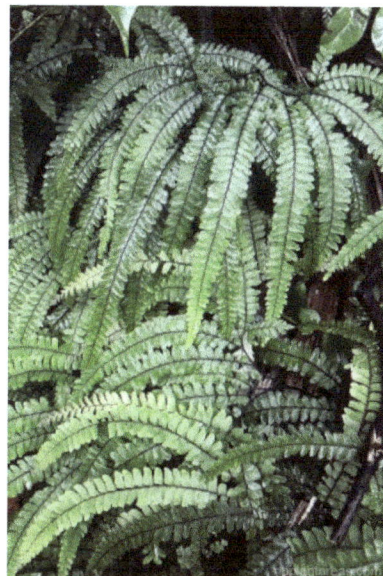

Photo: Gillian Gutridge, *Native Plants of the Northern Beaches, Sydney.* https://nbplantareas.com/

Among the more drought-tolerant and sun-tolerant of Sydney's locally native ferns. In times of drought it becomes sad and scruffy-looking, but it quickly puts out new fronds when moist conditions return. If you will not be able to provide supplemental watering, it is best to plant it in shade, where the soil will remain moist longer.

Often available from native plant nurseries, and it may also be available from commercial nurseries.

Allocasuarina distyla

Common name(s): Scrub She-oak

Max. height, usually: 2-3 m (up to 7 m in rich soil).

Max. width, usually: 3 m

Form: Pine-like shrub or small densely branched tree with blue-green "needles".

Soil: Sandy, well-drained soil; drought- and salt-tolerant.

Light: Full sun or light shade.

Flower season: Variable but mostly Jul to Sept.

Best features: Great screener or windbreak; stunning flowers and foliage; interesting cylindrical seed "cones" (on female individuals only); wind makes a nice sound through the branches.

Propagation: Easy from seed.

Native to: Sydney and Scotland Island; not PWSGF; see it on Northern Beaches bushwalks at Bangalley Head, Chiltern Trail, Cromer Heights, and others[Ω].

Distribution: In tall heath on sandstone hillsides; NSW and possibly also northeast Vic.

Other notes: She-oaks have their leaves reduced to small teeth at the top end of the ridged branchlets that make up the "needles". Plants are generally female or male but not both, so if you want fruits, you need to plant several.

This species has cylindrical cones, often with a short point at the apex.

Adult plants need no supplemental watering, and are very hardy, but seedlings need water up to a few feet tall. Responds well to pruning.

Needs no fertilisers because, like wattles, she-oaks can extract ("fix") nitrogen from the atmosphere thanks to symbiotic bacteria housed in nodules on their roots, as do members of the wattle and bean family.

If your garden has clay soil, consider the clay-tolerant *A. littoralis* (sun-loving) or *A. torulosa* (shade-loving) instead. Hybrids are common in the Sydney area between this species and *A. littoralis.*

Photos (above and below): Gillian Gutridge, Native Plants of the Northern Beaches, Sydney. https://nbplantareas.com/

Female flower cluster

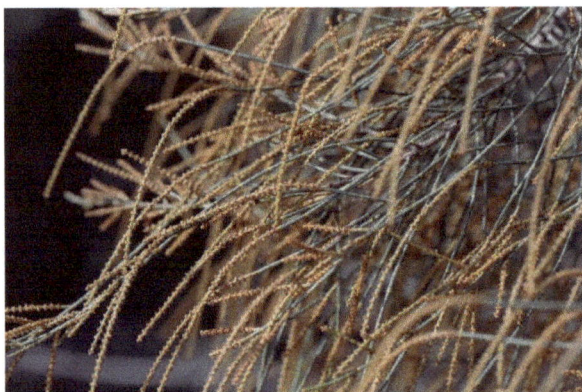

Male flowers

Ω   Gillian Gutridge, *Native Plants of the Northern Beaches, Sydney.* https://nbplantareas.com/

Allocasuarina littoralis

Common name(s): Black She-oak, Bull Oak

Max. height, usually: 12 m

Max. width, usually: 6 m

Form: Pine-like grey-green upright conical tree with male and female flowers on separate individuals; deeply fissured bark.

Soil: Prefers sandy, well-drained; tolerates clay and loam-type soils and very poor sandy soils. Do not plant near drains. Salt-tolerant. Tolerates short periods of drought. Does not tolerate water-logging.

Light: Prefers full sun; tolerates light shade.

Flower season: Mar to June; female flowers are wild-haired fat red clusters on older branches; male flowers are spikes at the end of branchlets that turn the whole tree an attractive copper red.

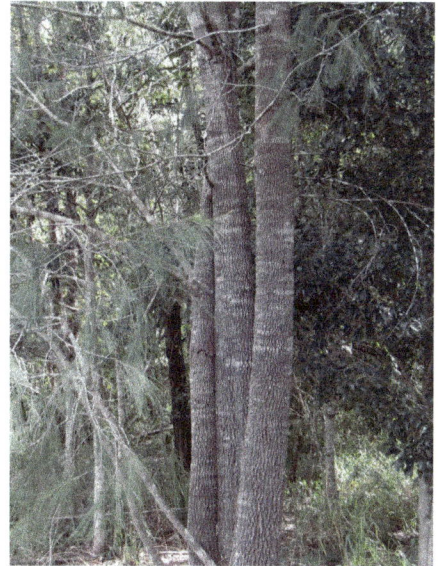
Photo: Neil Murphy, Eatons Hill, Qld

Best features: Fast-growing; tough and adaptable to less-than-ideal conditions; shares desirable attributes of other She-oaks, such as attractive flowers, pinelike cones and grey-green foliage, and the relaxing sighing sound the wind makes rustling through the "needles".

Propagation: Easy from seed.

Native to: Sydney and Scotland Island; a component of Dry PWSGF. Herbarium records show it as having been collected in Church Point, Newport, Avalon, and many other Pittwater locales.

Distribution: In woodland or tall heath, on poor soils in coastal and tableland regions; Tas, Vic, NSW and Qld.

Other notes: If growing for the fruits, plant a group as the sexes are on separate trees. Good windbreak. As is the case with other *Allocasuarinas*, though it looks like a pine tree, the "needles" are twigs, and the tiny teeth at the top of each twig section are the leaves. The cones are cylindrical (as opposed to *A. torulosa*). The tip of the cone has a flat or

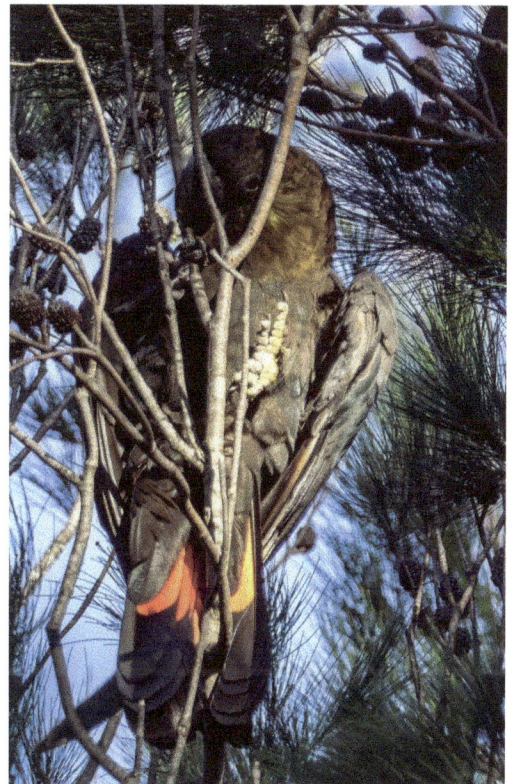
Photo: Kerri-Lee Harris, www.southernforestlife.net

blunt apex (as opposed to *A. distyla)*. Not a good choice for a sheltered, forested or otherwise shaded location; for that *A. torulosa* may be a better choice. If you have sandy soil and you prefer a smaller tree, you could consider *A. distyla*. See profiles for those species.

A favourite food tree of Glossy Black Cockatoos *(Calyptorhynchus lathami)*.

Allocasuarina torulosa

Common name(s): Forest Oak

Max. height, usually: 8 m in gardens (up to 30 m in forest).

Max. width, usually: 10 m when grown in open garden situations (narrower in forest).

Form: Small to medium-sized open-branched tree with weeping pine needle-like branchlets.

Soil: Almost any as long as it is not alkaline. Prefers moist humus-rich well-drained soils. Tolerates drought, wind and salt.

Light: Prefers light shade; tolerates full sun.

Flower season: Very small flowers blush rusty red along the needlelike branchlets on male plants in autumn to winter.

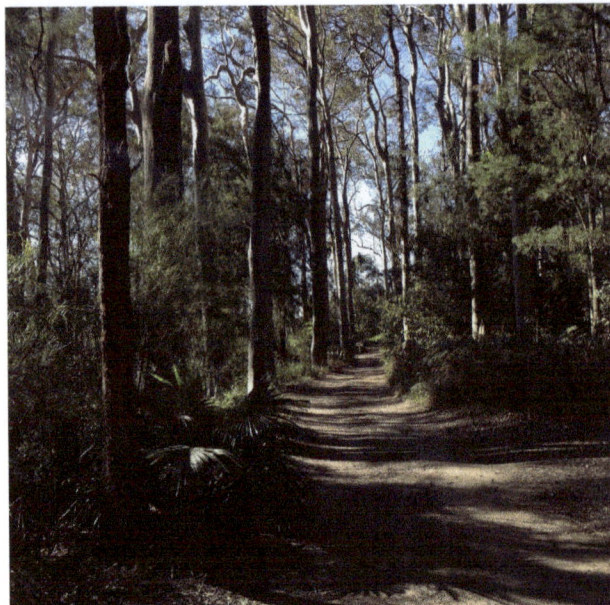
Photo: H Malloy

Best features: Fast growing; corky bark and weeping needle-like leaves are attractive.

Propagation: Seed, but as it sheds readily from the spherical fruits before or as the fruits fall, it is easier to dig up the plentiful small volunteer seedlings than germinate them yourself.

Native to: Sydney and Scotland Island. Typical of PWSGF.

Distribution: Understorey tree in forest along coast from Shellharbour north; NSW and Qld.

Other notes: Casts a pleasant, finely filtered shade and very useful for quickly providing light shade so that you can grow more sensitive plants. Long-lived when happy.

The seeds are a favourite of the Glossy Black Cockatoo. If you hear a chewing sound and occasional creaking squawks while walking through Scotland Island's Elizabeth Park, a pair may be feeding in the canopy nearby. Usually each tree has male or female flowers but not both, so if you want the fruits you need to plant a group.

Some species of *Allocasuarina* and *Casuarina* are thought to have properties that prevent or inhibit the development of some other plants beneath their canopies. Large older groves where Forest Oak dominates do seem to have reduced groundcover; however, this effect could be caused by the mulching effect of the buildup of dropped branchlets. Still, it may be best not to plant Forest Oak near vegetable or other non-native gardens.

Photo: Charles Dove, Australian Geographic Society

Arthropodium milleflorum

Common name(s): Pale Vanilla Lily

Max. height, usually: 1 m

Max. width, usually: 1.2 m

Form: Dark green, strappy leaves with dainty small flowers in panicles nodding along the arching stems.

Soil: Any soil; prefers moist, grassy, loamy sheltered slopes. Tolerates drought and the shallow soil on top of low rock outcroppings.

Light: Full sun, part sun, light shade, heavy shade. Said to become dormant if too dry (it recovers), so may be better in some shade.

Flower season: Pale mauve, white, pink, or blue flowers Nov to Feb.

Best features: Long flowering season. Though not large, flowers dangle and dance on long stems in a charming way. Tolerates drought due to its tuberous roots.

Propagation: Seed or division. Germination rate is high.

Native to: Sydney and also Scotland Island. Studies differ as to whether it is typical for PSGF[Ψ]. Nearest native records are from Cowan Creek and Barrenjoey.

Distribution: Wide distribution along the east coast, from Qld to SA and Tas, on sandstone rock ledges and moist grassy, sheltered slopes in open eucalypt forest, woodland, montane forest, and other grassland.

Photos (above and below): Australian National Botanic Gardens. http://www.anbg.gov.au/photo

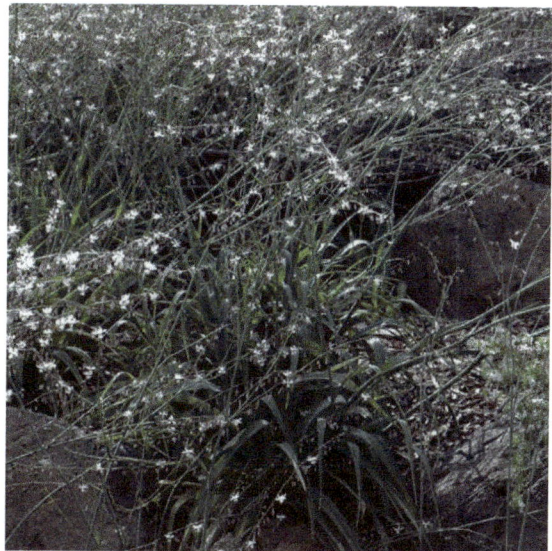

Other notes: Roots are tuberous but shallow, and are edible raw or roasted, but nearly without any taste. Even the bush turkeys don't care for them very much.

Not showy on its own. Good en masse in a meadow, rockery, or under trees. Self-seeds but does not become invasive, and excess plants are easily removed.

Ψ   Bell & Stables 2012 didn't record it in any site. OEH 2016 reported it in 14% of their PSGF sample sites.

Austromyrtus dulcis

Common name(s): Midgen Berry, Midyim Berry, Sand Berry, Silky Myrtle

Max. height, usually: 1 m

Max. width, usually: 1.5 m

Form: Spreading prostrate to low shrub.

Soil: Well-drained moist; prefers sandy loam. Moderately tolerant of drought. Does not tolerate waterlogging.

Light: Full sun, part shade or filtered shade; prefers afternoon shade.

Flower season: White star-shaped flowers with fluffy anthers spring to autumn; delicious berries late summer to autumn.

Best features: Sweet peppery or gingery edible berries, attractive reddish new growth.

Propagation: Easy from fresh seed or cuttings.

Native to: **Not native** to Sydney or Scotland Island, nor is it a component of PWSGF.

Distribution: Heath or dry sclerophyll forest on sandy soils or rainforest margins; coastal sites north from Urunga, NSW (near Coffs Harbour) north; also Qld.

Photo: Blue Mountains Botanic Garden

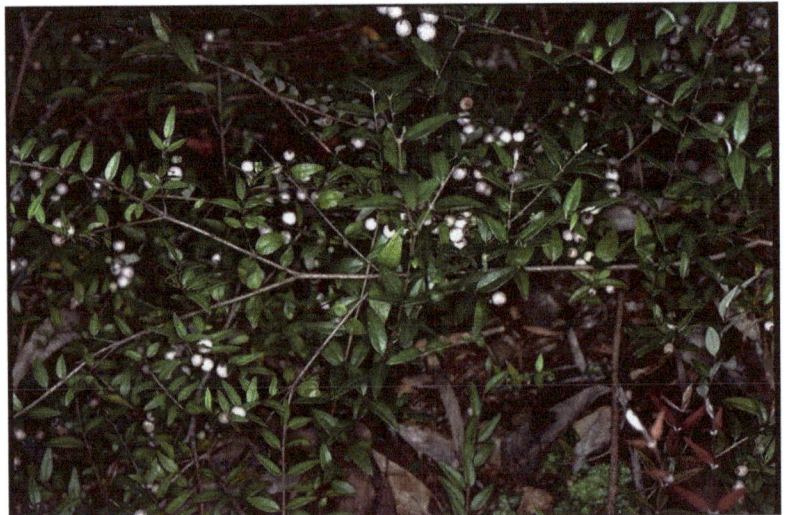

Photo: M Fagg, Australian National Botanic Gardens http://www.anbg.gov.au/photo

Other notes: Not a local Sydney native. I made an exception to my rule in including this species because it is such a useful, easy to grow garden plant, widely available, and (very important) it is not likely to be invasive, although I could be wrong. Purists had best avoid this species.

Add well-aged compost to soil, mulch and keep moist for a good supply of berries. Trim after harvesting to encourage bushiness. Can be grown as an informal low hedge.

Similar to *A. tenuifolia* (see next profile), except that species has narrower leaves and a more upright habit, requires a moister site, and is native to Scotland Island.

An attractive hybrid between the two species is sold commercially as "Copper Tops".

Austromyrtus tenuifolia

Common name(s): Narrow-leaf Midgen Berry, Midyim Berry, Narrow-leaf Myrtle

Max. height, usually: 1-1.5 m

Max. width, usually: 1-3 m

Form: Graceful small shrub with dense growth habit.

Soil: Tolerates wide range including clay; prefers moist areas.

Light: Full sun to semi-shaded.

Flower season: White flowers in spring, followed by edible fleshy white berries with purple spots.

Best features: Very adaptable. Both flowers and fruits are a feature. Useful for informal low hedging. Tasty berries with minty overtones.

Propagation: Cuttings (may be slow), seed which must be sown when fresh (from ripe berries).

Native to: Sydney and Scotland Island*. Not typical of PWSGF. Nearest native record is McCarrs Creek.

Distribution: In wet sclerophyll forests, often beside streams or in damp places in the Sydney Basin (Inner Sydney, Blue Mountains, Newnes Plateau, Campbelltown), usually near sandstone outcrop.

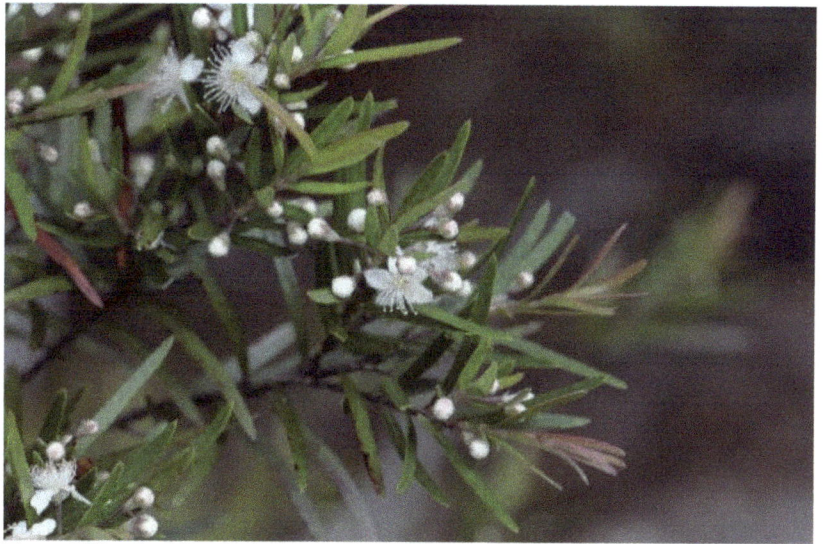

Photo: Gillian Gutridge, *Native Plants of the Northern Beaches, Sydney.*
https://nbplantareas.com/

In Ku-ring-gai Chase National Park. Photo: Peter Woodard
https://commons.wikimedia.org/w/index.php?
title=File:Rainforest_shrub_myrtle_smiths_creek.jpg&oldid=626286050
https://creativecommons.org/licenses/by-sa/4.0/deed.en

Other notes: Tolerates drought but flowers and fruits better if it receives plenty of water in the months leading up to its flowering.

Also consider *A. dulcis* (previous profile), which tolerates drier spots and has a more sprawling habit. It has a wider natural distribution but does not naturally occur south of Coffs Harbour.

An attractive hybrid between the two species is sold commercially as "Copper Tops".

---

*   Recorded as growing in NW gully in Craig Burton's study of the island 1978.

Bauera rubioides

Common name(s): River Rose, Dog Rose

Max. height, usually: 1.5 m

Max. width, usually: 3 m

Form: Tangled scrambling shrub with wiry stems.

Soil: Moist, well-drained sandy soil. Tolerates brief winter inundation.

Light: Prefers light shade or afternoon shade.

Flower season: Pink flowers mostly spring to summer (Nov), with sporadic flowers most of the year.

Best features: Pretty flowers, long flowering season; attractive fresh-looking whorled leaves; good for cut flowers in a shallow bowl.

Propagation: Seed or cuttings; easy.

Native to: Sydney but not Scotland Island, and not PWSGF. See it on local bushwalks Chiltern Trail, Deep Creek, and others[Σ]. Also Banks Track at Ku-ring-gai Wildflower Garden.

Distribution: Wet and often shaded situations; NSW, Qld, Vic, Tas, SA.

Photo: Gillian Gutridge, *Native Plants of the Northern Beaches, Sydney.* https://nbplantareas.com/

Photo: M. Fagg https://www.anbg.gov.au/photo/image-collection.html

Other notes: Slow-growing; requires moist soil to look its best. This may be one that only those with a southern or eastern exposure can grow easily. Well worth trying for gardens that are completely shaded during winter months, in a site that will be shaded during the summer. Amend clay soil with sand or aged compost, or grow in a pot. Flowers well in shade. If well-mulched to 5 cm deep, can take full sun with only moderate watering. Wilts when dry, but perks back up if watered soon after.

In the same family (Cunoniaceae) as *Callicoma* and *Ceratopetalum*, which also like the same moist conditions. All three are easy when their conditions are met.

Has been in cultivation for many years. A darker pink form is sometimes available. Widely available at native plant nurseries.

Σ   Gillian Gutridge, *Native Plants of the Northern Beaches, Sydney.* https://nbplantareas.com/

Billardiera scandens

Common name(s): Hairy Apple Berry, Apple Dumpling

Max. height, usually: Climber to 2 m when supported.

Max. width, usually: .5 m

Form: Small twining climber or scrambling shrub.

Soil: Well-drained sandy, clay or rocky soil. Tolerates drought but prefers moist conditions.

Light: Filtered sun to part shade.

Flower season: Pale yellow decorative bell-shaped flowers in spring, with sporadic flowers at other times.

Best features: Delicate-looking but hardy; well-behaved climber for small fences; new growth silky-hairy; edible berries.

Propagation: Seed, cuttings.

Native to: Sydney and Scotland Island. A component of Dry PWSGF, but also ubiquitous in other forest communities in the Sydney area.

Distribution: Open eucalypt forest and woodland; NSW, Qld, Vic, Tas.

Photos (above and below): Gillian Gutridge, *Native Plants of the Northern Beaches, Sydney.* https://nbplantareas.com/

Other notes: Fruits are edible if eaten when fully ripe, which reportedly does not happen until they are black and about to fall from the vine; said to taste like stewed apples.

When unsupported, makes a mounded groundcover to 1 m tall.

As a climber, it is charming and well-behaved. Does not overwhelm other plants.

Widely available at native plant nurseries.

Blechnum cartilagineum

Common name(s): Gristle Fern, Soft Water Fern

Max. height, usually: 1 m

Max. width, usually: Indefinite.

Form: Tufted fern spreading by running rhizomes to form colonies.

Soil: Prefers well-drained fertile, moist soil.

Light: Semi-shade to dappled shade.

Flower season: n/a

Best features: Bright pink new growth; graceful lush dark green fronds; hardy once established.

Propagation: Division.

Native to: Sydney and Scotland Island. Not a component of PWSGF. There is a large colony in Elizabeth Park visible from the footpath on the southern side. Can also be seen in the Irrawong Reserve, North Narrabeen[Ω].

Distribution: Widespread in open forest and rainforest; NSW, Qld, Vic, Tas.

Photos (above and below): Gillian Gutridge, *Native Plants of the Northern Beaches, Sydney.* https://nbplantareas.com/

Other notes: Hardy fern for large ferneries, shaded moist gardens, or beside water areas. Looks best when given supplemental water during dry times.

The shiny dark green leaves are extremely attractive. Sometimes the fronds get a bit nibbled at their tips; I wish I could say what it is that nibbles them. If it is insects, the nibbling could be kept to a minimum by ensuring that the ferns are not stressed by going dry for too long; stressed plants are more attractive to herbivorous insects.

Widely available at native plant nurseries.

Ω   Gillian Gutridge, *Native Plants of the Northern Beaches, Sydney.* https://nbplantareas.com/

Boronia pinnata

Common name(s): Fern-leaf Boronia

Max. height, usually: 1.5 m

Max. width, usually: 1 m

Form: Small shrub.

Soil: Well-drained, moist soil; does not tolerate either drying out or waterlogging. Protect from wind.

Light: Full sun to light shade.

Flower season: Pink flowers in spring.

Best features: Impossibly profuse 4-petalled starry flowers in hot pink, delicately glorious.

Propagation: Cuttings.

Native to: Sydney but not Scotland Island and not PWSGF. Can be seen on many Northern Beaches bushwalks including Chiltern North Trail, Chiltern Trail, Cromer Heights trails, and Katandra Bushland Sanctuary[Ω]. A sandstone-loving species.

Distribution: Endemic to NSW; moist sheltered places in dry sclerophyll forest and heath on sandstone; chiefly coastal districts.

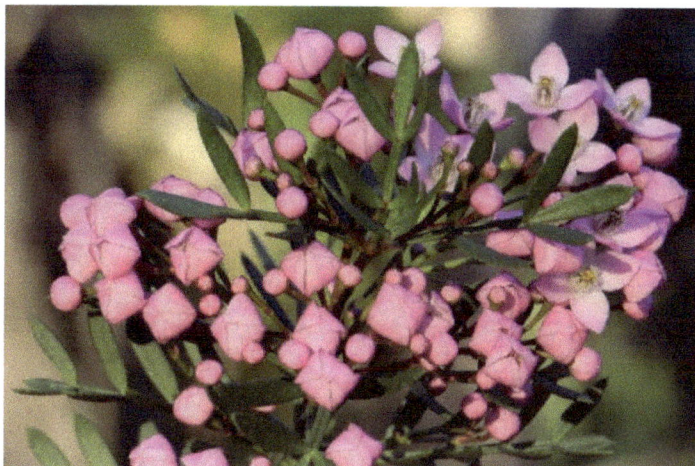

Photos (above and below): Gillian Gutridge, *Native Plants of the Northern Beaches, Sydney.* https://nbplantareas.com/

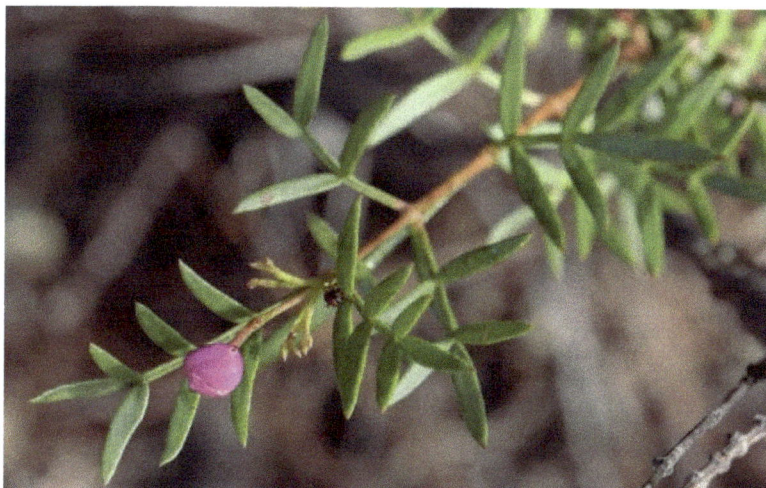

Other notes: Boronias are notoriously difficult to keep alive more than a year or two, but this species is tougher than most and can be long-lived in the right spot kept free of weeds, and with light trimming after flowering to keep it compact.

Grows very well in a pot, and if you have clay soil that is your best bet; move into the shade as necessary and to protect from drying winds.

Lightly scented but does not perfume the air like the justly more famous *Boronia megastigma*. Variable in form and habit.

Carried by some native plant nurseries.

Ω   Gillian Gutridge, *Native Plants of the Northern Beaches, Sydney.* https://nbplantareas.com/

Brachyscome graminea (formerly B. angustifolia)[*]

Common name(s): Grass Daisy

Max. height, usually: 70 cm

Max. width, usually: 30 cm to indefinite width as it spreads via stolons and/or suckers from the roots.

Form: Small, somewhat straggly groundcover with narrow, linear leaves; spreading by stolons and suckering from roots.

Soil: Any; prefers moist but tolerates drought if shaded.

Light: Full sun to part shade.

Flower season: White, mauve-pink or purple flowers on slender stalks all year, with peak Oct to May.

Best features: Long flowering season; grows well amongst native grasses, providing little pops of colour.

Propagation: Seed, cuttings, division.

Growing from clay embankment along road in Elizabeth Park. Also in photo: spotted gum seedling and *Tylophora barbata*. Photo: H Malloy

Native to: Sydney and Scotland Island. A component of Dry PWSGF, but not common enough to be typical.

Distribution: Widespread in coastal districts in open forests on moist ground, coastal marshes and damp cliff faces, and on the ranges at high altitude in freshwater swamps and streams in Qld, Vic, Tas, SA.

Other notes: The straggly form of Grass Daisy allows it to scramble over grasses to charming effect.

Many cultivars are available, e.g., pink flowers, compact form, etc.; however these are likely to be derived from a different species, which was formerly

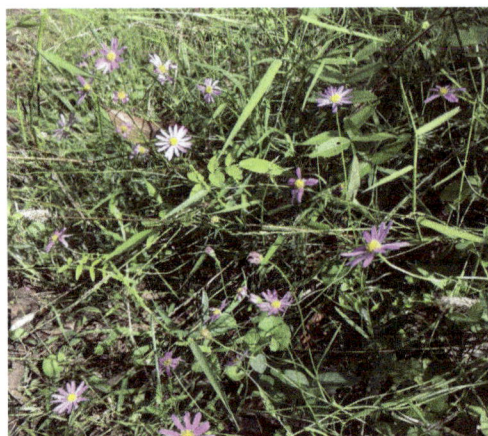

Scrambling over grasses in a shady meadow. Photo: H Malloy

known as *B. angustifolia* var. *heterophylla* and is now divided into several new species. One of these widely available cultivars is known as "Brasco Violet". It differs from *B. graminea* in its compact form and lobed leaves, and has a very different overall look from the Grass Daisy.

---

[*]   Formerly known as *B. angustifolia* var. *angustifolia* prior to a revision of Brachyscome in 2014 (P.S. Short, *Journal of the Adelaide Botanic Gardens* 28: 1-219). In the revision, the taxon formerly known as *B. angustifolia* var. *heterophylla* (which differs from *B. graminea* in its lobed leaves) was split into three new species: *B. triloba*, *B. brownii* and *B. sieberi*.

Breynia oblongifolia

Common name(s): Coffee Bush

Max. height, usually: 3 m

Max. width, usually: 1-1.5 m

Form: Small erect shrub with greyish green leaves.

Soil: Tolerates wide variety of soil as long as it is well drained. Prefers moist soil.

Light: Prefers light shade.

Flower season: Small greenish flowers in spring-summer, followed by orange or pink berries that turn black when fully ripe, and are said to be edible.

Photo: H Malloy

Best features: High habitat value. Striking growth pattern. The appearance of the leaves is strongly two-ranked, that is, alternately arranged on opposite sides of the stem. Stems and new growth are often reddish, providing good contrast with the dark green leaves. The larvae of a moth often create an interesting decorative pattern in the leaves.

Propagation: Seed, cuttings.

Native to: Sydney and Scotland Island. Typical of Dry PWSGF.

Distribution: Coastal tropical rainforests in North Qld and New Guinea through to cool eucalypt woodlands in south–eastern NSW to arid acacia woodlands in Western Qld.

Other notes: Supports many different animals that feed on

Photo: Gillian Gutridge, *Native Plants of the Northern Beaches, Sydney.* https://nbplantareas.com/

the leaves, berries and flowers including several moths and butterflies. Sometimes a plant gets completely defoliated by herbivores. They usually recover completely, but if it happens often, this can be an indication that the site is a little too sunny or too dry.

Can be cut to the ground annually, or kept as a hedge. If left uncut, it becomes an attractive small tree.

Brunoniella australis

Common name(s): Blue Trumpet, Blue Yam (a related Qld species has edible roots)

Max. height, usually: 15 cm

Max. width, usually: 20 cm

Form: Small herb with swollen succulent roots and furry leaves.

Soil: Well-drained soil; loves damp heavy soil; drought-tolerant thanks to its tuberous roots.

Light: Semi-shade.

Flower season: Blue-mauve flowers Oct to Jan.

Best features: Heart-melting dainty flowers much of the year; furry leaves.

Propagation: Seed, which is covered with specialised hairs that absorb water and produce a mass of sticky mucus when wet, aiding dispersal by small animals.

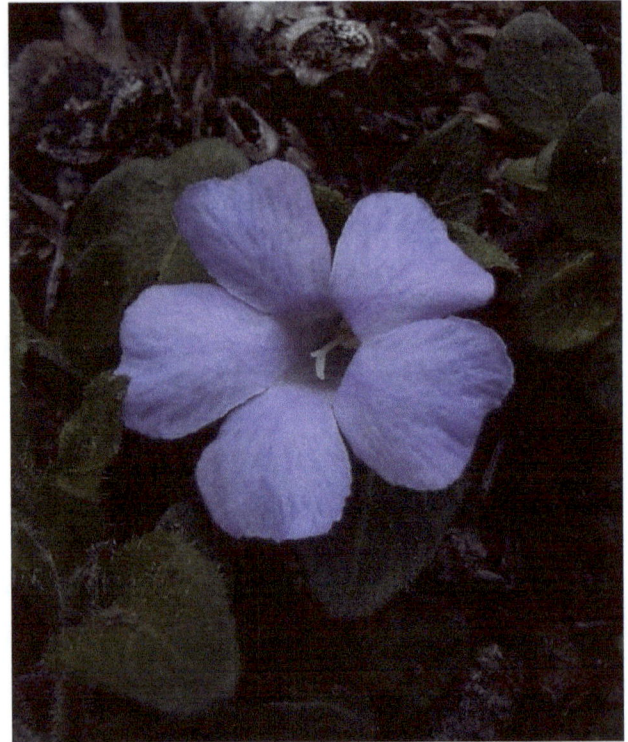

Photos (above and below): L von Richter, The Royal Botanic Gardens & Domain Trust

Native to: Sydney but not Scotland Island, and not part of PWSGF. Mostly inland, east of the Great Dividing Ranges. Nearest wild-collected records are KCNP and Hornsby. Common on moist clay soil in Cumberland Plain Woodlands, and Coastal Valley Grassy Woodlands.

Distribution: Sclerophyll forest and woodland; widespread, especially on slopes, north from Camden. Also Qld, NT, WA.

Other notes: Sometimes available from native plant nuseries. A cultivar called "Light Blue Trumpet" is available from some commercial nurseries.

Not to be confused with *Brunonia australis*, a completely different plant requiring full sun from west of the Blue Mountains.

Also consider *Brunoniella pumilio* (see next profile), a similar but smaller species that is native to coastal sandstone areas.

Brunoniella pumilio

Common name(s): Dwarf Trumpet

Max. height, usually: 10 cm

Max. width, usually: 20 cm

Form: Small herb with swollen succulent roots and smooth leaves with slightly raised veins.

Soil: Well-drained soil; prefers sandy soil; mulch well.

Light: Part shade; tolerates full sun.

Flower season: Blue flowers Oct to Jan.

Photos (above and below): Gillian Gutridge, *Native Plants of the Northern Beaches, Sydney.* https://nbplantareas.com/

Best features: Another heart-breakingly lovely little plant with lovely flowers that contrast well with the olive leaves.

Propagation: Seed, which is covered with specialised hairs that absorb water and produce a mass of sticky mucus when wet, aiding dispersal by small animals.

Native to: Sydney but not Scotland Island. Not considered part of PWSGF, but it is found in McKay Reserve on Palm Beach, parts of which contain PWSGF[Ψ]. It can be seen in the wild on several short bushwalk trails, including Turimetta Headland and Chiltern North Trail, but only following recent fire[Ω].

Distribution: Coastal sandstone areas, regenerating after fire; south from Myall Lakes in NSW, Vic.

Other notes: Seems to be dependent on recent fire in order to flower in the bush. In the garden, supplemental watering and a fertiliser designed for natives may coax it into flower.

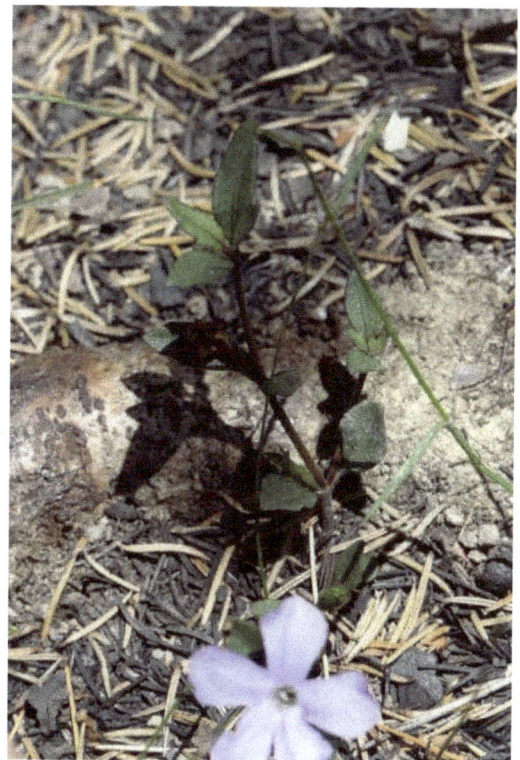

A cultivar called "Little Blue Trumpets" is sometimes available from some commercial nurseries. This may be the only practical way to obtain it as a garden plant, as it is not carried by most native nurseries. However, it would likely be a Vic form of the species, as the grower is located in Vic.

Also consider *Brunoniella australis* (see previous profile), a similar but larger species, with furry leaves, preferring heavy clay soil.

Ψ   Wikipedia.
Ω   Gillian Gutridge, personal communication.

Bulbine bulbosa

Common name(s): Bulbine Lily, Rock Lily

Max. height, usually: 50 cm

Max. width, usually: 30 cm

Form: Clumping herb with bulb-like tuber (corm) and hollow, fleshy leaves and spikes of flowers.

Soil: Well-drained, prefers on the dry side but supplemental watering required to prevent summer dormancy.

Light: Full sun or light shade.

Flower season: Yellow flower spikes Sept to Mar.

Best features: Fast-growing, long lived, very hardy; blue green leaves attractive even when not in flower.

Propagation: Seeds; division. Seeds are ripe beginning Oct to Nov. Flowers first year from seed. Store seed 2-3 months before planting, after which germination takes several weeks. If growing for naturalising, plant three or more plants as it reportedly has a self-sterility mechanism[*][Ψ]

Photo: Australian National Botanic Gardens
http://www.anbg.gov.au/photo

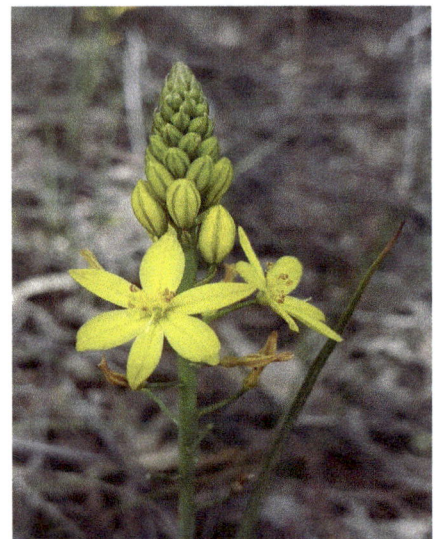

Native to: Sydney but not Scotland Island and not PWSGF. Nearest wild-collected record was from Parramatta in 19th century.

Distribution: Scattered throughout NSW in damp areas in woodland, grassland and sclerophyll forest; also Qld, Vic, Tas, WA.

Other notes: Requires watering during the hot months if you want to prevent it going dormant. With watering, new growth will be continually produced with no dormant period. Allow to dry out between waterings.

Looks best planted in drifts or colonies, as it grows in the wild.

Photo: Jenny aka Floydwafer, iNaturalist

---

[*]   The mechanism of self-sterility in *Bulbine bulbosa*: self-incompatibility or inbreeding depression. Archived September 12, 2009, at https://web.archive.org/web/20090912200610/http://www.aff.org.au/AFF2_Owen_Bulbine_talk.htm

[Ψ]   Facilitated Autogamy and Costs of Selfing in the Perennial Herb *Bulbine bulbosa* (Asphodelaceae) https://www.journals.uchicago.edu/doi/abs/10.1086/513488

Caesia parviflora*

Common name(s): Pale Grass Lily

Max. height, usually: 50 cm

Max. width, usually: 50 cm

Form: Tuft of strappy leaves with lily-like flowers.

Soil: Moist, well-drained sandy, loamy or heavy clay soil; tolerates drought due to its fleshy roots.

Light: Full sun, part sun, filtered sun; does not tolerate full shade.

Flower season: Small white to blue lily-like flowers, often striped, spring to summer.

Best features: Pretty; very hardy; long flowering season.

Propagation: No information readily available, but I am guessing seed, division.

Native to: Sydney and Scotland Island. A typical component of Dry PWSGF.

Distribution: Heath, woodland and dry sclerophyll forest, often on sandstone-derived soils; NSW, Qld, Vic, Tas, SA, WA.

Other notes: Dainty-looking but hardy plant for a weed-free native garden. The site needs to be weed-free in order for its charms to be seen, as the tufty leaves closely resemble grass when it is not in flower.

As a garden subject, it would do well in a rockery on a west-facing slope. I say this because there is a blue-flowered colony growing naturally in those conditions on Thompson Street, Scotland Island above Cargo Wharf, near the big rock. It is increasing despite asparagus fern and weedy grasses, for at least the five years I have lived nearby. *Caesia parviflora* var. *vittata* (pictured) is the more colourful of the two varieties, and is the variety on Thompson Street.

Photo: H Malloy

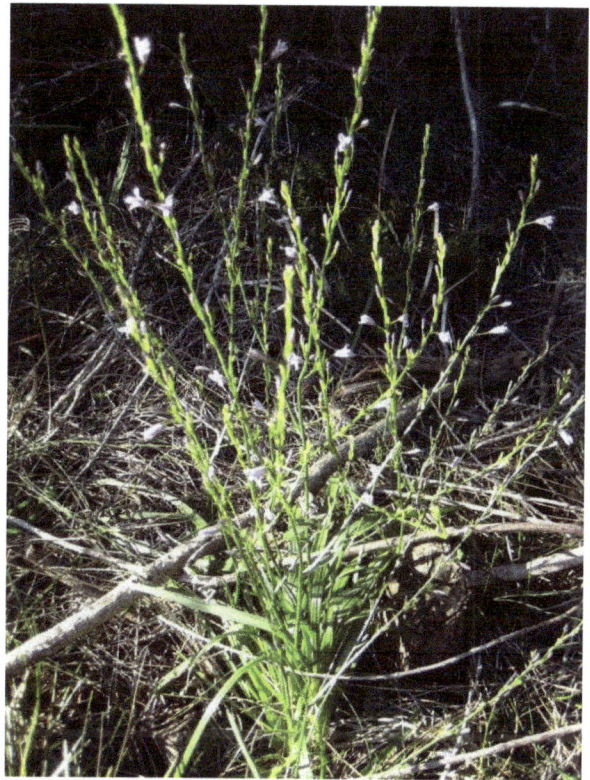

Photo: Gillian Gutridge, *Native Plants of the Northern Beaches, Sydney.* https://nbplantareas.com/

---

* There are two varieties recognised in NSW which are both Sydney local natives: *Caesia parviflora* var. *vittata* and *Caesia parviflora* var. *parviflora*. The two subspecies can hybridise, according to PlantNET.

Callicoma serratifolia

Common name(s): Blackwattle (but not related to true wattles)

Max. height, usually: 6-10 m

Max. width, usually: 3 m

Form: Bushy shrub or small tree.

Soil: Moist loamy soil, clay-based or sandy. Would benefit from additions of compost or mulch. Not drought or wind tolerant.

Light: Shade.

Flower season: White puff balls in spring.

Best features: Fast growing; good screener. Flowers are spectacular. Shiny large, thick, serrated, dark green leaves with whitish or rusty fuzz on underside are very attractive. Young foliage is pale bronze.

Growing in a sandstone gully at the southern boundary of its range, near Batemans Bay. Photo: Bateman's Bay Bushwalkers. http://baybushwalkers.org.au/little-forest-plateau-2/

Propagation: Cuttings in autumn, seeds which germinate readily when fresh (seeds ripe Dec-Jan). The fruits are small hairy capsules produced in globular clusters. Each capsule contains 2 or 3 small seeds which are released when ripe (technically the ovary separates into carpels which then open along the inner edge).

Native to: Sydney but not Scotland Island. Not found in PWSGF. Nearest wild-collected record is dated 1969 from Katandra Bushlands Sanctuary where it was common along a creek.

Distribution: In protected moist gullies usually in close proximity to creeks, along the coastal areas of NSW from the Braidwood district to south-east Qld.

Other notes: Beautiful anywhere, but may be best in gullies; elsewhere may need supplemental watering to prevent wilting in hot, dry spells. The leathery leaves droop and hang vertically to reduce water loss, but recover after the dry spell is over.

The striking dark green leaves provide welcome contrast with the more typical narrow native leaf forms of grevilleas or phebaliums, making it an attractive background plant for a bed of those kinds of plants. They would all appreciate a little extra water during drought.

Available at most native plant nurseries.

Centella asiatica

Common name(s): Asiatic Pennywort, Gotu Kola, numerous regional names

Max. height, usually: 20 cm

Max. width, usually: Indefinite.

Form: Groundcover creeping by stolons.

Soil: Moist; tolerates waterlogging.

Light: Full sun to part shade; does not tolerate full shade.

Flower season: Insignificant green flowers summer to autumn.

Best features: Hardy groundcover for moist places.

Propagation: Division.

Native to: Sydney and Scotland Island. Not a component of PWSGF. Nearest wild-collected record is from Long Reef in 1982.

Distribution: Grows mainly in damp places in coastal districts; NSW, Qld, Vic, WA, SA. Also grows in swampy areas in many regions of the world, including North America, Africa, Asia, and Pacific Ocean islands.

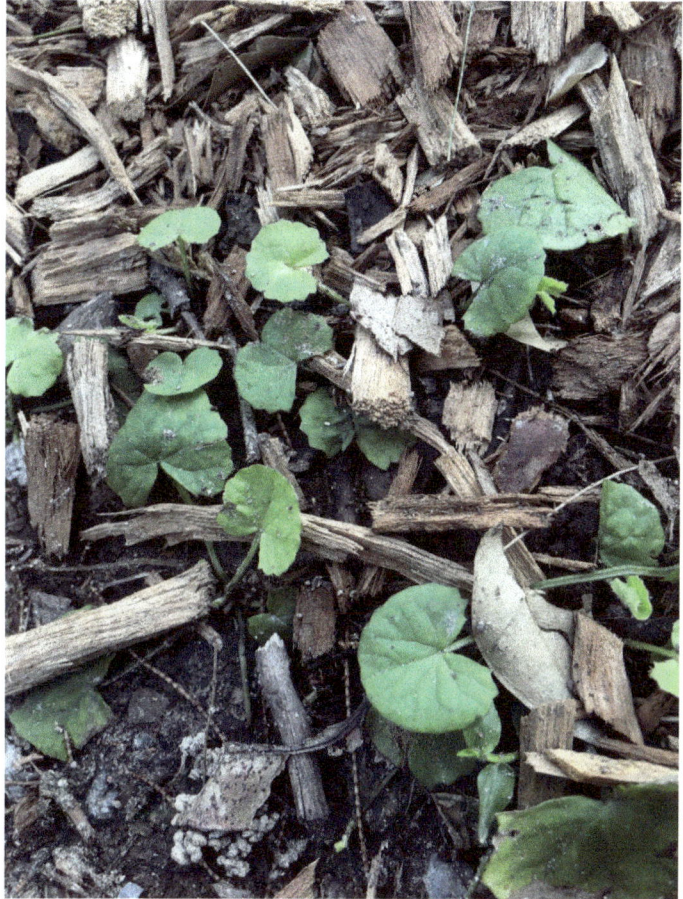
Photo: H Malloy

Other notes: Leaves resemble the leaves of *Viola hederacea.*

Can be invasive in well-watered garden situations. Generally not a problem in native gardens that are not excessively watered, and a valuable groundcover where its conditions are met.

Does not tolerate much foot traffic, so not a good lawn substitute.

Many culinary uses in southeast Asia. Many traditional medicinal uses for various disorders and minor wounds, none so far confirmed by modern scientific methods. May cause drowsiness and have adverse effects on liver function.

Dodgy internet sources often confuse Asiatic pennywort with a distantly related non-native herb with wide global spread, *Hydrocotyle bonariensis* (not to be confused with *H. sibthorpioides*, a native groundcover). *H. bonariensis* is a familiar weed of Australian beaches, and easily distinguised from Asiatic pennywort by its shiny peltate leaves (*peltate*: the leaves sit perpendicular to their stems like little tables).

The genus *Centella* is in the carrot family, whereas the superficially similar genus *Hydrocotyle* was moved to the ivy family in 2009 as a result of DNA analysis.

Ceratopetalum gummiferum

Common name(s): New South Wales Christmas Bush

Max. height, usually: 5 m

Max. width, usually: 4 m

Form: Tall shrub or small upright tree.

Soil: Well-drained but moist; prefers sandy, so plant on a slope if your soil is clay-based to avoid root rot.

Light: Full sun or semi-shade.

Flower season: White flowers late Nov, followed by the Christmas-time display of the red "flowers" which are the enlarged papery sepals surrounding the seed capsules.

Photos (above and below): Gillian Gutridge, *Native Plants of the Northern Beaches, Sydney.* https://nbplantareas.com/

Best features: Pretty white flowers followed by pretty pink "flowers"; attractive trifoliate leaves with fine serrations year round, with pinkish new growth.

Propagation: Seed, cuttings.

Native to: Sydney and Scotland Island. Not a component of PWSGF. Nearest wild-collected record is Bilgola, in dry sclerophyll forest.

Distribution: NSW; heath or moist gullies, from Ulladulla to Evans Head; mostly on sandstone or old sand dunes. Frequently cultivated.

Other notes: When young, it is a rounded shrub, but in good conditions can grow to a 10 m tree.

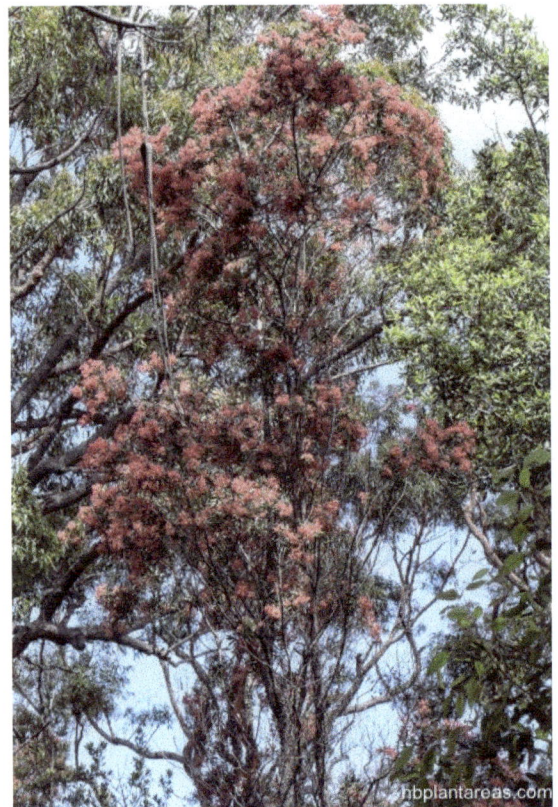

Dig in well-aged compost when planting if soil is very poor. Mulch annually to help keep roots cool and moist. Benefits from annual feeding with a slow-release fertiliser. Related to *Callicoma serratifolia*, with similar cultivation requirements.

Responds well to pruning after flowering by 1/3 if a smaller bushy habit is preferred, or try "Johanna's Christmas", which is a naturally occurring dwarf cultivar. Widely available in nurseries.

Cheilanthes sieberiana[Ω]

Common name(s): Mulga Fern, Rock Fern, Poison Rock Fern

Max. height, usually: 30 cm

Max. width, usually: 10 cm

Form: Small fern forming clumps or colonies.

Soil: Sandy, clay or loamy soil; tolerates poor drainage; tolerates drought.

Light: Full sun to dappled shade.

Flower season: n/a

Best features: Delicate-looking but tough as nails (for a fern).

Propagation: Spores, division.

Native to: Sydney and Scotland Island; not part of PWSGF. Nearest wild-collected record is from Narrabeen.

Distribution: Widespread in arid as well as non-arid areas, in exposed rocky habitats, in rock crevices or shelter of rocks, open forest or woodland, throughout much of NSW; also all other Australian states, Lord Howe Island, Norfolk Island, New Zealand and New Caledonia.

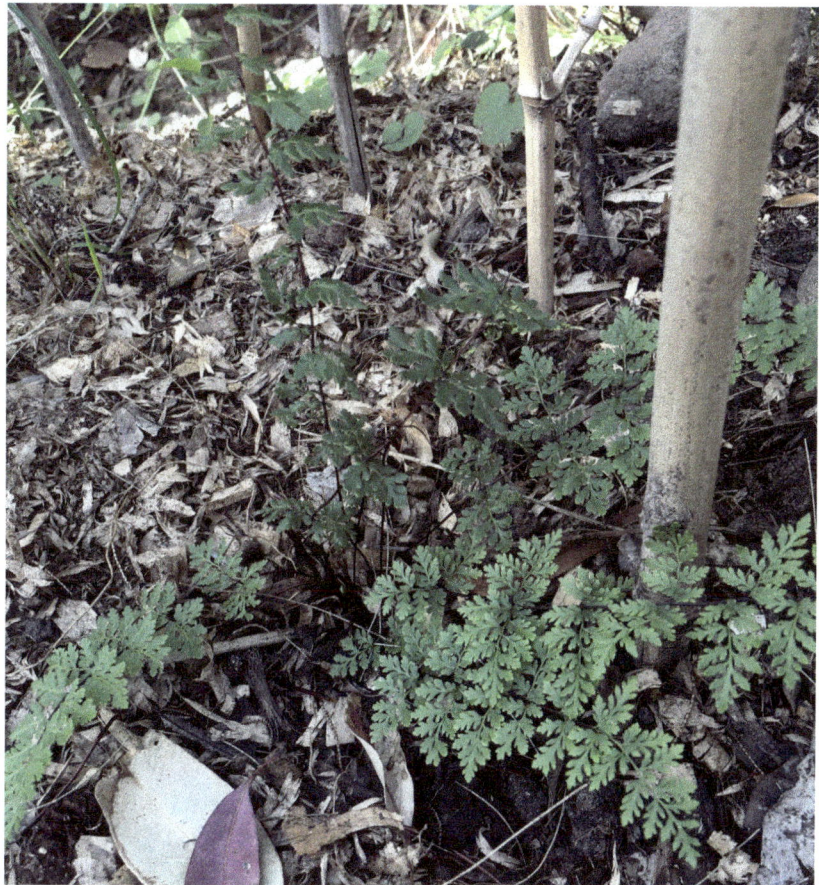

Photo: H Malloy

Other notes: Small, tough fern with appealing dainty, lacy texture. It is possible that not everyone would find it appealing; I have seen it described as harsh. It needs a perfectly weeded site to set off its charms. On top of that, it does not compete well with weeds, and the fronds are easily broken, so it is best sited in a protected location.

Ideal for sunny rockeries or as underplanting for large, openly branching shrubs.

Not available from local native nurseries but you might find it from a specialist fern nursery. Or you may have it already; I have found it several times on my block, and have seen it on damp Scotland Island road reserves, where it can be seen growing in sunny places amongst the weeds.

The genus is of interest for its species' adaptation to arid conditions. The leaves of *C. lasiophylla* (found in western NSW) and many other species curl up as if dead in dry times, and revive rapidly with the return of moisture, thanks to a thick covering of thirsty hairs and scales.

Ω   Full name: *Cheilanthes sieberiana* subsp. *sieberi*

Clematis aristata

Common name(s): Traveller's Joy, Wild Clematis, Goat's Beard, Old Man's Beard (names also applied to northern hemisphere species)

Max. height, usually: 6 m with support.

Max. width, usually: 2 m as groundcover when unsupported.

Form: Vine climbing by means of petioles (leaf stem) and petiolules (leaflet stems) that twine.

Soil: Moist well-drained soil, protected from wind; prefers sandy or loam soils.

Light: Dappled sun.

Flower season: White flowers Sept to Dec.

Best features: Spectacular in flower, with profuse flowers followed by fluffy seedheads (bit like a dandelion); exuberant climber.

Propagation: Seed.

Native to: Sydney and Scotland Island. Studies differ as to whether it is a component of PWSGF[Ω].

Distribution: Widespread on the coast and ranges, in moist or sheltered sites, usually in forest; NSW, Qld, Vic, Tas, WA.

Other notes: Vigorous and rampant climber that can smother other plants; needs regular pruning to keep it under control as a garden subject, if the site is moist and fertile. Can withstand heavy pruning. Best on a fence or trellis well away from other structures or plants unless you want the whole lot covered with Clematis.

C. aristata. Photos (above and below): Gillian Gutridge, *Native Plants of the Northern Beaches, Sydney.* https://nbplantareas.com/

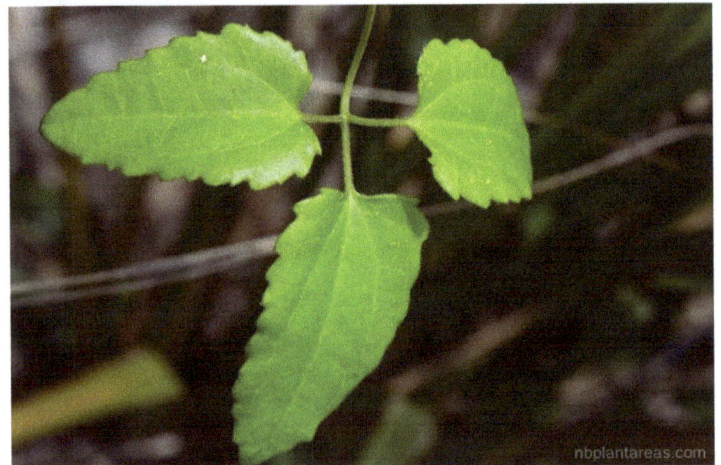

Plants are usually male or female but not both; this arrangement prevents self-fertilisation. Seedlings have leaves that are attractively variegated with a silvery appearance, for a short time.

There is a similar species, *C. glycinoides,* which occurs in similar habitat in NSW, Qld and Vic. The two are hard to differentiate and often occur together in the same location. *C. glycinoides* tends to have less toothing in the leaves and is found in drier areas. The other differences require examining the flowers.

Ω   Bell & Stables 2012 don't report it. OEH 2016 reports it as typical of PSGF.

Clerodendrum tomentosum

Common name(s): Hairy Clary, Downy Chance Tree, Lolly Bush

Max. height, usually: 4 m when unpruned.

Max. width, usually: 1.5 m

Form: Upright shrub.

Soil: Well-drained sandy, clay or loamy soil. Drought-tolerant.

Light: Part shade.

Flower season: White flowers Oct to Feb.

Best features: New leaves velvety; showy white flowers (though not profuse), showy red and green fruit ripening to red and black.

Photos (above and below): Gillian Guttridge, *Native Plants of the Northern Beaches, Sydney.* https://nbplantareas.com/

Propagation: Seed (slow), cuttings.

Native to: Sydney and Scotland Island. Studies differ as to its part in PWSGF.[Σ]

Distribution: Margins of rainforest; widespread in coastal district; NSW, Qld, WA.

Other notes: Often used in bush regeneration work, as it functions

naturally as a bird-dispersed pioneer species. Pollinated by moths with long tongues, if the length of the white floral tube is anything to go by.

Not particularly fast-growing. Responds to pruning, which results in more abundant flowers and fruit. Seems to prefer moist soil, though it is very hardy. Mature specimens can be spectacular.

You may have seedlings of it already if your block is near bushland; look for dark, soft, furry, slightly lobed leaves.

Available from some native plant nurseries.

[Σ]   Bell & Stables 2012 doesn't report it. OEH 2016 reports it as diagnostic for PSGF.

Commelina cyanea

Common name(s): Scurvy Weed, Native Wandering Jew

Max. height, usually: 20 cm

Max. width, usually: Spreads indefinitely.

Form: Sprawling stems with thick fleshy roots emerging at the nodes; tolerates drought.

Soil: Prefers moist loam or clay-based soil.

Light: Prefers half shade; tolerates full sun if moist.

Flower season: Vivid blue flowers spring to autumn, each flower only lasting a day but opening in a steady succession.

Best features: Bright saturated blue colour contrasts well with other wildflowers; fast-growing pioneer species for rehabilitating degraded soil; habitat value for native bees and other invertebrates.

Photo: H Malloy

Propagation: Cuttings and seed, but it is so widespread and fast-growing that generally no action is needed.

Native to: Sydney and Scotland Island; part of PWSGF flora.

Distribution: In moist forest or woodland; sometimes as weed in vegetable gardens; NSW, Qld.

Other notes: When non-native weeds are removed from disturbed areas, often Scurvy Weed colonises the ground so fast that it crowds out other small native groundcovers, forming monocultures over large areas. This situation will generally resolve itself with no assistance required during the cooler months, as Scurvy Weed dies back or grows very weakly in cold weather, giving other plants a chance to establish themselves. Overall, it makes an excellent choice for rehabilitating degraded soil.

Don't let Scurvy Weed encroach in vegetable gardens. Unlike many other native plants, it grows very well with the extra moisture and nutrients of veggie gardens, and it is labour-intensive to remove it where it is not wanted in the short term.

Young shoots are reportedly edible raw or cooked; the name "Scurvy Weed" dates from the days of European settlers when it was used to combat Vitamin C deficiency. The leaves are certainly palatable to a variety of wildlife, as evidenced by the ragged appearance they take on, which limits their attractiveness as a garden plant. But when grown among other plants which camouflage the nibbled leaves, the vivid flower colour more than makes up for its dishevelled state.

Not often carried by native plant nurseries, probably because there is no call for it as it is so ubiquitous. You could place an order to have some grown for you, or dig some up from a friend's property.

Commersonia (formerly Rulingia) hermanniifolia

Common name(s): Wrinkled Kerrawang

Max. height, usually: 1.5 m

Max. width, usually: 2 m

Form: Prostrate or trailing shrub.

Soil: Most reasonably drained soils; drought-tolerant once established.

Light: Full sun to light shade; too much shade inhibits flowering.

Flower season: Pink and white star-like flowers in spring beginning July.

Best features: Intricately detailed flowers and deep green, glossy, wrinkled leaves.

Propagation: Seed, cuttings.

Native to: Sydney but not Scotland Island. Not part of PWSGF. Can be seen on Bangalley Head coastal walk, North Avalon.[Σ] A sandstone-loving species.

Distribution: Endemic to NSW: coastal areas from Broken Bay to Botany Bay, and south to Jervis Bay.

Other notes: Popular and has been in cultivation for many years, so nurseries generally carry it under the old name *Rulingia hermanniifolia (*the name change was made in 2011).

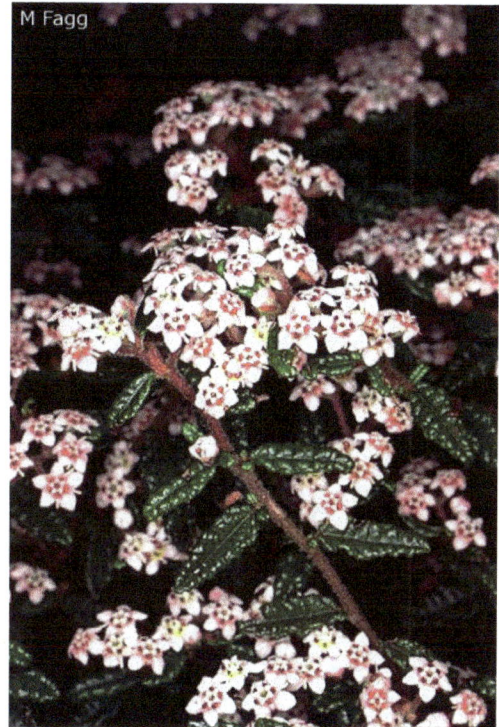

Photo: M Fagg, Australian National Botanic Gardens

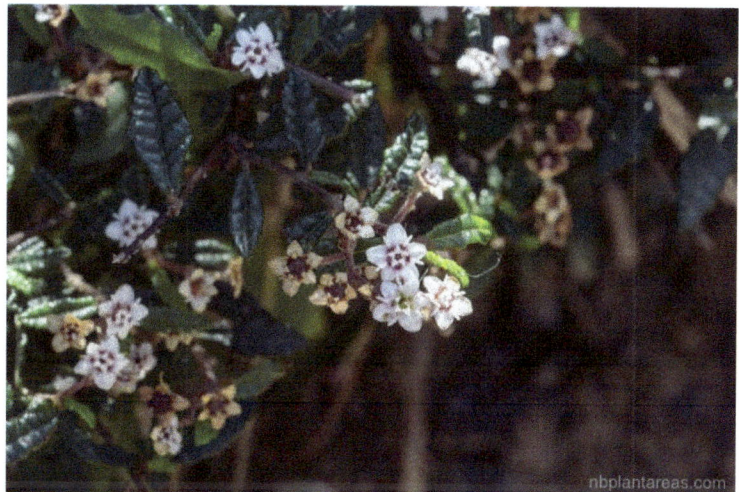

Photo: Gillian Gutridge, *Native Plants of the Northern Beaches, Sydney.* https://nbplantareas.com/

The growth form is naturally trailing and it is well suited for rock gardens, or flowing gracefully down rocky slopes. The flowers are fascinating, with an intricate checkered pattern. Even when not in flower, the dainty wrinkled leaves and trailing stems are strikingly beautiful.

If your garden has clay soil, plant it on a slope to ensure it does not get waterlogged, or grow it in a wide, low pot where you can give it perfect drainage and better admire the flowers. It is very easy to grow in a pot.

Σ   Gillian Gutridge, *Native Plants of the Northern Beaches, Sydney.* https://nbplantareas.com/

Cordyline stricta

Common name(s): Slender Palm Lily or Narrow-leaved Palm Lily

Max. height, usually: 2-3 m; can reach 5 m

Max. width, usually: 1 m for each stem, and multiple stems can form a patch any number of meters wide.

Form: Cluster of stems that can sprawl or arch, each topped with a cluster of strappy leaves.

Soil: Well-drained. Prefers moist but is very drought-tolerant.

Light: Prefers dark, moist gullies but tolerates full sun.

Flower season: Small white to purple flowers are produced in large clusters (panicles) to 40 cm long, in winter and spring, from upper leaf axils, followed by black berries.

Best features: Foliage, form, flower heads and berries. Its tall, narrow growth makes it

Photos (above and below): Jess McGowan

useful as a screen plant near doors. Looks kind of like a palm, but a lot more manageable.

Propagation: Seed, cuttings, division. Seed is said to germinate readily.

Native to: Sydney but not Scotland Island*, and not PWSGF. Nearest wild-collected record was from Bilpin in 1978.

Distribution: Rainforests and wet sclerophyll forests along coast from southern border of Qld to the Sydney region.

Other notes: Can be grown indoors in a pot. Reshoots readily, so can be pruned to any height.

Does not require supplementary watering after establishment.

---

* There are some recent "garden escapes" in Elizabeth Park on the south side of the footpath.

Coronidium (formerly Helichrysum) scorpioides*

Common name(s): Button Everlasting

Max. height, usually: 20 cm

Max. width, usually: 20-30 cm

Form: Erect unbranched woolly-hairy perennial herb spreading from underground stems to form a mat.

Soil: Moist, well-drained soil.

Light: Light shade.

Flower season: Yellow flowers with curling papery bracts, Sept to Dec.

Best features: Long flowering season; long lasting flowers.

Propagation: Seed, cuttings, division. Seed should be planted in autumn or spring, as long as 2-3 months have passed since the seeds were released (seeds may be dormant when fresh). Seed does not last long in storage.

Photo: H Malloy

Native to: Sydney but not Scotland Island and not PWSGF. Recorded as wild-collected in Mona Vale in 1945.

Distribution: In well-drained open forest to heathy woodlands, rarely grasslands or heathland. Widespread and common through south-eastern Australia near the coast, Qld, NSW, SA, Tas.

Other notes: Attracts butterflies.

Photo: Harry Rose 2016 https://www.flickr.com/photos/macleaygrassman/32675812296
https://creativecommons.org/licenses/by/2.0/

Good as a drift under established trees. New shoots appear in autumn, after the original plant stops flowering for the season.

---

* *Helichrysum* is now recognised as a genus of African and Eurasian species. Australian members have been reclassified into a number of groups including *Coronidium*.

Correa alba

Common name(s): White Correa

Max. height, usually: 1.5 m

Max. width, usually: 1.5 m

Form: Small rounded shrub.

Soil: Prefers sandy soil but tolerates most reasonably drained soils including clay; very tolerant of salt spray; tolerates drought once established. Does not tolerate waterlogging.

Light: Full sun; tolerates semi-shade, with flowering reduced somewhat.

Flower season: Chiefly Apr to June, with some flowers sporadically all year.

Best features: Fast-growing; attractive silvery woolly leaves and stem; pretty flowers in winter.

Propagation: Cuttings; seeds are difficult.

Native to: Sydney but not Scotland Island. Not a component of PWSGF. Nearest wild-collected records are Avalon 1957 and Barrenjoey 1946.

Distribution: Sandy and rocky situations near sea; in NSW chiefly south from Port Stephens; also Vic, Tas.

Other notes: Tip prune to keep it symmetrical if desired; tends to sprawl.

There are pink forms available, which can grow larger than the white form, up to 2 m. The pink form is said to be less reliable.

Widely available and many cultivars are available commercially, including a prostrate form by the name of "Star Showers", a compact form, and a small-statured form with a longer flowering period (autumn to spring).

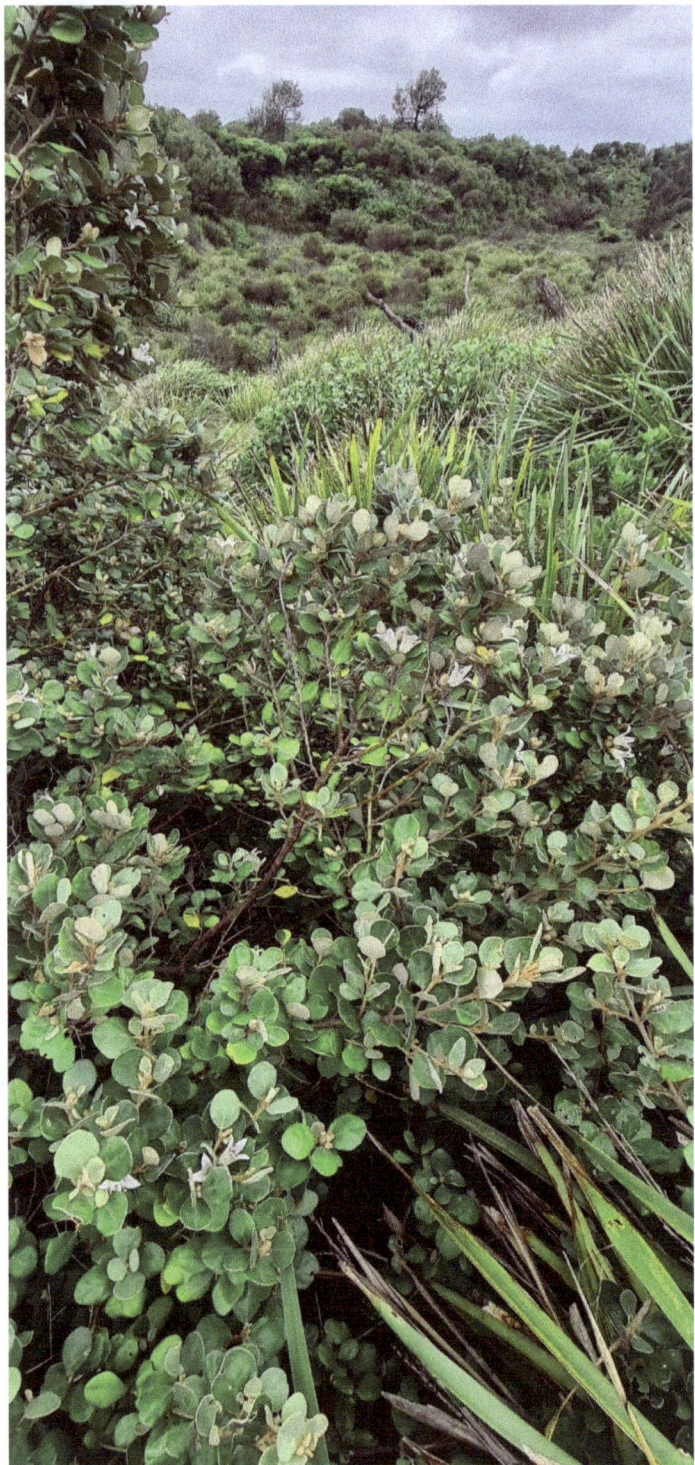

Photo: Jenny aka Floydwafer, iNaturalist

Correa reflexa

Common name(s): Common Correa or Native Fuchsia

Max. height, usually: Varies from prostrate to 1.5 m

Max. width, usually: .5 m to 1 m

Form: Prostrate or upright shrub with rusty-woolly stems.

Soil: Practically any soil including clay; prefers sandy soil with good drainage.

Light: Some shade; prefers dappled with afternoon shade.

Flower season: Red and green (sometimes all green) flowers Apr to Sept and intermittently throughout year.

Best features: Striking flowers in the off-season; tidy habit.

Propagation: Easy from cuttings.

Native to: Sydney but not Scotland Island. Not a component of PWSGF. A sandstone-loving species. Can be seen at Bangalley Headland (green-flowered form), Deep Creek track and Katandra Bushland Sanctuary[Ω].

Distribution: Dry sclerophyll forest and heath on sandstone or dunes; NSW, Qld, Vic, Tas, SA.

Other notes: Unusually for a sandstone-loving species, it is very adaptable to garden situations. Survives neglect, but appearance suffers. Mulch with rich, well-aged compost, and provide regular, deep watering. Tip-prune in late spring, after its main flowering period is over. Avoid pruning after mid-summer so as not to cut off any incipient flower buds that are gearing up for the main flowering in winter.

Photos (above and below): Gillian Guttridge, *Native Plants of the Northern Beaches, Sydney*. https://nbplantareas.com/

Highly variable in leaf and flower, even within the same populations. There are about 20 distinct forms or varieties across its wide range. The two occurring in NSW are *reflexa* and *speciosa*; *reflexa* is the one seen locally in the Northern Beaches (shown in photos). It is said to be hardier in gardens than other varieties, and its shape is attractive even when it is not in flower.

Most native plant nurseries carry it. Many cultivars and hybrids are available commercially, but you may have more success with our local variety rather than named cultivars from commercial nurseries, which may originate from far away.

Ω   Gillian Guttridge, *Native Plants of the Northern Beaches, Sydney*. https://nbplantareas.com/

Corymbia maculata

Common name(s): Spotted Gum

Max. height, usually: 30 m (up to 45-60 m).

Max. width, usually: 15 m

Form: Medium to tall tree.

Soil: Well-drained.

Light: Full sun when mature, but seedlings require light shade.

Flower season: White flowers in winter.

Best features: Attractive bark; prolific flowers attract many nectar-feeding animals.

Propagation: Seed. Volunteer seedlings can be easily transplanted up to the 3-leaf stage into pots for planting out in more appropriate places in autumn. Seedlings easily recognised by rough magenta fuzz on the first few true leaves and the kidney-shaped seed leaves.

Self-seeds readily, but seedlings expire on sites that have been stripped of natural groundcover. Seedlings need the shade and protection of undergrowth when young, and so natural regeneration is not often seen on residential blocks.

Native to: Sydney and Scotland Island. The very essence of both Dry and Moist PWSGF.

Distribution: Endemic to open forest along coast of NSW up to Qld, with a disjunct population in Vic.

Other notes: Bark sheds in early summer and can be collected for mulch, compost additive, or paths. The very deep roots of Spotted Gums do not compete with the shallower roots of native grasses and groundcovers, so you can plant close to the trunks.[*][†]

Slow-growing, and young trees have the appearance of attractive shrubs for many years, with large shiny dark green leaves.

A 59 m specimen known as "Old Blotchy" in Termeil, NSW with a diameter of 3.4 m is estimated to be in excess of 400 years old.[‡]

Photo: H Malloy

Rainbow lorikeet feeding on nectar in the flowers. Photo: Christine Ashe http://christmashills.blogspot.com

Spotted Gum Seedlings. Photo: H. Malloy 2022

---

[*]   https://era.daf.qld.gov.au/id/eprint/3902/4/Spotted%20gum%20final%20factsheet_update%20May%202017.pdf

[†]   https://agroforestry.net.au/main.asp?_=Spotted%20Gum

[‡]   https://anpsa.org.au/the-largest-spotted-gum-in-the-world/

Crinum pedunculatum

Common name(s): Swamp Lily, River Lily or Mangrove Lily

Max. height, usually: 2 m

Max. width, usually: 2-3 m

Form: Large bulb-forming strap-leaved plant, with big bunches of flowers on long stalks.

Soil: Tolerates almost any soil as long as it is moist, including clay and poorly drained. Salt and drought tolerant.

Light: Prefers dappled shade, but will grow in full sun (but then requiring supplemental water).

Flower season: Sweetly fragrant white flowers Nov to Mar.

Best features: Dramatic form; exuberant flowers.

Propagation: Seed; bulbils; division of bulbs.

Native to: Sydney but not Scotland Island and not PWSGF. Nearest wild-collected record is Minnamurra River (Illawarra region) in 1970.

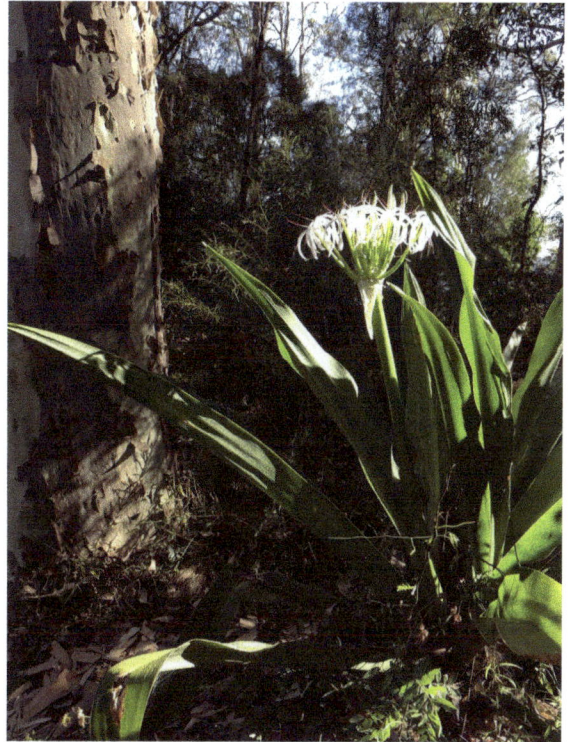

Photo: H Malloy

Distribution: Swamps and stream banks in coastal districts and on offshore islands; NSW, Qld, NT.

Other notes: Prone to attack by slugs and snails as well as caterpillars. Can thrive in dry spots, as long as it is shaded by trees, shrubs and groundcover, or well mulched.

Over time, each rosette develops a naked "trunk". It is soft, not woody, and the plant can be easily rejuvenated by lopping it off at ground level. A new shoot will arise from the bulb, though it may take a few years to flower again afterwards.

The flowers have the characteristics of coevolution for pollination by sphinx moths, a family of large, often attractive moths with a long tongue. This includes pale flower colour, long floral tube containing nectar, flowers remaining open at night, and sweet fragrance.[*] But as far as I know, no one has seen sphinx moths on this particular *Crinum* species.

Convolvulus Hawkmoth (*Agrius convolvuli*) – a sphinx moth common in the Sydney area – could in theory pollinate the flowers, or perhaps the species is self-pollinating. Photo: Carol and Trevor Deane. http://butterfliesdorrigo.weebly.com/agrius-convolvuli-convolvulus-hawk-moth.html

---

[*] J.C. Manning and D. Snijman, 2002. Hawkmoth-pollination in *Crinum variabile* (Amaryllidaceae) and the biogeography of sphingophily in southern African Amaryllidaceae. *South African Journal of Botany* 68: 2. https://www.sciencedirect.com/science/article/pii/S0254629915304221

Crowea saligna

Common name(s): Willow-leaf Crowea

Max. height, usually: 1 m

Max. width, usually: 1 m

Form: Small shrub with angled branches.

Soil: Prefers well-drained moist, but reasonably drought-tolerant once established. Prefers loam, sandy loam, or sandy soil; tolerates clay. Does not tolerate waterlogging. Plant on a slope if your soil is clay-based.

Light: Prefers part shade; tolerates full sun if well watered. Best with afternoon shade.

Flower season: Bright pink large flowers late autumn to winter, sometimes also in spring.

Best features: Large flowers in the "off" season, aromatic foliage, tidy habit.

Propagation: Cuttings. Seed is erratic.

Native to: Sydney and Scotland Island. Not part of PWSGF. Can be seen on many Northern Beaches bushwalks, including Chiltern Trail, Cromer Heights, Deep Creek, and Terrey Hills.

Distribution: Endemic to Sydney and Blue Mountains, in sclerophyll forest or heaths.

Other notes: Can be hard to establish though it is hardy once established, so plant several, mulch, and water carefully (too much is as bad as not enough). Adding well-aged compost when planting can be helpful. Lightly prune after flowering to maintain bushiness.

Photos (above and below): Gillian Gutridge, *Native Plants of the Northern Beaches, Sydney.* https://nbplantareas.com/

Available from native nurseries, though it can be hard to find it in stock.

Many cultivars and/or hybrids available commercially, such as "Poorinda Ecstasy", "Rosy Glow", "Large Flower" and "Festival". "Poorinda Ecstasy" is said to be hardier than other forms. As a general rule, however, the local native form is to be preferred, as it is more likely to do well and not accidentally hybridise with the local forms.

Cullen tenax

Common name(s): Emu-foot, Native Lucerne, Tough Scurf-pea

Max. height, usually: .5 m

Max. width, usually: 1.5 m

Form: Slender trailing native pea with lush green fan-shaped leaves.

Soil: Prefers moist, heavy clay soil; drought-tolerant.

Light: Full sun, part sun, filtered sun.

Flower season: Bluish pea flowers in spikes Aug to Mar.

Best features: Unusual palmately divided leaves; long flowering season; host plant for three (or more) beautiful species of butterfly.

Propagation: Seed, which remains viable 10+ years.

Native to: Sydney but not Scotland Island. Not a component of PWSGF. Nearest wild-collected record is Collaroy, 1968.

Distribution: Widespread, in forest or grassland, on heavy soils; NSW, Qld, Vic.

Photos (above and below): Garry Sankowsky, www.rainforestmagic.com.au

Other notes: This plant is a rarity – a species that actually prefers heavy clay soil and may be unhappy on lighter soil. It is also rare in the sense that it is generally only the keenest of native plant (or butterfly) enthusiasts who have heard of it. It is hard to even find seeds of it for sale, let alone plants.

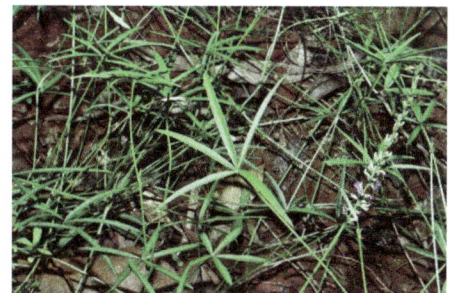

Forms rounded mounds, with the flowers held above the foliage. Flower is a little similar to *Glycine,* but larger and better presented as a garden subject. A larger-leaf form is found west of the Dividing Range[Σ].

Main host plant in Eastern Australia for a showy, beautiful butterfly, the Chequered Swallowtail (*Papilio demoleus*).

Palatable to livestock, which perhaps accounts for its current relative scarcity, given how widespread it is (or once was) on the east coast. Liable to removal when mistaken for a weed ("too pretty to be a native"), or mown (it readily grows amongst grass). A herbarium collection made in 1968 in Collaroy carries the notation "found covering a moderate area – regarded as weed to be eradicated".[*]

Σ   Pers. comm. from Patricia Gardner, Toowoomba, Quyeensland

*   https://images.ala.org.au/image/details?imageId=103e0655-c867-4908-b3b6-cdcb6159981e

Cyanthillium (formerly Vernonia) cinerarea[Ψ]

Common name(s): Iron Weed, Fleabane, Purple Fleabane

Max. height, usually: 50 cm

Max. width, usually: 20 cm

Form: Annual or short-lived perennial herb.

Soil: Most soils, wet or dry; tolerates drought and poor soils.

Light: Full sun, light dappled shade.

Flower season: Purple-mauve flowers summer to autumn.

Best features: Tolerates harsh conditions; leaves are a pleasing ashy dark green, with purplish undertones that pick up the flower colour.

Photos (above and below): H Malloy

Propagation: Seed.

Native to: Sydney and Scotland Island[Σ]. Not reported as part of PWSGF, but it has been reported for two vegetation communities similar to PWSGF in the Lake Macquarie district[Ω]. Nearest wild-collected records are from Avalon in 1957 and KCNP in 1951.

Distribution: Found in most of the world's tropical regions, frequently as a weed of waste places, but also in moist forest and rainforest.

Other notes: Authorities disagree as to whether this plant is native or introduced to Australia[Φ]. I think the issue is whether people assisted its arrival or not.

It is said to originate from tropical Africa and Asia, where there is a long history of using the leaves as a cooked vegetable, and for many different medicinal purposes, especially in India.

I am not sure if it is a good garden candidate, as it appears to self-seed. But it does not seem to be invasive, and it definitely has some appeal.

Ψ *Cyanthillium cinereum* var. *cinereum* since 1990, as per NSW Flora Online. The name *Vernonia* is also still widely used.

Σ It is possible it has only arrived on the island in the last five or so years, as it has not appeared in any previous surveys.

Ω Bell, S.A.J. (2016) *Volume 2: Vegetation Community Profiles, Lake Macquarie Local Government Area. Working Draft v2.* Unpublished Report to Lake Macquarie City Council. March 2016. Eastcoast Flora Survey.

Φ Les Robinson's *Field Guide to the Native Plants of Sydney* treats it as native. See NSW Flora Online for more information.

Cymbopogon refractus

Common name(s): Barb Wire Grass, Native Lemon Grass

Max. height, usually: 1 m

Max. width, usually: .5 m

Form: Clumping grass.

Soil: Prefers sandy loam. Tolerates any soil, including infertile and clay-based. Very drought tolerant, and tolerant of eroded sites.

Light: Prefers full sun; tolerates partial shade.

Flower season: Flowers all year, but mainly spring to autumn.

Best features: Blue-green leaves with purple base, turning orange-brown in autumn. Striking seed heads on arching stems. Long lived. Lemony-orangey scent when crushed (useful for tea).

Propagation: Seed. Unusually for a native grass, it does not have a dormancy period, and fresh seed will germinate readily.

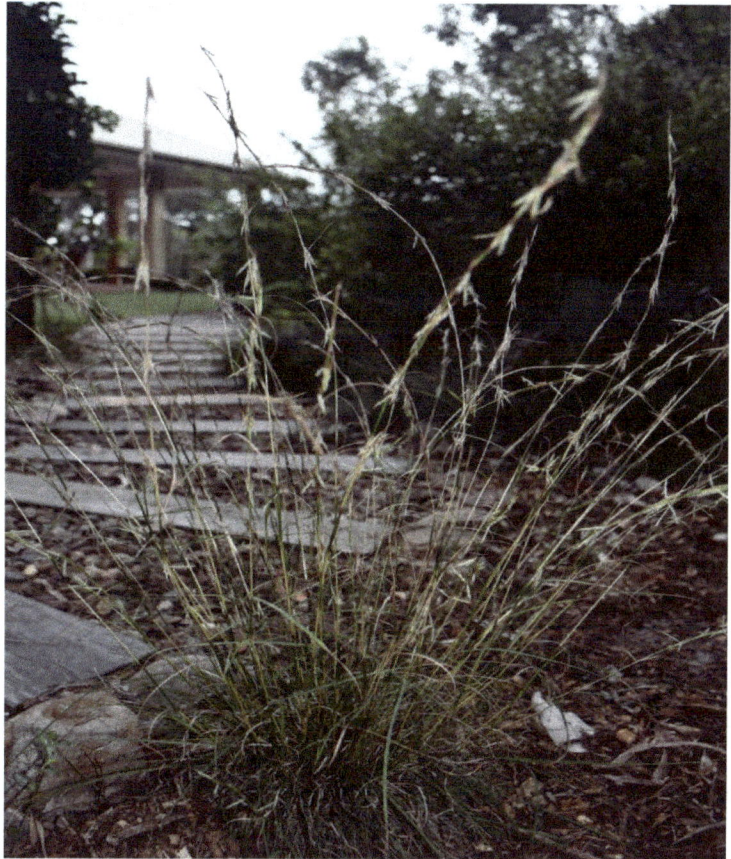

Photo: Jude Tulloch, Marcus Beach Bushcare Association, Qld.
https://mbba.org.au/cymbopogan-refractus-barded-wire-grass/

Native to: Sydney and Scotland Island. A component of Dry PWSGF, but not typical.

Distribution: Widespread in the eucalyptus forests and woodlands of eastern Australia, especially on lighter soils of low fertility; rare in northern NT.

Other notes: Can cut back after flowering to allow emergence of new growth. Similar in size and form to Kangaroo Grass. Attractive when planted with Kangaroo Grass or by itself in a group.

Does not need any fertilising but appreciates supplemental watering during drought.

Grows most actively in the warm season (C4 grass), and very little if any in the winter.

Despite the name, leaves and seed heads are soft, not raspy or sharp.

Davallia solida var. pyxidata

Common name(s): Hare's Foot Fern

Max. height, usually: 60 cm

Max. width, usually: Creeps indefinitely.

Form: Fern with creeping rhizomes.

Soil: None; normally grows on rocks or trees. To grow in the ground, choose a well-drained position in shade and replace most of the original soil with well-aged bark, coir peat and sand in equal measures, simulating the detritus that accumulates in tree crevices. Drought-tolerant.

Light: Prefers dappled morning sun to full shade; tolerates part sun as long as it has overhead shade.

Flower season: n/a

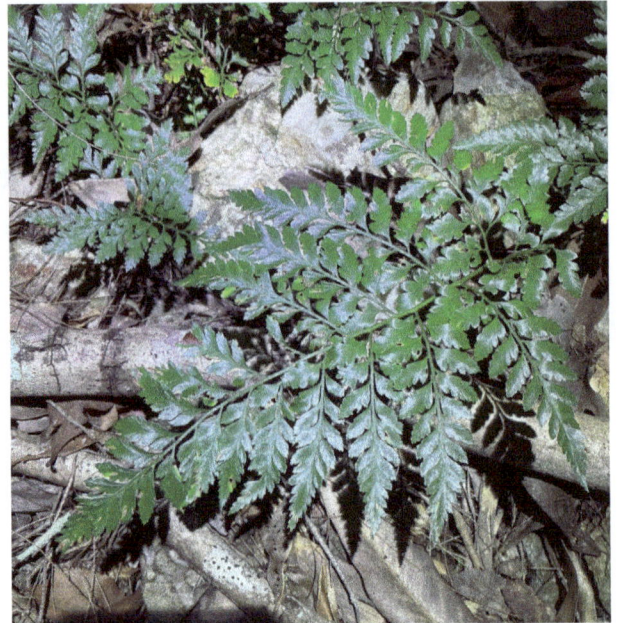

In Spring MountainReserve (near Brisbane). Photos (above and below): Greg Tasney, iNaturalist. https://creativecommons.org/licenses/by-sa/4.0/

Best features: The creeping rhizomes poke out of the soil and are covered with long, pointed brown scales, giving the overall appearance of a hare's or rabbit's foot (or perhaps a giant spider). The finely divided, dark green leaves are attractive in their own right.

Propagation: Break off pieces of rhizome containing a few leaves each and lay on prepared suitable soil-free medium in shaded place.

Native to: Sydney and Scotland Island. Not PWSGF. Nearest wild-collected records are Church Point, Newport and KCNP.

Distribution: Widespread rainforest epiphyte, also on rocks in open forests; NSW, Qld, Vic, Tas.

Other notes: Popular as a houseplant, in coir-lined wire baskets, allowing the furry rhizomes to creep over the edges and hang down like dangling legs.

On Scotland Island it grows in Elizabeth Park and in several road reserves – a good reason to adopt your road reserve and keep it weeded.

Available at some native plant nurseries. Be wary of buying at general nurseries because they may sell you one of the 50 non-native species in the genus.

Dendrobium kingianum

Common name(s): Pink Rock Orchid

Max. height, usually: 30 cm

Max. width, usually: 30 cm

Form: Lithophytic (rock-growing) orchid.

Soil: None; normally grows on rocks. When grown in pots or in the ground, prefers orchid-growing bark or loose, fast-draining detritus such as aged bark pieces, coconut shell chips, woodchips, charcoal etc. (not soil)

Light: Full sun to dappled shade.

Flower season: Delicately scented pink flowers in spring.

Growing in Sherwood Nature Reserve, near Coffs Harbour. Photo: Geoff Derrin. https://creativecommons.org/licenses/by-sa/4.0/

Best features: The most beautiful plant you can possibly grow for the least amount of effort.

Propagation: Division, or pull off the keikis (aerial bulbils that form on shoots after flowering finishes) when they have developed leaves and a few roots and pot them up.

Native to: Sydney but not Scotland Island and not PWSGF. Nearest wild-collected record is from Wahroonga (near Hornsby), 1945.

Distribution: Grows on rocks or occasionally on soil and very rarely on trees in open forest to woodland and in exposed situations; NSW, Qld.

Other notes: Widely cultivated. The qualities that allow it to grow on sheer rock faces make it one of the hardiest of orchids. In a garden, it is easiest in unglazed terracotta pots but looks best when grown on rocks, logs or old stumps. Fertilise every two weeks after flowering with a weak organic fertiliser, and water regularly through the active growing period, which is Aug to Mar. Withhold water and fertiliser in autumn and winter for best flowering; otherwise it puts its efforts into new shoots at the expense of flowers.

Avoid using high-nitrogen fertilisers at any time, as it is said that they promote the growth of keikis (pups or offshoots) at the expense of new flowering shoots (unless you want new keikis of course).

Widely available from native plant nurseries, orchid specialists and commercial nurseries. Or (best) ask a neighbour who has one to give you a keiki (pup).

Dendrobium linguiforme (also known as Dockrillia linguiformis)[Ω]

Common name(s): Tongue Orchid

Max. height, usually: 4 cm

Max. width, usually: Spreads indefinitely.

Form: Epiphytic or epilithic orchid.

Soil: None; normally grows on rocks. Can be planted in orchid-growing bark.

Light: Part sun to dappled sun.

Flower season: Sprays of delicate-looking white flowers in spring.

Best features: Interesting leaves; lovely fragrant flowers; easy care.

Propagation: Division.

Native to: Sydney and Scotland Island. Not part of PWSGF.

Distribution: Grows on rocks and trees, usually in sclerophyll forest, also in rainforest and in exposed rocky sites; NSW, Qld.

Other notes: The leaves are modified to store water; each leaf has longitudinal furrows on the upper surface which allow it to shrink during dry weather and expand when rain returns.

Growing in Katandra Bushland Sanctuary. Photos (above and below): Gillian Gutridge, https://nbplantareas.com

Even hardier than *Dendrobium kingianum,* but its creeping nature makes pot culture impractical; it keeps trying to climb out of the pot. Within the normal distribution of the plant, it can simply be tied to a slab, tree, or rock and left in a fairly open location, until the roots adhere to the support. Water lightly every morning during spring and summer, and move to a shadier spot if it shrivels.

[Ω] Also known as *Dockrillia linguiformis* var. *linguiformis*, a name which is not recognised by the Australian Plant Name Index.

SYDNEY LOCAL NATIVE

Dianella caerulea var. producta

Common name(s): Blue Flax Lily or Paroo Lily

Max. height, usually: 1.3 m

Max. width, usually: 1.3 m or indefinite.

Form: Tufted strappy-leaved plant with creeping rhizomes and attractive blue flowers as well as blue berries.

Soil: Any. Drought-tolerant and tolerant of moderate waterlogging. Prefers moist well-drained. Tolerates salt and wind.

Light: Prefers full sun or part sun; tolerates shade but flowering and growth will be less.

Photo: Brian Walters, Australian Native Plants Society (Australia). https://anpsa.org.au/native-plant-profiles/

Flower season: Blue-violet flowers in spring, follwed by edible blue-violet berries.

Best features: Incredibly tough and hardy; strappy leaves provide nice contrast in the garden; nice flowers and fruit.

Propagation: Seed or division. You can pull up unwanted shoots and pot them into tubestock pots; they will grow new roots within a few weeks, if watered well and kept out of direct sun.

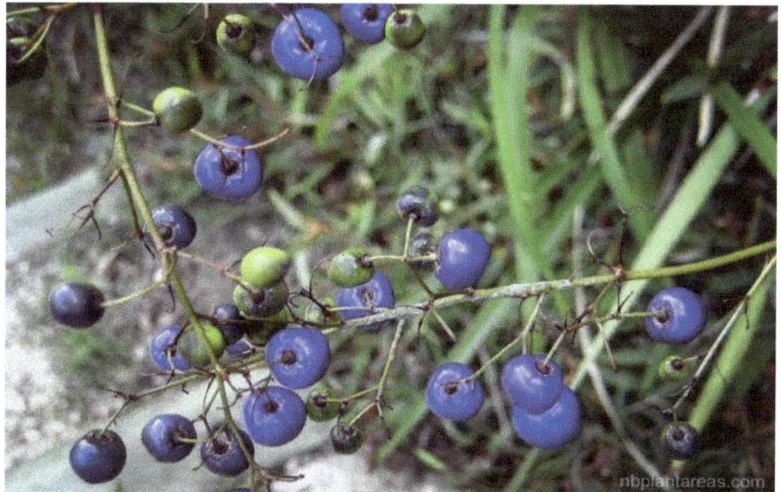

Photo: Gillian Gutridge, *Native Plants of the Northern Beaches, Sydney.* https://nbplantareas.com/

Native to: Sydney and Scotland Island. Typical component of Dry PWSGF.

Distribution (for our variety): Chiefly on rocky hillsides in NSW, Qld.

Other notes: The vividly blue-purple berries are edible but rather tasteless. Better to leave them for the King Parrots and Eastern Rosellas, who relish them. Requires no supplemental watering.

Works well to soften the look around the base of large trees such as Spotted Gums, which have deep roots and tend not to compete with groundcover planted around their bases.

Works well as an edge-definer along paths or bordering large garden beds. In such locations, it may be necessary to restrict its spread by pulling up excess shoots, because it spreads at a moderate pace; this is very easily done and the shoots can be potted up into tubestock pots.

Dichelachne crinita

Common name(s): Longhair Plume Grass

Max. height, usually: 1.5 m

Max. width, usually: .5 m

Form: Clumping grass.

Soil: Prefers sandy soil but tolerates most soils; tolerates drought.

Light: Full sun (i.e. at least four hours of direct sun).

Flower season: Fluffy green to purple-tinged seed heads in late spring to summer.

Best features: Long-lasting dramatic cream-coloured hairy plumes remain on the plant after the seed has ripened.

Propagation: Seeds.

Native to: Sydney but not Scotland Island and not PWSGF. Nearest wild-collected record is Dee Why in 1932.

Distribution: Open and cleared areas in grassland to woodland on sand or soils derived from sandstone. Native to all states of Australia; also New Guinea, Norfolk Island, Kermadec Islands and New Zealand.

Photos (above and below): Bungalook Nursery, Victoria

Other notes: Best in mass planting. Remove plumes in late summer to encourage new growth.

Unlike many other grasses, its period of greatest growth is the cooler months, so you will not see much new growth after the flowering period is over in summer – until the temperature begins to fall in March.

When it is too shaded, the stems tend to fall over and recline on the ground, which is not very attractive. Because of this, it is best for sites where it gets at least four hours of direct sun each day.

Most native plant nurseries carry it on their stocklists.

For shadier sites, consider the equally beautiful but less flamboyant *D. rara*. It has a spray of delicate florets most of the year rather than a condensed plume, and grows up to 1.3 m. *D. rara* is native to Scotland Island and is available at some native plant nurseries.

Dichondra repens

Common name(s): Kidney Weed

Max. height, usually: 4 cm

Max. width, usually: 2 m

Form: Groundcover with creeping habit, roots forming at the nodes.

Soil: Prefers clay or clay-based soils, moist with medium to high levels of nutrients. Will tolerate sandy, poor soil. Drought resistant when established.

Light: Prefers shaded. Will grow in sunny spots with supplemental watering. Leaves grow smaller with higher light levels.

Flower season: Small starry green to white flowers at all times of the year, which are usually concealed by the leaves.

Best features: Kidney-shaped leaves with appealing downy texture and sculpted veins are generally attractive year round.

Photo: H Malloy

Propagation: Division.

Native to: Sydney and Scotland Island. Studies differ as to whether it is a component of PWSGF or PSGF.[*]

Distribution: All areas of Australia.

Other notes: A member of Convulvulaceae, the morning glory family.

Good lawn or living mulch alternative but will not stand up to heavy traffic.

Attractive when grown as a dense mat without any other species present, but also combines well with other groundcovers for a more natural tapestry-style look. It is well-behaved and does not overwhelm other small plants.

---

[*]   Bell & Stables 2012 did not report it. OEH 2016 reported it as present in 18% of their sites, but also present in non-PSGF sites.

Dodonaea pinnata

Common name(s): Fern-leaf Dodonaea

Max. height, usually: 1.5 m

Max. width, usually: 1 m

Form: Shrub.

Soil: Well-drained; prefers sandy; tolerates drought.

Light: Dappled shade.

Flower season: Insignificant flowers in early spring, followed by (on female plants only) red papery winged fruits.

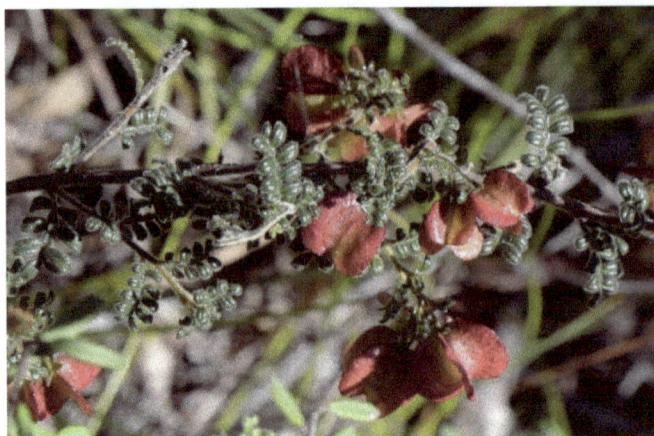

Photo: Gillian Gutridge, *Native Plants of the Northern Beaches, Sydney.* https://nbplantareas.com/

Best features: Appealing furry fernlike foliage; decorative red winged fruit contrasting well with foliage.

Propagation: Seed, cuttings.

Native to: Sydney but not Scotland Island and not PWSGF. Can be seen on several Northern Beaches bushwalking trails – Chiltern, Cromer Heights, and Deep Creek[Σ].

Distribution: Endemic to NSW, in dry sclerophyll forest on sandstone-derived soils confined to Nepean and Hawkesbury R. systems.

Other notes: Not well known in cultivation and I have only just become acquainted with it. *D. pinnata* would be a real winner in the garden if it turns out to be even half as easy as *D. triquetra*, which is extremely hardy (but not such a looker). As its range is so restricted, it is probably a sandstone-loving species.

Sometimes available at native plant nurseries.

On the Chiltern Track, Ku-ring-gai NP. Photo: Marita Macrae

Σ   Gillian Gutridge, *Native Plants of the Northern Beaches, Sydney.* https://nbplantareas.com/

Dodonaea triquetra

Common name(s): Hop Bush

Max. height, usually: 3 m

Max. width, usually: 1-2 m

Form: Erect shrub, with separate plants for male and female.

Soil: Prefers sandy, well-drained soil; tolerates clay. Extreme waterlogging can kill it. Very drought resistant.

Light: Full sun, semi-shade.

Flower season: Insignificant flowers in early spring, followed by (on female plants only) papery winged fruits.

Best features: Fast-growing screen. The bunches of winged fruits (female plants only) are often red-tinged and very decorative.

Propagation: Seed.

Native to: Sydney and Scotland Island. Studies differ as to whether it is a component of PWSGF or PSGF.[*] Occurs in KCNP. Can be seen on numerous bushwalking trails such as Bangalley Head, Chiltern, and Deep Creek[Ω].

Distribution: NSW, Qld and Vic; dry and wet sclerophyll forest usually in sand or sandstone, along east coast.

Other notes: Plants are usually either male or female but not both. The decorative winged fruits form on female plants regardless of whether or not the flowers have been pollinated. Seeds are relished by King Parrots.

Pioneer plant which grows abundantly after bushfire. Older plants can become leggy it not tip-pruned from a young age.

Photo: Jenna aka Floydwafer, iNaturalist

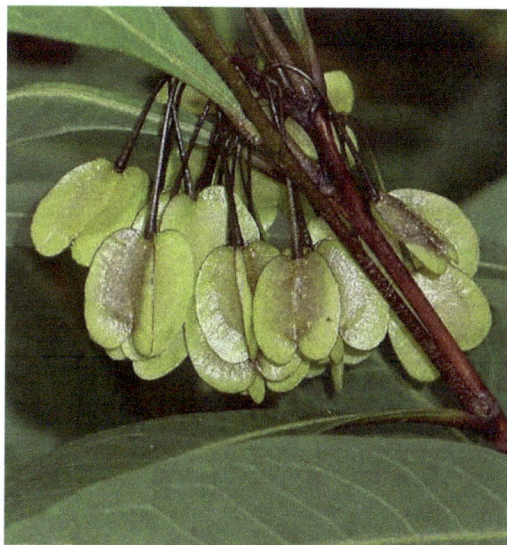
Photo: Robert Whyte, Save Our Waterways Now

Best to plant more Hop Bushes after your first ones are starting to get leggy, as they are not long-lived. Or plant slower-growing shrubs at the same time as your Hop Bushes, so they can take over when the fast-growing Hop Bushes run out of steam.

---

[*]   Bell & Stables 2012 did not report it. OEH 2016 reported it as present in 18% of their sites, but also present in non-PSGF sites.
[Ω]   Gillian Gutridge, *Native Plants of the Northern Beaches, Sydney.* https://nbplantareas.com/

Doodia aspera

Common name(s): Prickly Rasp Fern

Max. height, usually: .4 m

Max. width, usually: spreads indefinitely via creeping rhizomes.

Form: Ground-cover fern with leathery, textured leaves held upright.

Soil: Clay, loam, or sandy; prefers humus-rich, moist, well-drained acidic soil; relatively drought-tolerant, for a fern anyway.

Photo: Bill de Belin http://nativeplants-sydney.blogspot.com/2013/07/

Light: Prefers light shade with protection from afternoon sun.

Flower season: n/a

Best features: New fronds are bright pink, turning to deep green as they age.

Propagation: Division; spores.

Native to: Sydney but not Scotland Island. A component of Moist PWSGF, but not typical.

Distribution: Widespread, in tall open forest and rainforest margins; NSW, Qld, Vic.

Other notes: There is a sizable colony in Elizabeth Park on Scotland Island, along the footpath. Grows particularly well under large trees when leaf litter is left on top of them. If you are planting to a new spot, dig some well-aged compost into the soil beforehand, and mulch well.

Prune the old growth away at the end of winter to prompt lots of pink new fronds to develop, and allow them to be seen well. Don't wait too long if you are going to do it, or else you risk cutting off developing spring fronds. Also puts out a smaller new flush of leaves if there are summer rains.

Readily grows from spores and it is worth checking when you buy nursery tubestock to see if you got some free rasp ferns with them. Also check around for baby ferns in any forgotten half-filled pots you have laying around.

In a garden situation, can grow so well that it kills small shrubs, so site it with care.

Doryanthes excelsa

Common name(s): Gymea Lily

Max. height, usually: 4 m when in flower.

Max. width, usually: 2.5 m

Form: Very large clump or rosette of sword-shaped fibrous leaves.

Soil: Prefers deep, well drained, moist soils with added organic matter; drought- and wind-tolerant.

Light: Prefers full sun; tolerates part shade.

Flower season: Spring; flowering spike begins in winter, on plants at least 8 years old. Seed pods ripen in mid- to late summer.

Best features: Dramatic form, both in and out of flower.

Propagation: Seed; division.

Native to: Sydney but not Scotland Island. Not a component of PWSGF. Can be seen at Katandra Bushland Sanctuary.

Distribution: Endemic to NSW, in dry sclerophyll forest and woodland on sandstone and partly clay soil, mostly in Sydney region, but with three isolated northern populations in North Coast region.

Other notes: As the plant grows, its strong roots contract to pull the

Photo: Wikimedia Commons, user: Eug. https://creativecommons.org/licenses/sa/1.0/

growing point of the rosette down under ground. This keeps it from developing a naked trunk, and helps it to survive bushfire. It also explains why the plants do better in deep soil.

Does well on Scotland Island, including on the clay soils of waterfront properties.

Echinopogon ovatus

Common name(s): Forest Hedgehog-grass

Max. height, usually: 70 cm

Max. width, usually: 15 cm to indefinite.

Form: Clumping grass spreading by underground stems, stems reclining.

Soil: Prefers moist, well-drained.

Light: Dappled shade.

Flower season: Spring to summer.

Best features: Soft bristly roundish flowerheads are attractive.

Propagation: Seed.

Native to: Sydney and Scotland Island[*]. A similar species, *E. caespitosus*, is present but not typical in Dry PWSGF.

Distribution: Wet sclerophyll woodland and by creeks; widespread in all Australian states; also New Guinea, Lesser Sunda Islands, New Zealand.

Other notes: The stems are bent at the joints and recline on the ground when not supported. Good with an upright shade-loving grass, such as *Poa affinis*, to help hold up the floppy stems.

Leaves and stems are raspy to the touch, so perhaps not too good along paths. The raspiness, which is caused by tiny teeth pointing only in the downwards direction, helps it to hang onto other plants to stay upright. When it is growing on its own, its stems grow much shorter, and its curling leaves can be seen.

E. caespitosus, a very similar species, would in theory make a better garden subject, as its stems do not lie down on the ground. However, it is not shade-tolerant, and *E. ovatus* does better in the shaded conditions on my block.

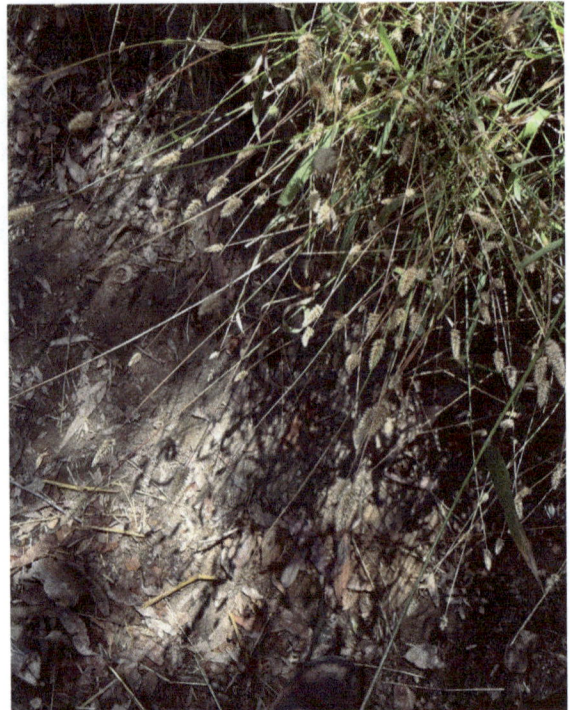

Growing along fire trail at top of Scotland Island. Photo: H Malloy

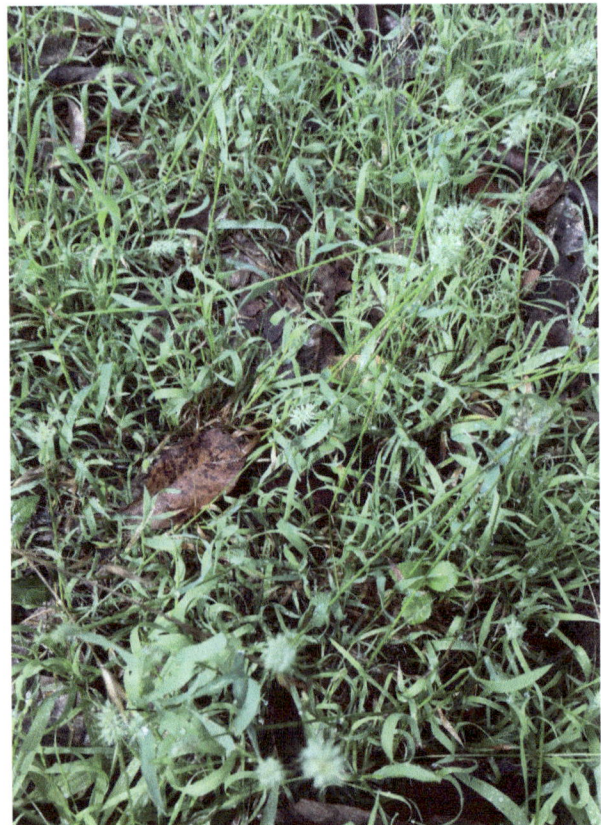

Growing as a nearly pure patch along Fitzpatrick Trail. Photo: H Malloy

---

[*] Not recorded in previous surveys of the island. However, *E. caespitosus* was recorded, a very similar species. It is likely that both are present.

Elaeocarpus reticulatus

Common name(s): Blueberry Ash

Max. height, usually: 3-15 m

Max. width, usually: 3-5 m

Form: Small tree or tall shrub, generally with a narrowly conical shape. Plants growing under tall trees frequently have the top lopped off by falling branches, in which case the shape is more rounded.

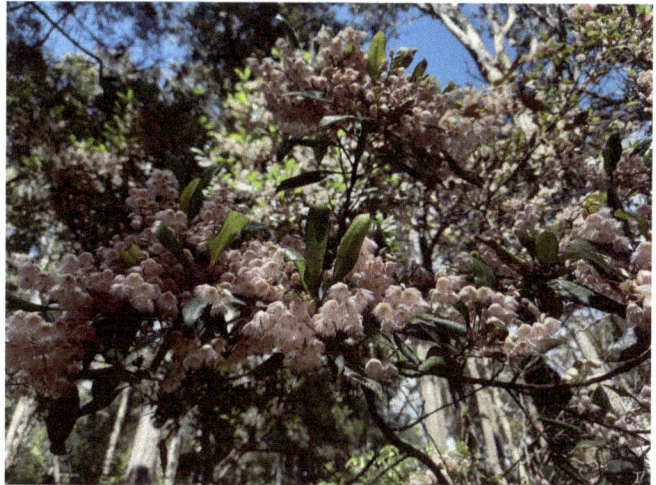

Pink-flowered tree in Catherine Park, Scotland Island. Photo: Lew Walker

Soil: Prefers humus-rich moist soil, but is very tolerant of less than ideal situations. Tolerates dry ridges as long as the soil is clay-based. Tolerates drought. Does not tolerate waterlogging.

Light: Prefers dappled shade but tolerates full sun and heavy shade.

Flower season: Profuse fringed flowers in late spring, usually white but occasionally pink.

Photo: Australian National Botanic Gardens
http://www.anbg.gov.au/photo

Best features: Lovely flowers followed by bright blue long-lasting fruit (drupes). Dying leaves turn a brilliant red and are retained on the tree a long time, providing good contrast with the dark green leaves, and new growth is pinkish; pretty blue berries.

Propagation: Cuttings, taken in autumn while it is still warm. Seeds take more than 18 months to germinate.

Native to: Sydney and Scotland Island. Typical of Dry PWSGF.

Distribution: Wide range of environments, from moist gullies through to rocky ridge outcrops and sandy coastal scrubs, occurring all along the east coast of Australia from Fraser Island, Qld down to Flinders Island, Tas.

Other notes: Watch for spitfire (sawfly) larvae, which can quickly defoliate the whole plant. Plants can fully recover from defoliation, but it may take a few years.

Responds well to pruning and reportedly can be hedged.

There are a couple of dark pink-flowered trees on West Head, and a couple of pale pink-flowered trees on Scotland Island along the stairs from Robertson Road down to Catherine Park. Pink forms are sometimes available in native plant nurseries.

The white form is widely sold, and there are numerous cultivars available at commercial nurseries.

Fruit are relished by cockatoos and currawongs.

Entolasia marginata

Common name(s): Right-angle Grass, Bordered Panic Grass

Max. height, usually: 30 cm

Max. width, usually: Indefinite

Form: Spreading grass, leaf size highly variable but at least 2 mm wide.

Soil: Moist well-drained soil; prefers sandy.

Light: Dappled or part shade.

Flower season: Green flowers throughout the year, esp. Oct to May.

Best features: Fresh green-coloured leaves are held stiffly at right angle to stems, providing interesting visual texture.

Propagation: Division

Native to: Sydney and Scotland Island. Typical of Dry PWSGF.

Distribution: In scrub in slightly damper areas on sandy or sandstone-derived soils in NSW; also Qld, Vic.

The leaves form a criss-cross pattern. Photo: H Malloy

Other notes: Spreads by very short rhizomes. Looks good in a shaded meadow mixed with other shade-loving grasses, or in small clumps where the crisscross pattern created by the leaf angle can be admired.

Aerial stems sometimes elongate and clamber upwards as much as 2 m through undergrowth it encounters, so best sited away from shrubs. Best in infertile soils (i.e. not too near a septic system); it can get rampant with too much nutrients.

Grows actively in summer; in winter it is mostly dormant (C4 grass).

Similar to *E. stricta*, and both are common in Elizabeth Park on Scotland Island. *E. stricta* is very badly behaved in a garden situation and not to be recommended. It is extremely common on the dry north-facing slope where the 2019 hazard-reduction burn was, where it is the dominant plant. Compared to *E. marginata*, when both are growing side-by-side in shaded conditions, *stricta* is more wiry; forms smaller clumps; often grey-green; with stems bent at the joints many times; leaves narrower than 2 mm; leaves tending to wither on older stems, giving the appearance of being a leafless tuft of stems; sometimes with leafy tufts at the nodes. Other differences are technical and require a microscope (fertile floret 1 mm shorter than the upper glume, if you want to know).

Epacris longiflora

Common name(s): Fuchsia Heath, Native Fuchsia, Scarlet Epacris or Cigarette Flower

Max. height, usually: 1 m

Max. width, usually: 1 m

Form: Spreading shrub.

Soil: Tolerates most soils as long as drainage is good, including clay loam; prefers sandy loam; does not tolerate drought.

Light: Dappled shade.

Flower season: Red and white flowers year round, with peak late summer.

Photos (above and below): Gillian Gutridge, *Native Plants of the Northern Beaches, Sydney*. https://nbplantareas.com/

Best features: Outrageously decorative and prolific off-season flowers – up to 100 per stem; sharply pointed leaves for small bird habitat.

Propagation: Cuttings; take care as roots are very fine.

Native to: Sydney but not Scotland Island and not PWSGF. Can be seen on many local bushwalk trails – e.g., Chiltern, Cromer Heights, Deep Creek, and Katandra Bushland Sanctuary[Ω].

Distribution: NSW and Qld, in sandy soils on wet cliff faces and wet coastal heath to woodland margins. Particularly common along seepage lines on sandstone.

Other notes: One of the most beloved of Sydney's wildflowers. In cultivation for some 200 years.

A member of the heath family. As for other members of the family, protect from root disturbance as the roots are very fine; avoid transplanting unnecessarily. Mulch to help retain soil moisture and inhibit weeds. Weeds too close to the plant can cause excess humidity which can lead to its death, but as it is best to minimise soil disturbance, it is better to prevent the weeds from growing. Mix well-aged compost into the soil before planting. Feed with well-aged compost or a native fertiliser annually in spring. Protect from wind and don't let it dry out completely.

Natural habit is straggly and spreading. If this is not desired, it can be tip-pruned to a more formal rounded shrub shape; responds well to pruning. Grows well in a pot, which shows off the arching stems to best advantage, as long as the drainage is good and you remember to water it.

Looks great with correas, which enjoy the same conditions.

Ω   Gillian Gutridge, *Native Plants of the Northern Beaches, Sydney*. https://nbplantareas.com/

Eucalyptus punctata

Common name(s): Grey Gum

Max. height, usually: 35 m

Max. width, usually: 5 m

Form: Tall tree where soil is fertile (e.g., the clay-based soil of Scotland Island).

Soil: Well-drained.

Light: Full sun; but seedlings need shade.

Flower season: White flowers Dec to Mar.

Best features: Attractive tan and grey bark, with shades of salmon-orange when bark is freshly shed in summer.

Propagation: Seed.

Native to: Sydney and Scotland Island. Not typical of PWSGF due to its frequency being low everywhere it occurs. Nearest wild-collected records are from McCarr's Creek, Church Point and Ingleside.

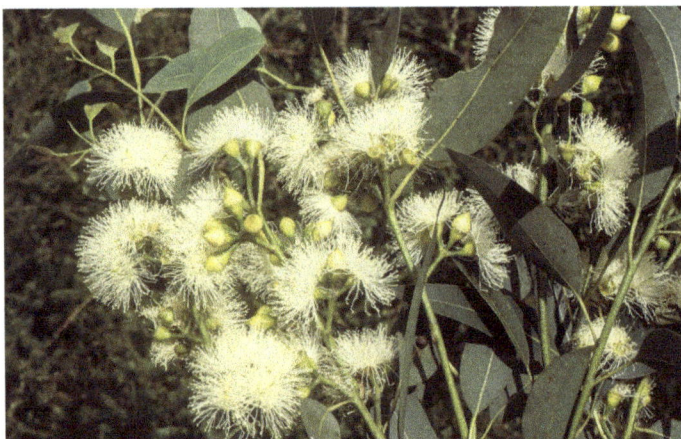

Photo: Alan Fairley https://resources.austplants.com.au/plant-database

Distribution: Ranges and near coastal areas from near Gympie in Qld, to near Nowra in NSW, most commonly on transition zone soil types between sandstone and shale, mainly on the coast and tablelands, extending into the western slopes.

Other notes: Koalas and possums relish the tender new leaves. Flying foxes and lorikeets feed on the flowers.

Readily self-seeds if there is a mature tree in the vicinity, and the seedlings can be dug up and potted (see photo). Seedlings are similar to Spotted Gum but narrower in all parts, and without the magenta fuzz, and much less hardy.

Photo: Alan Fairley https://resources.austplants.com.au/plant-database

Grey Gum Seedlings. Photo: H Malloy

Eupomatia laurina

Common name(s): Bolwarra, Native Guava, Scented Laurel, Copper Laurel

Max. height, usually: 5 m

Max. width, usually: 3 m

Form: Shrub or small tree.

Soil: Damp and humus rich but moderately well drained; sandy, clay, or loamy.

Light: Part shade to dappled shade; tolerates full sun but only if well watered.

Flower season: White flowers in summer.

Best features: Heavily perfumed flowers, very sweet, urn-shaped berries; glossy foliage – coppery in winter and spring.

Photos (above and below): Gillian Gutridge, *Native Plants of the Northern Beaches, Sydney*. https://nbplantareas.com/

Propagation: Seed.

Native to: Sydney but not Scotland Island and not PWSGF. Nearest wild-collected records are Clareville on the Barrenjoey peninsula and Narrabeen. Can be seen at Katandra Bushland Sanctuary[Ω].

Distribution: Widespread in or near warmer rainforest and moist eucalypt forest on the coast and lower ranges in NSW, Qld, Vic; also New Guinea.

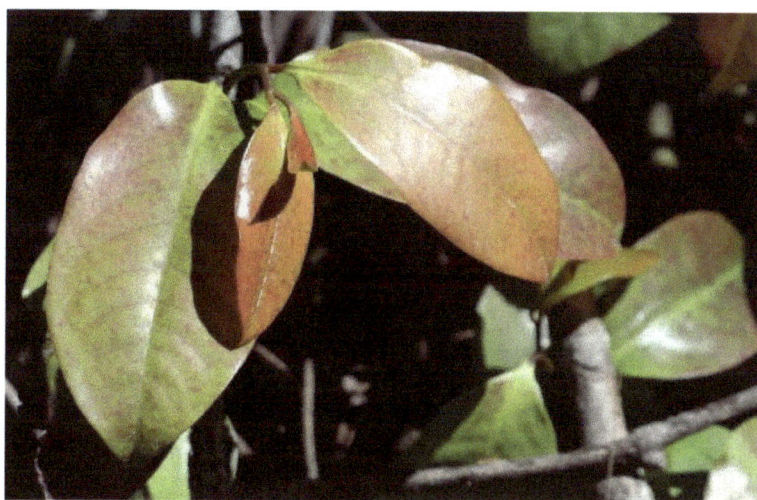

Other notes: Eupomatia is the only genus in the relict family Eupomatiaceae, a legacy of Gondwana. The other two species are endemic to small areas of eastern Australia. The Australian Botanic Garden says that fruits are "quite good" to eat raw, which is not much of an endorsement[Ψ]. They are creamy in texture but full of small seeds. Pollinated by small weevils.

Benefits from mulching and additional water in dry periods; this is a rainforest-loving plant. Best with protection from the afternoon sun. Would best suit a tropical-themed or rainforest-themed garden.

Most native plant nurseries carry it.

Ω   Gillian Gutridge, *Native Plants of the Northern Beaches, Sydney*. https://nbplantareas.com/
Ψ   https://www.australianbotanicgarden.com.au/plants/flowering-calendar/eupomatia-laurina?m=12

Eustrephus latifolius

Common name(s): Wombat Berry

Max. height, usually: 6 m if supported.

Max. width, usually: 3 m if unsupported.

Form: Twining plant or scrambling groundcover, stems to 6 m long.

Soil: Not fussy; drought-tolerant once established.

Light: Prefers dappled sun.

Flower season: White to pale pink flowers with fringed margins in spring and summer.

Best features: Fast-growing, light, delicate twiner; charming flowers, colourful orange fruit in winter.

Propagation: Fresh seed.

Native to: Sydney and Scotland Island. A typical component of both Dry and Moist PWSGF.

Distribution: NSW in sclerophyll forest, woodland, heath and on margins of rainforest; widespread, from coastal districts to the ranges; also Qld, Vic, Pacific Islands, and Malesia.

Photos (above and below): Gillian Gutridge, *Native Plants of the Northern Beaches, Sydney*. https://nbplantareas.com/

Other notes: Leaf width varies, sometimes within the same population. Attractive when allowed to climb small trees. As it is small and light, it rarely causes a problem.

The tuberous roots are edible either raw or baked, and wombats are said to like them too. The stems can be used as twine once stripped of leaves.

Superficially resembles Scrambling Lily (*Geitonoplesium cymosum*; see profile*)*, which occurs in roughly the same range and habitat, but is placed in a different plant family, and differs in many ways. Both are common on Scotland Island and often grow together.

More popular in cultivation than Scrambling Lily. Most native plant nurseries carry it.

Ficinia (formerly Isolepis) nodosa

Common name(s): Knobby Club Rush; Knotted Club Rush

Max. height, usually: 1 m

Max. width, usually: .8 m

Form: Grass-like sedge growing in tufts.

Soil: Any; tolerates waterlogging as well as drought; prefers coastal locations; tolerates salt and wind.

Light: Prefers full sun; tolerates light shade.

Flower season: Knobby pink heads of small flowers develop in early summer (e.g., Jan) followed by 1.5 cm spherical seed heads which remain on the stem.

Photo: Oz Trees https://www.oztrees.com.au/product/ficinia-nodosa-knobby-club-rush/

Best features: Cute knobby seedheads; fast-growing.

Propagation: Readily self-seeds if happy; clumps can be divided.

Native to: Sydney but not Scotland Island. Not a component of PWSGF. Nearest wild-collected records are Barrenjoey and Narrabeen Lakes.

Distribution: Coastal backdunes, in sandy salty soil and salt marshes; NSW, Qld, Vic, Tas, WA, SA. Also New Zealand, Africa.

Other notes: Requires moist soil for establishment but after that is quite drought-tolerant.

Commonly used in filtration beds and ponds, and to stabilise sand movement. Widely used in roadside plantings in coastal areas.

In the garden, best when planted in massed groups, to accentuate the ornamental knobby seedheads.

Would be great planted alongside gully torrents, rain diversion ditches, or a water feature, provided it is sunny enough. Looks good with *Gahnia melanocarpa* and *Juncus usitatus* – other grasslike plants that enjoy the same conditions. These species will all self-seed when conditions are moist enough. Once the young "volunteer" plants have developed sufficiently, they become hardy and can withstand dry conditions very well.

Prune back to the ground every 3-4 years to freshen it up.

Available at most native nurseries.

Gahnia melanocarpa

Common name(s): Black Fruit Saw-sedge

Max. height, usually: 1.2 m

Max. width, usually: 2 m

Form: Grass-like plant with arching leaves.

Soil: Any well-drained; tolerates temporary waterlogging; tolerates drought.

Light: Prefers filtered sun; tolerates heavy shade.

Flower season: Spring-summer.

Best features: Dramatic arching leaves, shiny black fruit which dangle like beads from the seedheads when ripe, shade-tolerant, no maintenance required.

Propagation: Seed, division. Seed is difficult.

Native to: Sydney and Scotland Island. Studies differ as to whether it is a component of PWSGF[Ω]. Nearest wild-collected records are from Elanora Heights and North Bilgola Head.

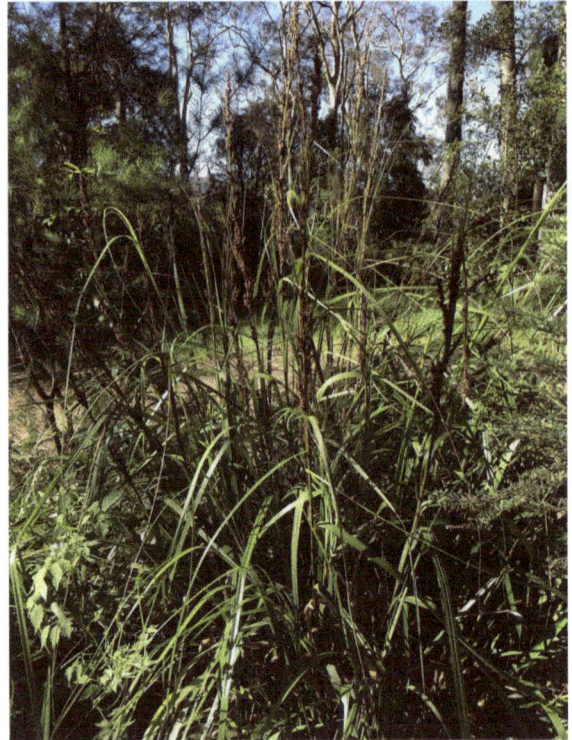

Along Fitzpatrick Trail. Photo: H Malloy

Distribution: Wet sclerophyll forest or rainforest margins; widespread on coast; NSW, Qld, Vic.

Other notes: Not generally grown in gardens, and little information is available on its cultivation.

Gahnia melanocarpa is the species we have native on Scotland Island, and is well suited for protected, partly shaded conditions. For hot, dry positions, *G. sieberiana* may be a better choice, and it is seen in gardens more frequently than *G. melanocarpa*.

Leaf edges are saw-toothed and sharp enough to cut the skin. But there is no need for maintenance, as old foliage naturally drops and rots down. Gahnias have a preference for wet conditions, and this species does

Photo: Martin Purvis. https://www.purvision.com/

very well alongside gully torrents or road runoff, though they can also tolerate drought very well. Looks great with Dianella*s*, which also like the same conditions.

Gahnia species are larval hosts for the beautiful Swordgrass Brown butterfly (*Tisiphone abeona*).

Some native plant nurseries carry it.

Ω   Bell & Stables 2012 report it as an uncommon component of Moist PWSGF. OEH 2016 do not report it at all.

Geitonoplesium cymosum

Common name(s): Scrambling Lily

Max. height, usually: 8 m if supported.

Max. width, usually: n/a

Form: Slender scrambling, twining vine.

Soil: Not fussy. Prefers moist but tolerates dry soil.

Light: Prefers dappled sun; tolerates full sun and full shade.

Flower season: White delicately fragrant flowers in spring and summer, followed by succulent black fruit.

Best features: Dainty, star-like flowers; shiny black fruit.

Propagation: Seed.

Native to: Sydney and Scotland Island. Typical component of both Dry and Moist PWSGF.

Distribution: Widespread in NSW in coastal districts in moist eucalyptus forests, sparse rainforests and creek banks, and also on the ranges; also Lord Howe Island, Qld, Vic, Pacific Islands and Malesia.

Photos (above and below): Gillian Gutridge, *Native Plants of the Northern Beaches, Sydney.* https://nbplantareas.com/

Other notes: Wide- and narrow-leaved forms occur, but the form generally seen in the Sydney region is narrow-leaved.

Resembles Wombat Berry (*Eustrephus latifolius)*, which occurs in same range and habitat, but it is placed in a different plant family, and differs in numerous ways. In the Sydney region, vines with narrow leaves tend to be Scrambling Lily, and vines with wider leaves tend to be Wombat Berry. Scrambling Lily develops multi-stemmed thickets with larger, tougher stems than those of Wombat Berry, with a striated or sandpapery texture on even the smallest stems. Some find this habit untidy.

Scrambling Lily can be allowed to climb small trees and will not overwhelm them unless they are very young. It is best sited away from shrubs and young trees, and is probably best avoided for small gardens.

The shoots are edible when boiled or raw from the vine, a fine substitute for asparagus.[*] Roots are fibrous and not edible like the tubers of Wombat Berry.

Less popular in cultivation than Wombat Berry. Most native plant nurseries carry it.

---

*   https://pfaf.org/user/Plant.aspx?LatinName=Geitonoplesium+cymosum81

Geranium homeanum

Common name(s): Rainforest Crane's-bill

Max. height, usually: 1 m

Max. width, usually: 2 m

Form: Prostrate scrambling perennial herb with thick, branched taproot.

Soil: Moist well-drained. Drought-tolerant due to thick root.

Light: Full sun to part shade

Flower season: Pale pink flowers Oct to Mar.

Best features: Flowers over a long period; dependable groundcover for dry sites. Leaf shape contrasts well with other groundcovers.

Propagation: Seed.

Native to: Sydney and Scotland Island. Not typical of PWSGF. Nearest wild-collected record is Dee Why, 1950.

Distribution: Widespread in sclerophyll forest and on the margin of rainforest, usually in damper sites, in NSW, Qld, and Vic.

Other notes: Seeds are shot from the plant with force when ripe, quickly colonising bare soil.

Can become rampant where soil is overly moist and fertile (e.g., clay soil), but excess growth is easily controlled. Best combined with other groundcovers on such fertile sites to keep it in check.

Plants tend to remain smaller and daintier on drier, less fertile soils (e.g, sandy). On very dry sites it can behave like an annual, regenerating from seed after rains.

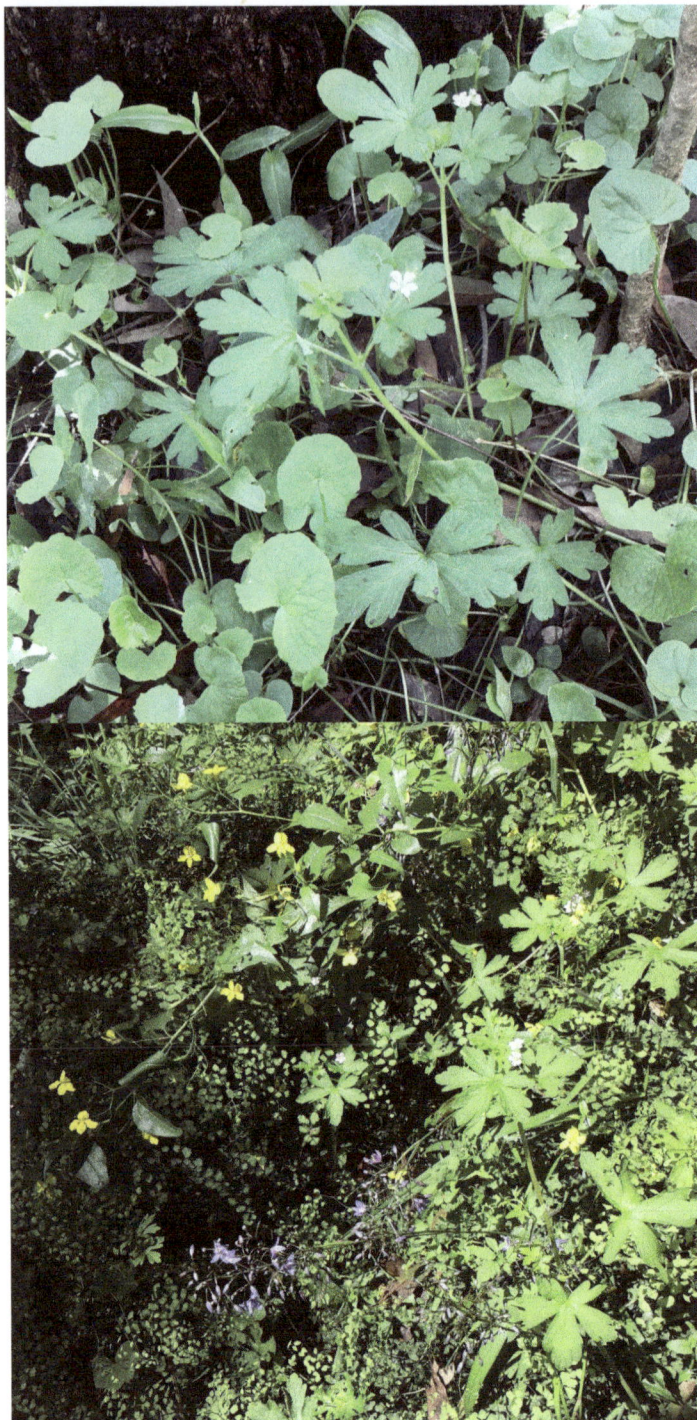

Growing with *Dichondra repens* and *Centella asiatica* (top). With *Goodenia ovata, Dianella caerulea,* and Maidenhair Ferns (bottom). Photos: H Malloy

Glochidion ferdinandi

Common name(s): Cheese Tree (the fruits resemble miniature wheels of cheese)

Max. height, usually: 8 m, though in rainforest conditions it can reach 30 m

Max. width, usually: 3 m

Form: Woody shrub or small tree.

Soil: Any; prefers moist well-drained; drought-tolerant once established.

Light: Full sun, light shade.

Flower season: Flowers are inconspicuous; pink to deep red pumpkin-shaped fruit open to reveal bright red seeds, Nov to Apr.

The "cheese" fruits are green until they ripen. Photo: H Malloy

Best features: Red fruits are relished by parrots and many other birds; provides dense shade.

Propagation: Seed, which must be fresh, and which may take up to four months to germinate.

Native to: Sydney and Scotland Island. Typical component of both Dry and Moist PWSGF.

Distribution: Rainforest as well as drier locations including coastal wet sclerophyll forest; NSW, Qld, NT, WA.

Other notes: Fast-growing and foliage is dense, so it can quickly provide relatively dense shade, if that is what is desired. Here is a downside to this gung-ho species: as is also true of some of our other rainforest species, it is a bird-dispersed "opportunist" or coloniser, meaning that young plants are seen very frequently, in sheltered moist positions as well as hot dry ones where they look ragged and scruffy, and grow slowly. If you look around your block, you may find that you already have quite a few scruffy 'volunteers'. Even the scruffy ones seem to survive and eventually (in theory) bear more cheese fruits.

A mature tree provides quite dense shade. Photo: H Malloy

For best-looking foliage and fastest growth, plant in a moderately shaded spot and provide generous supplemental water. If you can water it, or you have a sheltered spot for it, you may find it worthwhile to grow it for the fruits, which attract King Parrots and Currawongs. Rainbow Lorikeets are said to eat the new leafy growth.

Also consider Scentless Rosewood (*Synoum glandulosum*), which has a similar look but is hardier in hot dry locations.

Glycine **clandestina**

Common name(s): Small-leaf Glycine

Max. height, usually: n/a

Max. width, usually: n/a

Form: Small twiner or scrambler.

Soil: Moist soils tolerating poorly drained soil in winter, in moist grassy areas of forests; tolerates drought.

Light: Semi-shade to dappled shade.

Flower season: Crowded sprays of 5-13 pea flowers; white, pink or violet with a white spot, main flowering Oct to Apr, but some flowers all year, as moisture permits.

Best features: Long flowering period; not a head-turner, but sweet in its way: small, delicate-looking decorations draped over other understorey plants in a cool shaded location.

Propagation: Seed.

Native to: Sydney and Scotland Island. Typical of Dry PWSGF.

Distribution: Widespread from coast to subalpine situations, in NSW, Qld, Vic, Tas, SA.

Other notes: As a member of the legume family, it is a nitrogen-fixer and therefore beneficial to the soil.

Leaflet shape and degree of hairiness extremely variable.

Its light stems don't weigh down the plants it climbs on, though it can be a little unsightly if there is a lot of it.

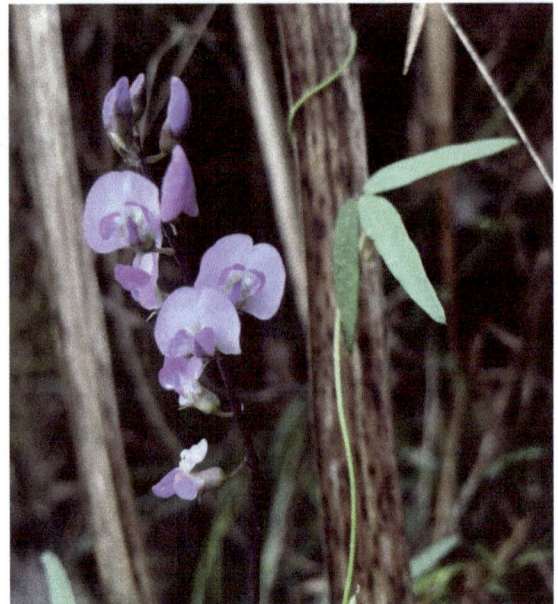

Photos (above and below): H Malloy

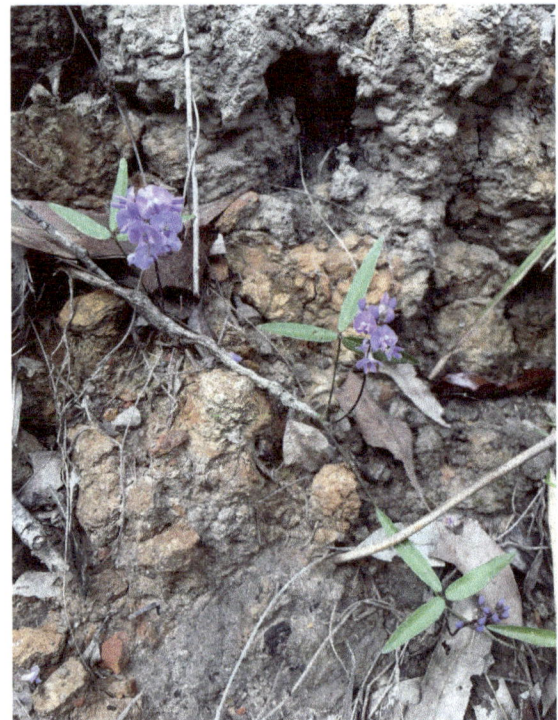

Similar to *G. microphylla*, which also occurs on Scotland Island, but in that species the middle leaflet normally has a longer stem (petiolule) than the other two. *G. microphylla* favours moister positions and can root at the nodes, making it valuable when rehabilitating eroded soil.

Neither *G. clandestina* nor *G. microphylla* are generally available from native nurseries, but if anyone wants them and doesn't already have them growing in their garden, they can come and get some from my block.

Goodenia ovata

Common name(s): Hop Goodenia

Max. height, usually: 1 m

Max. width, usually: 1-3 m

Form: Small upright shrub.

Soil: Clay, loam, sand; tolerates moderate drought.

Light: Light shade, half shade; tolerates full sun but plants grown in full sun may be short-lived (seems to get a virus).

Flower season: Brilliant yellow flowers all year, with a peak Oct to Mar.

Best features: Fast growing; cheerful flowers most of the year.

Propagation: Seed, cuttings (very easy).

Native to: Sydney and Scotland Island. Studies differ as to whether it is a component of PWSGF*. Nearest wild-collected records include KCNP, Mona Vale, and Church Point.

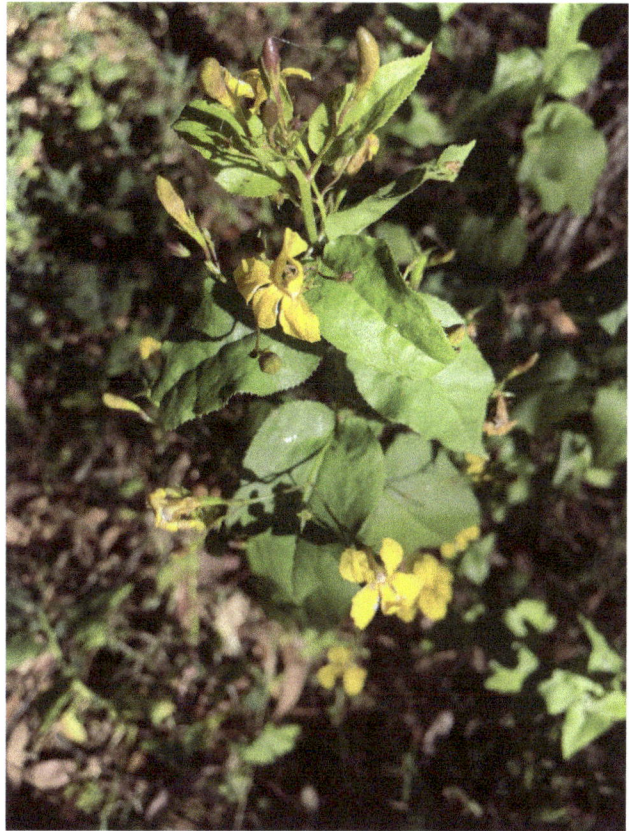

Photo: H Malloy

Distribution: Widespread in all mainland states except Western Australia, usually in open forest and woodland, sometimes in exposed rocky situations near sea.

Other notes: A good filler plant. Responds to light pruning. Combines well with *Dianella* and *Indigofera*, which bloom at the same time in spring.

When mass-planted, could provide quick cover for ground-nesting birds such as the Buff-banded Rail.

Gets straggly over time if not pruned. Tip pruning from a young age is preferred, and can extend its life.

Widely available at native nurseries. A low-growing form known as "Gold Cover" is also available. The low form reputedly prefers full sun but is less drought tolerant than the tall form.

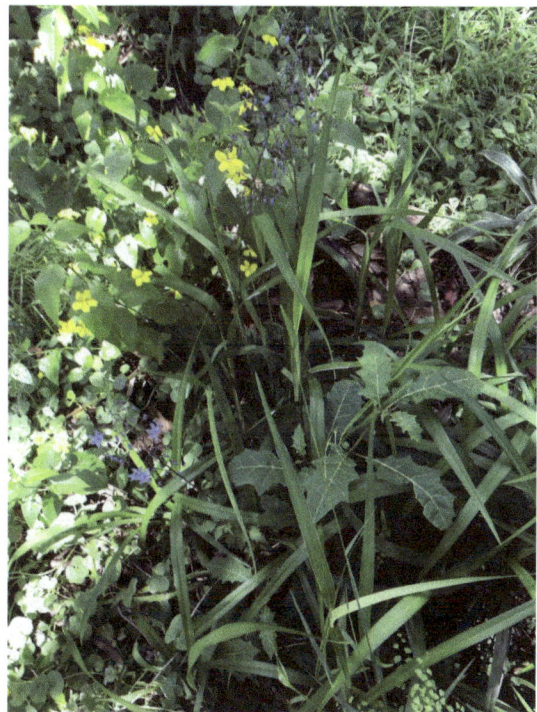

Growing with *Dianella* and *Solanum prioniphyllum*.
Photo: H Malloy

---

* Bell & Stables 2012 did not report it. OEH 2016 reported it as present in 18% of their sites.

Grevillea arenaria[*]

Common name(s): Sand Grevillea, Hoary Grevillea, Nepean Spider Flower

Max. height, usually: 2 m

Max. width, usually: 2 m

Form: Bushy shrub with hairy-silky grey-green leaves.

Soil: Any well-drained; drought-tolerant.

Light: Filtered sun.

Flower season: Pink and green flowers most months, peaking July to Nov.

Best features: Grey-green foliage; shade-tolerant; low maintenance.

Propagation: Seed, cuttings.

Native to: Sydney but not Scotland Island. Not a component of PWSGF. Nearest wild-collected records are from Ingleside, North Elanora, and Narrabeen.

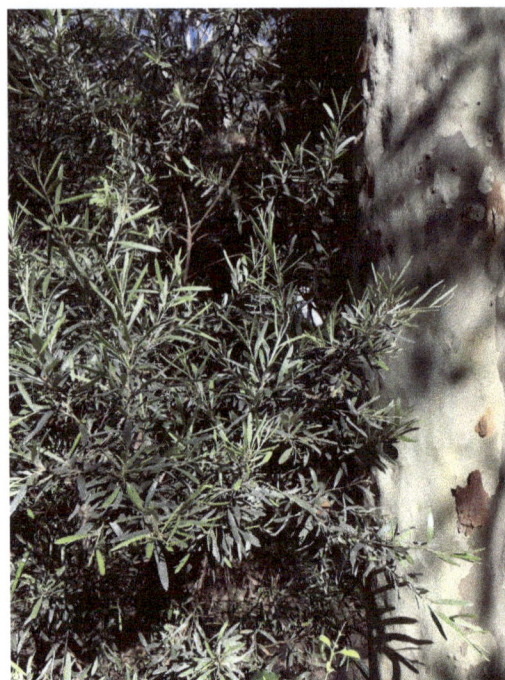
Photo: H Malloy

Distribution: Woodland associations in NSW, in a range of shallow stony soils over various substrates including sandstone, granite, rhyolite and occasionally limestone; mainly on the eastern side of the Great Dividing Range and adjacent subcoastal ranges.

Other notes: I have included this plant mostly because it is one of the few grey-green species that I know of that are shade-tolerant. It even tolerates clay soil, and is also very low maintenance as it does not require pruning to look good.

On the down side, the flowers are small and not showy, and on some plants (including mine) they are mostly green.

The growth is dense and it is a good screener, with foliage down to the ground even on old specimens. When planted with other dense shrubs, it creates a thicket that (in theory) could help to discourage Noisy Miners and provide a haven for smaller birds.

Some native plant nurseries carry it.

---

[*]   Full name: *Grevillea arenaria* subsp. *arenaria*.

SYDNEY LOCAL NATIVE

Grevillea linearifolia

Common name(s): White Spider Flower, Linear-leaf Grevillea

Max. height, usually: 1.5 m

Max. width, usually: 1 m

Form: Upright spreading shrub.

Soil: Prefers moist sandy soil, but adaptable to any free-draining soil; tolerates drought.

Light: Full sun to light shade.

Flower season: White flower clusters, occasionally tinged pink, appearing most of the year if sufficient moisture is available, with a peak Aug to Dec.

Best features: Long flowering season, fast growing, self-rounding shape.

Propagation: Seed, cuttings. Seeds are quickly shed when ripe; to catch them, tie a reusable tea bag over each flower cluster when flowers have fallen and seed pods begin to swell.

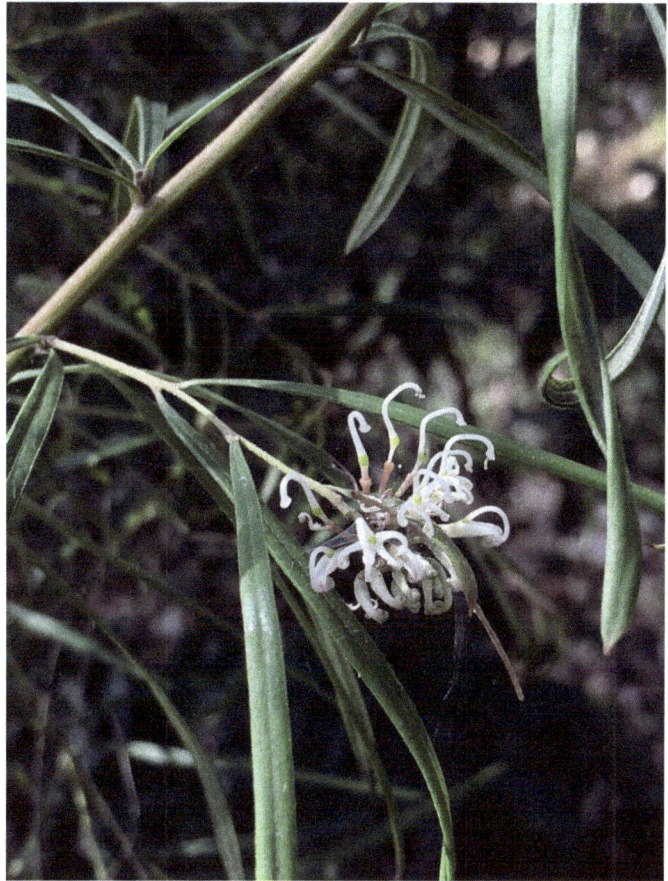
Photo: H Malloy

Native to: Sydney but not Scotland Island. Not typical of PWSGF. Nearest wild-collected record is near the Bahai temple on Mona Vale Road, on Sydney sandstone.

Distribution: Dry sclerophyll forest, woodland and heath, mostly in well-drained semi-shaded to open sites, mostly in sandy soils over sandstone, primarily in the Greater Sydney Basin, from Gosford and Putty area to the Parramatta River and Port Jackson, then with disjunct populations near Nowra and Ulladulla as well as Lawson in the Blue Mountains.

Other notes: Not a "wow" plant, but a good fast-growing screen plant.

Growth is dense and form is self-rounding with no pruning or other maintenance needed. Can prune to make it more compact and symmetrical.

Pinkish and/or compact forms exist, though they may be hard to track down.

Carried by most native nurseries.

Grevillea sericea[*]

Common name(s): Pink Spider Flower

Max. height, usually: 2 m

Max. width, usually: 1-2 m

Form: Vigorous shrub with angular branches and slightly prickly grey-green leaves.

Soil: Well-drained; prefers sandy soil. If your soil is clay-based, plant on a slope. Does not tolerate any waterlogging. Dislikes alkaline soil.

Light: Full sun to part-shade; tolerates heavy shade.

Flower season: Prolific light pink (sometimes deep pink, red-pink, mauve or white) flowers, mainly July to Jan but with some flowers at other times.

Best features: Long flowering period, attractive flowers.

Photo: Brian Atwell, Macquarie University

Propagation: Seed, cuttings. Seeds should be nicked with a sharp knife prior to sowing to improve germination.

Native to: Sydney but not Scotland Island. Not a component of PWSGF. Nearest wild-collected records are KCNP, Bilgola, Angophora Reserve, Avalon, and Careel Head.

Distribution: Heath and shrubby sclerophyll woodland and open forest, in sandy soils; endemic to NSW, and widespread throughout the Sydney Basin.

Other notes: Popular in cultivation and generally successful in soils of reasonable drainage.

Dense growth makes it a good screener or informal hedge. Responds well to pruning, though it doesn't require maintenance unless a more compact shape is desired. As is the case for all members of its family (Proteaceae), do not give it high phosphorus fertiliser.

Bees find the flowers very attractive (native as well as European bees). Great habitat for small birds.

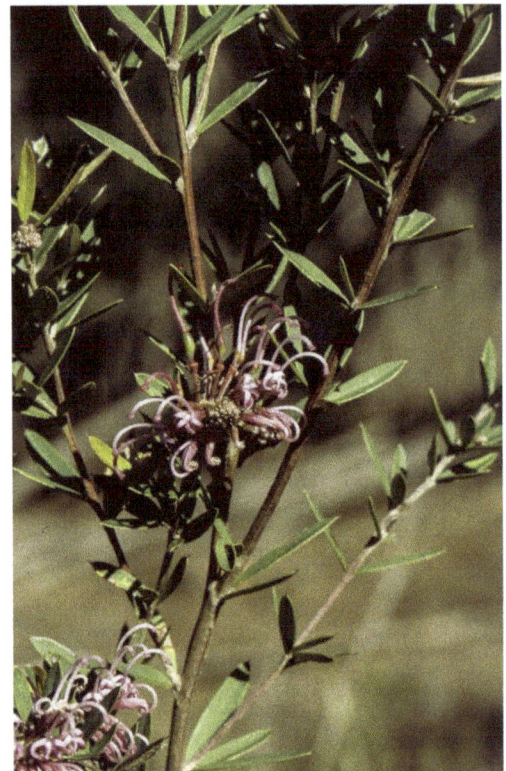

Photo: Alan Fairley
https://resources.austplants.com.au/plant-database/

There is a popular cultivar "Collaroy Plateau" with brighter pink flowers, which is a hybrid with *G. speciosa* (Red Spider Flower).

---

[*] Full name *Grevillea sericea* subsp. *sericea*. The other subspecies *(riparia)* grows in flood-zones in the lower Blue Mountains.

SYDNEY LOCAL NATIVE

Grevillea speciosa

Common name(s): Red Spider Flower

Max. height, usually: 2 m

Max. width, usually: 2 m

Form: Small to medium sized, densely bushy shrub with slightly prickly leaves.

Soil: Well-drained sandy. Grows naturally in wet sandstone heath as well as drier areas, so it may possibly tolerate clay soil; tolerates drought but needs regular watering to keep flowering.

Light: Full sun to light afternoon shade.

Photos (above and below): Gillian Gutridge, Native Plants of the Northern Beaches, Sydney. https://nbplantareas.com/

Flower season: Bright red or deep pink flowers in spring, with some flowers most of the year.

Best features: One of the most brightly coloured of Sydney's wildflowers; prickly leaves; good screener as it is densely bushy.

Propagation: Cuttings.

Native to: Sydney, mostly north of the harbour, but not Scotland Island; not part of PWSGF.

Distribution: Moister areas of dry sclerophyll forest or heath; sandy soils on Hawkesbury Sandstone; endemic to Central Coast region, from Gosford to Port Jackson (Sydney Harbour).

Other notes: A sandstone-loving, sun-loving species which is reported to be hardy in most garden situations. If you have clay soil, plant on a slope or on a mound of hilled-up soil, or pass it up for another more reliably clay-tolerant species. Dig in well-rotted compost before planting. Mulch well and do not disturb roots after establishment. Benefits from tip pruning, especially after the spring flush of flowers; pruning helps to keep the plant densely branching and increases flowering. Generally needs no fertiliser.

Slightly prickly leaves provide habitat for small nectar-feeding birds, which also visit the brilliant large dangling clusters of flowers or pick off the many insects that visit the flowers.

Medium- to slow-growing; it may take several years for it to reach a height of one metre[Ω].

Widely available at native plant nurseries.

[Ω]   https://resources.austplants.com.au/plant/grevillea-speciosa/

Gymnostachys anceps

Common name(s): Settler's Twine, Boorgay

Max. height, usually: 3 m

Max. width, usually: 2 m

Form: Tuft of long, narrow very tough grass-like leaves, with creeping rhizome, forming small clumps.

Soil: Moist well-drained soil; tolerates drought once well established.

Light: Dappled shade.

Flower season: All year; many tiny green flowers on wiggly spikes in clusters at end of long stem, followed by blue-black fruit.

Best features: Shade-loving strappy-leaved plant.

Propagation: Fresh seed, which takes up to 5 months to germinate; division.

Native to: Sydney and Scotland Island. An uncommon component of Dry PWSGF and a typical component of Moist PWSGF.

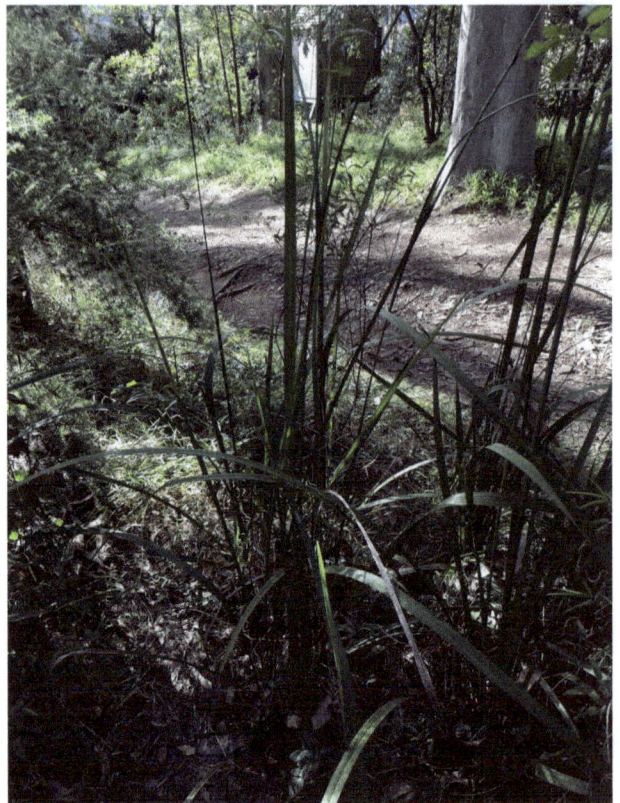

Photo: H Malloy

Distribution: NSW in rainforest and wet sclerophyll forest; coastal districts and escarpment ranges; also Qld.

Other notes: Leaves are fibrous and can be used as a strong twine. A member of the aroid family, but a strange one; it lacks the spathe typically found in the family (e.g., in *Anthurium* species).

Does not usually form clumps of multiple tufts, but rather forms colonies of individual tufts via a creeping rhizome. Appropriate as a garden plant in a rainforest setting under large trees, where it can develop stately tall tufts. A smaller, less messy alternative to *Cordyline stricta* when a palmy look is wanted. Good choice near a shaded water feature, though it is not actually a water plant.

Tolerates abuse, but not at its best without shade, regular water and protection from wind. Where these are provided, it is an elegant, low-maintenance plant with structural and curiosity value.

Birds are said to eat the blue-black fruits, and disperse the seeds.

Not generally available at native or commercial nurseries, but you may be lucky enough to have it already, courtesy of the birds. It is common in shaded areas of Elizabeth Park on Scotland Island.

Hakea sericea

Common name(s): Silky Needle Bush

Max. height, usually: 3 m

Max. width, usually: 3 m

Form: Large spreading, bushy shrub with no lignotuber.

Soil: Well-drained; very drought tolerant.

Light: Full sun to part shade.

Flower season: Fragrant white or pink flowers in May to Oct, with a peak in July to Aug. The flowers smell like honey or almonds (but don't get your nose too close to the sharp leaves).

Best features: Fast growing; divine fragrance; winter flowers; prickly habit; interesting knobbly fruits.

Propagation: Seed

Native to: Sydney and Scotland Island. Studies differ as to whether it is a component of PWSGF[*].

Distribution: Southeast Qld to southeast NSW.

Other notes: Dramatic shrub with a look reminiscent of conifers, but the needle-like leaves

Photo: Neil Murphy, Eatons Hill, Qld

Photo: Gillian Gutridge, Native Plants of the Northern Beaches, Sydney. https://nbplantareas.com/

are sharper and more rigid than conifer needles. Best sited well back from paths and trails unless a deterrent is desired, in which case it could be used to make an impressive and strong hedge.

A clump of three or more would provide safe nest sites to small birds. Good screener and windbreak.

White is the usual flower colour, but a pink form is sometimes available. Apparently it is a naturally occurring form and comes true from seed.

The knobbly, pointed fruits accumulate over the plant's lifetime, opening up when plant is burned or dies. The fruits will also open and release seeds if cut off with secateurs and brought indoors. Place in a bowl for a few days to catch the seeds – two winged seeds per fruit. The seeds are large, easy to handle and germinate within a few weeks.

An environmental weed in some countries, including South Africa, New Zealand and Portugal. It is best not planted outside its natural range.

---

[*]   Bell & Stables 2012 report it as an atypical component. OEH 2016 don't report it.

Hardenbergia violacea

Common name(s): Purple Coral Pea, False Sarsaparilla and Waraburra

Max. height, usually: Climber with wiry stems up to 2 m long; height depends on what it is climbing.

Max. width, usually: Depends on what it is climbing; with no support, it can cover an area of around 2 m.

Form: Loosely twining sub-shrub or shrub with no climbing tendency at all; climbing forms rarely causes damage to the host plant (may not be true of all cultivars).

Soil: Well-drained; prefers sand or loam-based soil, but tolerates light clay; does not tolerate waterlogging. Drought-tolerant.

Light: Full sun to part shade; does not flower well in heavy shade, and plants may be short-lived in shade.

Flower season: Usually purple or violet, sometimes pink, white or other colours, Aug to Nov.

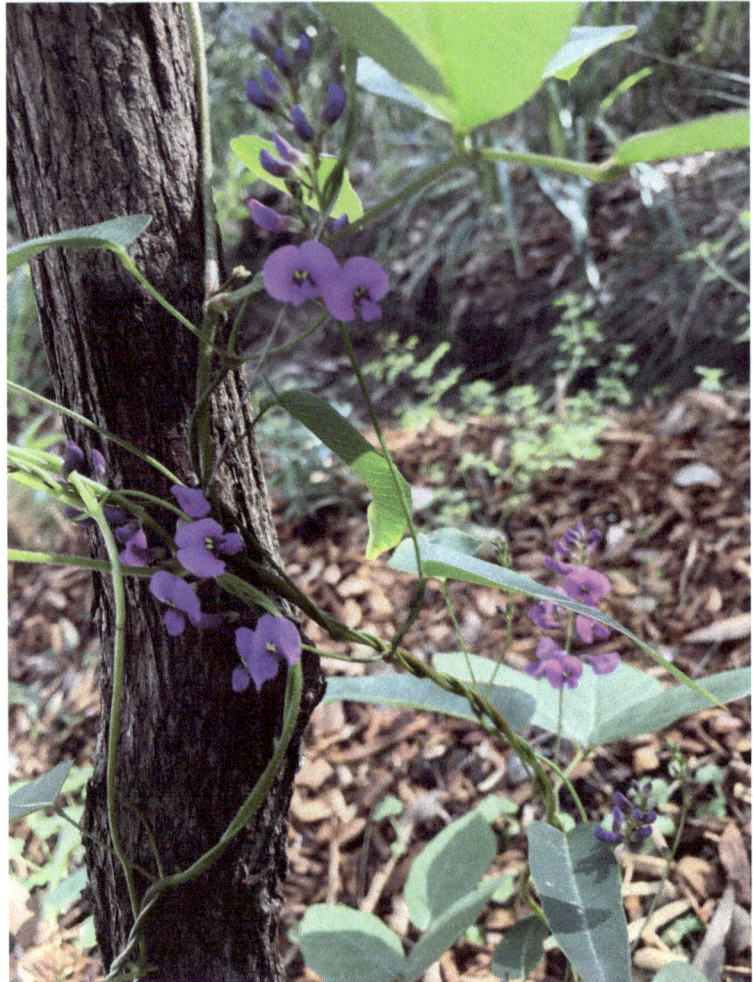

Growing with Kennedia rubicunda (flowers not shown). Photo: H Malloy

Best features: Spectacular flowers.

Propagation: Seed, which remains viable for many years; cuttings.

Native to: Sydney and Scotland Island. Typical of Dry PWSGF.

Distribution: Open forests, woodlands and undisturbed areas, in eastern parts of Qld, NSW, and Vic and southern SA, with one population in Tasmania.

Other notes: Responds well to pruning.

Many cultivars available, including non-climbing ones (e.g., "Mini Haha"). As *Hardenbergia* is very widespread over a broad range of conditions, cultivars may not be adaptable to our local conditions if they are from a different area, or conversely, cultivars may outshine local forms.

I have seen several pink-flowering plants in Scotland Island's Elizabeth Park, but I don't know if plants grown from seeds from those plants would have pink flowers. But the purple is so pretty, why would anyone want anything else?

Looks great with the deep red flowers of *Kennedia rubicunda* (see profile).

Hibbertia aspera*

Common name(s): Rough Guinea Flower

Max. height, usually: 60 cm

Max. width, usually: 50 cm

Form: Bushy small shrub, but it can become a scrambling-vine type shrub if planted with other climbers and given a support to climb. Can form a good suckering groundcover over time.

Soil: Prefers soil with good drainage. If your soil is clay-based, plant on a slope. Somewhat salt tolerant.

Light: Full to part sun.

Photo: https://resources.austplants.com.au/plant-database/

Flower season: Prolific bright yellow flowers in spring and early summer.

Best features: A blaze of colour when in flower, for a lengthy flowering period.

Propagation: Stem cuttings; division of root suckers. Seeds are unreliable.

Native to: Sydney but not Scotland Island. Studies differ as to whether it is a component of PWSGF^Ψ. Nearest wild-collected records are Newport, 1946 and Elanora Heights, 1958.

Distribution: NSW, in sclerophyll woodland or forests mainly in coastal areas, in a wide range habitats; somewhat salt tolerant; also Qld, Vic.

Other notes: Relatively easy to grow and hardy, but needs attentive watering while establishing.

Flowers are very numerous when it is in flower, and like some other species of *Hibbertia*, may also have intermittent flowers year round after the main flowering period. The tiny roundish leaves which cover the wiry stems are attractive even when the plant is not in flower.

When young, makes a good fill-in plant for a rock garden. When mature, it is a scrambler, and can eventually grow into an attractive scrambling groundcover under mature trees. If planted near a trellis with other climbers, it scrambles over and amongst the other plants and adds its own blaze of colour during its flowering period. Provides safe nesting sites for small native birds.

Prune when young if bushier growth is desired.

Hybrids are known between *H. aspera* and *H. empetrifolia* (see profiles). The latter of these is native to Scotland Island.

---

*   Full name: *Hibbertia aspera* subsp. *aspera*. There is another subspecies occurring in NSW, but it does not occur in the Sydney (Central Coast) region.

Ψ   Bell & Stables 2012 record it as an uncommon component of Dry PWSGF. OEH 2016 do not record it.

Hibbertia dentata

Common name(s): Toothed Guinea Flower, Trailing Guinea Flower or Twining Guinea Flower

Max. height, usually: 2 m twining with support.

Max. width, usually: 1 m when grown as groundcover.

Form: Nonvigorous twining or trailing vine.

Soil: Moist clay, shale, or sandstone-based soil with good drainage and protection from wind. Somewhat salt tolerant.

Light: Prefers part shade; tolerates sun and full shade.

Flower season: Winter to spring.

Best features: Bright yellow flowers contrast well with dark green to bronze foliage; flowers well in shade.

Propagation: Unlike most other members of the genus, easy from seed; also cuttings taken in early spring. Seed pods mature from Nov to Jan and split open to release the seeds. Often self-seeds, and the seedlings can be dug up and potted or moved elsewhere.

Photo: Jenny aka Floydwafer, iNaturalist

Native to: Sydney and Scotland Island. An uncommon component of Dry PWSGF[Ψ] or a typical component of PSGF,[Ω] depending on which study you consult.

Distribution: Mainly in open forest or on margins of rainforest; widespread on the coast and coastal ranges; NSW, Qld, Vic.

Other notes: If pruning is desired, for example when growing as groundcover, can be pruned in late winter back to nodes close to the center of the plant. Avoid tip pruning, which is said to make them rangier. Would work as a groundcover under gum trees, though when grown that way it might need some supplemental water.

Not prone to smothering the plants it climbs or scrambles on, unlike its sibling species *Hibbertia scandens* (see profile).

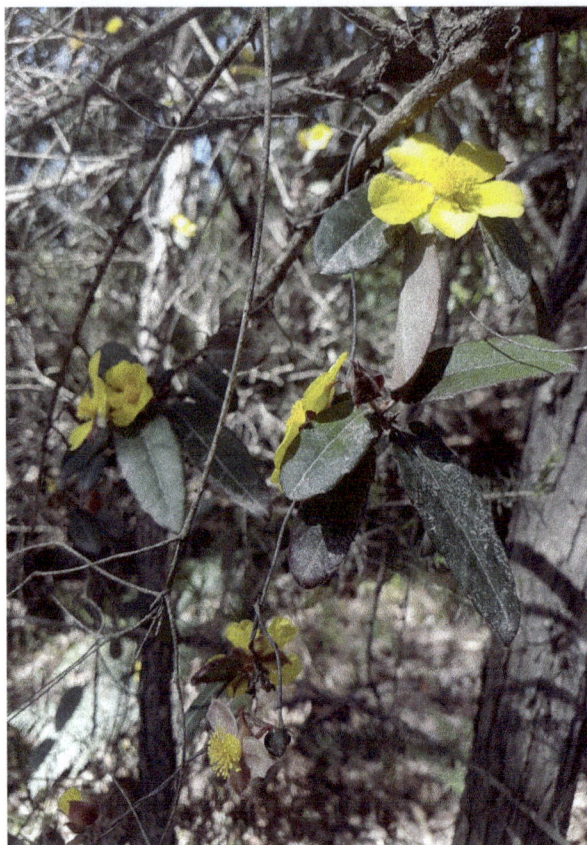

Ψ   Bell & Stables 2012.
Ω   OEH 2016.

Hibbertia empetrifolia*

Common name(s): Trailing Guinea-flower, Tangled Guinea-flower

Max. height, usually: 1 m

Max. width, usually: 2 m (to 3.5 m in garden situation).

Form: Reclining or spreading shrub with wiry or trailing stems, sometimes scrambling over other vegetation.

Soil: Moist well-drained sandy, loamy or clay soil; tolerates drought.

Light: Light shade to partial shade.

Wild specimen in modest summertime bloom. Photo: H Malloy

Flower season: Bright yellow flowers Aug to Feb, with peak Sept to Oct.

Best features: Long flowering season; decorative flower shape; red stems and tidy dark green leaves year round.

Propagation: Cuttings, which are said to strike readily when taken Jan to Feb. Seed germination unreliable.

Native to: Sydney and Scotland Island[Ω]. Studies differ as to whether it is a component of PWSGF[Ψ]. Nearest wild-collected records are Angophora Reserve and KCNP. Also Barrenjoey Headland in wet heath.

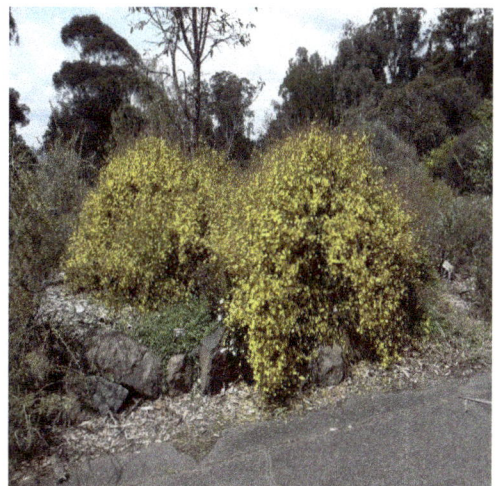
Cultivated specimen in prolific springtime bloom. Photo: M. Fagg https://www.anbg.gov.au/photo/image-collection.html

Distribution: Woodland and moist forest in NSW; also Qld, Vic, Tas.

Other notes: Very hardy and long-lived. Not readily available at nurseries (as yet).

Sometimes hybridises with the much smaller *Hibbertia aspera* (see profile), which I have not seen growing naturally on Scotland Island and which does not appear in any vegetation study of the island that I am aware of.

---

[*] Full name is *Hibbertia empetrifolia* subsp. *empetrifolia*, but as it is the only subspecies occuring in NSW, the short name is reasonably clear. There is one other subspecies, *radians*, which occurs in SA and is much lesser known.

[Ω] Has not been recorded in any vegetation survey of Scotland Island that I know of, but I have seen it in numerous locations in Elizabeth Park as well as "volunteering" in Ann Dennis' native plant garden on Scotland Island.

[Ψ] Bell & Stables 2012 don't report it. OEH 2016 report it as a typical component.

Hibbertia procumbens

Common name(s): Spreading Guinea Flower

Max. height, usually: 20 cm

Max. width, usually: 1 m

Form: Prostrate spreading small shrub, often forming mats.

Soil: Prefers moist well-drained humus-rich sandy soil (similar to heath or open scler-ophyll forests on ridgetops). Tolerates ex-posed, disturbed sites including gravel.

Light: Full sun to part shade.

Flower season: Profuse bright yellow flowers Oct to Dec, with intermittent flowering through Mar.

Best features: Bright flowers intermittently throughout summer after spring peak is over; hardy groundcover.

Propagation: Cuttings.

Native to: Not Sydney and not Scotland Island. Not a component of PWSGF. Nearest native site is several locations near Gosford. May also occur in Vic and Tas, or those could be of a different undescribed species.

Photo: H Malloy

Distribution: Rare in NSW; Central Coast region near Somersby, Kulnura and Mangrove Mountain.

Other notes: Though it is endangered in NSW, it is easy to grow, and widely available in commercial nurseries as well as online. Beware that commercial nurseries may carry the forms from Vic and Tas, where it is abundant, rather than the endangered NSW form. Local forms are more likely to succeed, and specialised native nurseries are almost always a safer bet than commercial nurseries. Purists wanting to plant only Sydney local native plants should avoid this species.

I became acquainted with this plant from Stony Range Botanical Garden nursery. The volunteers who sold it to me assured me that it is dependable and long-flowering in their own home gardens. It is pretty and appears to be a hardy garden plant and very useful for fill-in, rock gardens, or general groundcover. I have planted it near several plants of *Prostanthera denticulata* (see profile), a low-growing island native that is covered in purple flowers in spring, when the *Hibbertia procumbens* will be a blaze of yellow.

Hibbertia scandens

Common name(s): Snake Vine, Climbing Guinea Flower, Golden Guinea Vine ("guinea" being the name of an old British gold coin)

Max. height, usually: 3 m when supported.

Max. width, usually: 5 m when grown as groundcover.

Form: Twining vine.

Soil: Sand, clay, or loam with reasonable drainage; drought-tolerant; tolerates salt-laden winds.

Light: Prefers full sun; tolerates light shade.

Flower season: Large yellow flowers spring to summer and sporadically throughout the year.

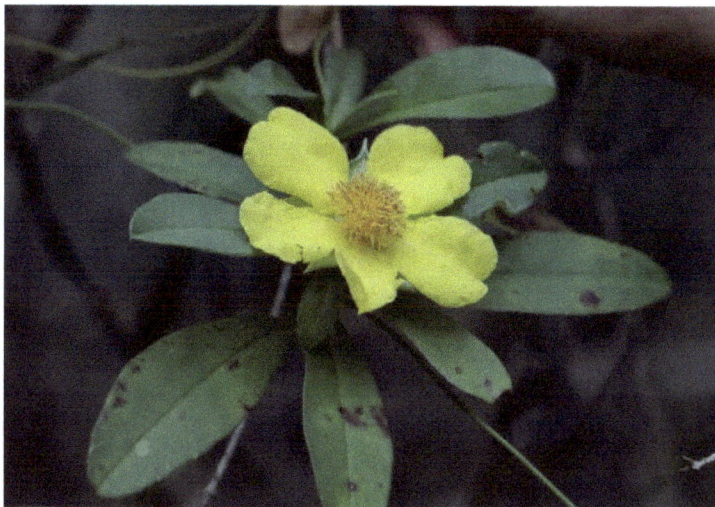

Photo: Gillian Gutridge, *Native Plants of the Northern Beaches, Sydney.*
https://nbplantareas.com/

Best features: Dense growth; flowers contrast well with foliage; flowers are followed by attractive red fruits.

Propagation: Cuttings; seed, which is slow to germinate.

Native to: Sydney and Scotland Island. Not a component of PWSGF.

Distribution: Coastal areas of Qld, NSW and far northeast Vic; in dune forest, wet sclerophyll woodlands, shrublands, and heath, often on sandy soil.

Other notes: Very hardy plant, and vigorous; can smother smaller plants. Foliage is dense and it is often grown as a groundcover to cover embankments. Will climb if it encounters a shrub or support. Can be trained over a sturdy support to provide dense shade, or to provide screening. Growth does not become unattractively rampant as with many other climbers, and little maintenance is needed. Vines become woody and thickened over time, so the support needs to be very sturdy.

Some people (myself included) find the flower's mothball-like smell a little unpleasant; others can't smell it.

Flowers best in full sun. For shaded conditions, *Hibbertia dentata* (see profile) is a better choice.

Very common in cultivation and widely available.

Homalanthus (formerly Omalanthus) populifolius

Common name(s): Bleeding Heart, Native Poplar, Queensland Poplar

Max. height, usually: 6 m

Max. width, usually: 4 m

Form: Bushy shrub or small tree.

Soil: Prefers humus-rich or moist soil but very adaptable.

Light: Full sun or part shade; young plants are very tolerant of shade, so it can be grown indoors when young.

Flower season: Yellow-green to red insignificant flowers Sept to Dec, followed by seed capsules Dec to Mar.

Photo: Margaret R Donald. https://creativecommons.org/licenses/by-sa/4.0/

Best features: Extremely fast-growing; shapely crown of attractive heart-shaped leaves; red older leaves give a pop of colour.

Propagation: Seed, which ripens in late summer, but have a long dormancy period.

Native to: Sydney but not Scotland Island. Not part of PWSGF. Nearest wild-collected records are Northbridge and Sailor's Bay. Frequently seen in local gardens as a "volunteer" through bird dispersal.

Distribution: NSW, Qld in regrowth or on margins of most types of rainforest, also in moist situations in eucalypt forest; widespread in coastal areas, also on the ranges.

Other notes: A pioneer rainforest species and a good candidate for revegetating disturbed sites quickly, but note that it grows so fast it bears seed within two years, which means you may end up with more of it than you had planned.

Favourite host plant for Australia's largest moth, the Hercules moth (*Coscinocera hercules*). Fruits are eaten by birds including honeyeaters, currawongs and silvereys, some of which might be responsible for the seedlings that I have seen from time to time in Elizabeth Park and along Fitzpatrick Trail on Scotland Island. They are not hard to pull up.

Larvae of the Hercules moth. The adults are also eye-catching. https://creativecommons.org/licenses/by/3.0/deed.en

Hovea acutifolia

Common name(s): Purple Bush Pea, Pointed-leaf Hovea

Max. height, usually: 3 m

Max. width, usually: 1-2 m

Form: Medium- to tall-size shrub or small tree with open branching.

Soil: Most well-drained soils; appreciates mulch. Tolerates clay soil, drought and salt spray.

Light: Prefers dappled to part shade; tolerates full sun.

Flower season: Masses of large purple pea-like flowers in spring.

Photo: Brian Walters, Australian Native Plants Society (Australia). https://anpsa.org.au/native-plant-profiles/

Best features: Fast-growing, good screener; large flowers followed by interesting ovoid seed pods; attractive leaves with rusty fuzz underneath; stem also has the same rusty fuzz.

Propagation: Seed, cuttings. Seed remains viable for many years.

Native to: Sydney but not Scotland Island. Not part of PWSGF. Nearest wild-collected records are from Lane Cove National Park and Mt Riverview (near Blaxland).

Distribution: Rainforest margins or other damp sheltered sites; coastal NSW and Qld.

Other notes: Beautiful plant year round.

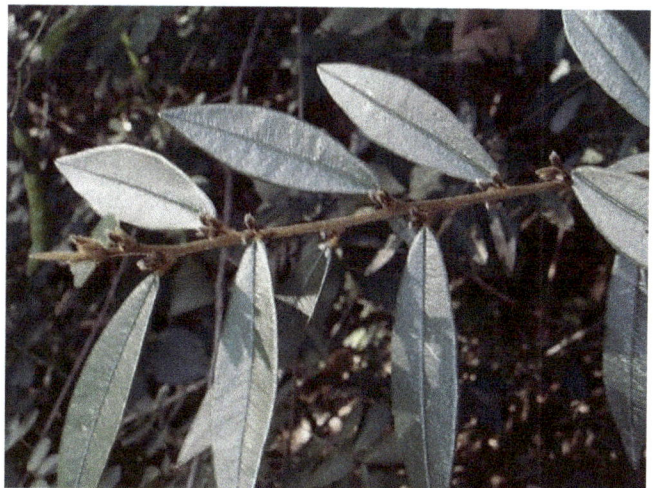

Photo: T.M. Tame, The Royal Botanic Gardens & Domain Trust

Short-lived; useful garden life is five to seven years, but it is easy to propagate so that you always have some in peak form. Often self-seeds if the soil remains undisturbed. Responds well to a light pruning after flowering, but unfortunately that does not appreciably extend its life. Young pods are said to be edible. Pods ripen to black and click or pop audibly when they open to release the seeds. Very attractive to a wide variety of critters including birds, wasps, bees, butterflies and spiders.

Also consider *Hovea longifolia* (see profile) if you have very well-drained soil and want a daintier-looking plant.

Popular plant for native gardens for many years and available at most native plant nurseries.

Hovea longifolia

Common name(s): Long-leaf Hovea, Rusty Pods

Max. height, usually: 3 m

Max. width, usually: 1-2 m

Form: Medium- to tall-size shrub with a narrow spread and open branching.

Soil: Very well-drained soil; prefers sandy or enriched sandy loam.

Light: Part-shade.

Flower season: Large purple pea-like flowers Aug to Oct.

Best features: Large flowers followed by interesting ovoid seed pods; attractive leaves with golden fuzz underneath; stem also has the same golden fuzz.

Propagation: Seed, cuttings. Seed remains viable for many years.

Native to: Sydney but not Scotland Island. Not part of PWSGF. Nearest wild-collected records are from Galston Gorge and Muogamarra Nature Reserve (Hawkesbury Sandstone).

Distribution: Shaded creek slopes and banks; coastal NSW.

Other notes: Best planted in a group of three or more, as each plant is usually somewhat narrow. This gives the appearance of a wider, spreading shrub or thicket.

Plant on a slope away from any runoff to ensure it is very well drained, especially if your soil is clay-based, as this is a sandstone-loving species. Also consider *Hovea acutifolia* (see profile), which is clay-tolerant.

Photo: In Narooma, NSW. Jenny aka Floydwafer, iNaturalist

Prune lightly after flowering to make it more compact, if that is desired. May be short-lived in the garden. Grows easily from seed and may self-seed in good conditions.

Available at some native plant nurseries.

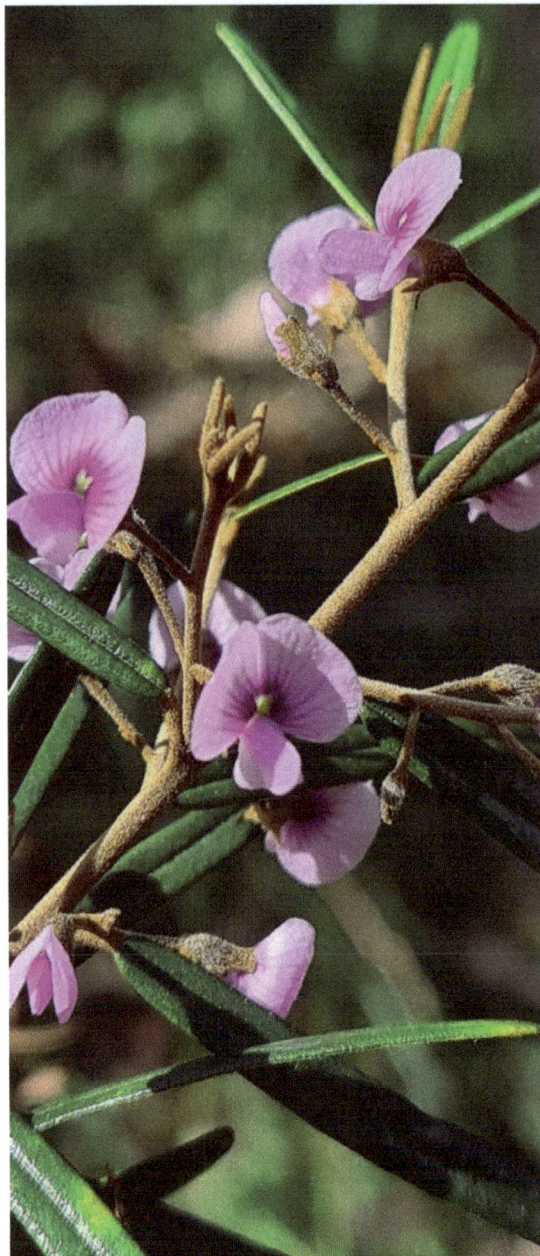

Hydrocotyle sibthorpioides (formerly H. peduncularis)

Common name(s): Pennywort

Max. height, usually: 15 cm

Max. width, usually: Indefinite.

Form: Slender herb with creeping stems above and below ground.

Soil: Moist sand, clay or loam.

Light: Light to heavy shade.

Flower season: Insignificant flowers spring to autumn.

Best features: Fast-growing groundcover; very shade-tolerant.

Propagation: Division; seeds are produced but collecting them is not feasible.

Native to: Sydney and Scotland Island. Not a component of PWSGF.

Distribution: Sclerophyll forest in NSW, Qld, Vic, Tas; also as garden weed.

Other notes: When growing on its own, can really gallop and cover large areas quickly during wet weather, including sunny areas, but dies back when dry weather comes (the same is true for *Viola banksii*).

Best when growing with other groundcovers, to provide biodiversity and visual relief, and to prevent the galloping effect. See Index section for a list of other groundcovers – creeping and otherwise.

Photo: Harry Rose https://www.flickr.com/photos/macleaygrassman/9005097983/ https://creativecommons.org/licenses/by/2.0/

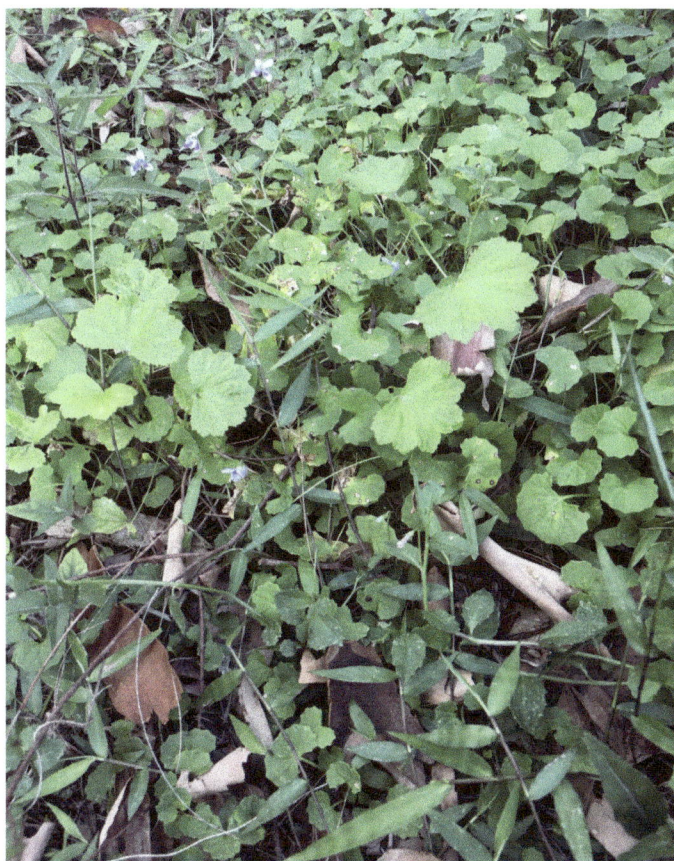

Behaving itself when grown with other groundcovers: *Pseuderanthemum variabile, Viola hederaceum, Oplismenus imbecilis, Lobelia purpurascens* (Pratia). Photo: H Malloy

Indigofera australis

Common name(s): Australian Indigo

Max. height, usually: 2 m

Max. width, usually: 2 m

Form: Upright shrub, tending to arch or straggle in one direction, but can be trimmed into a symmetrical shape.

Soil: Most well-drained soils are acceptable as long as it is not alkaline; tolerates drought once established; does not tolerate waterlogging.

Light: Prefers light shade; tolerates full sun; does not flower well in deep shade.

Flower season: Prolific pink flowers, ranging to soft purple, Aug to Oct.

Best features: Spectacular flowers contrasting well against the leaves; blue-green leaf colour year round, usually unblemished and fresh-looking.

Propagation: Seed.

Native to: Sydney and Scotland Island. Not a component of PWSGF. Can be seen on bushwalks at Bangalley Head.

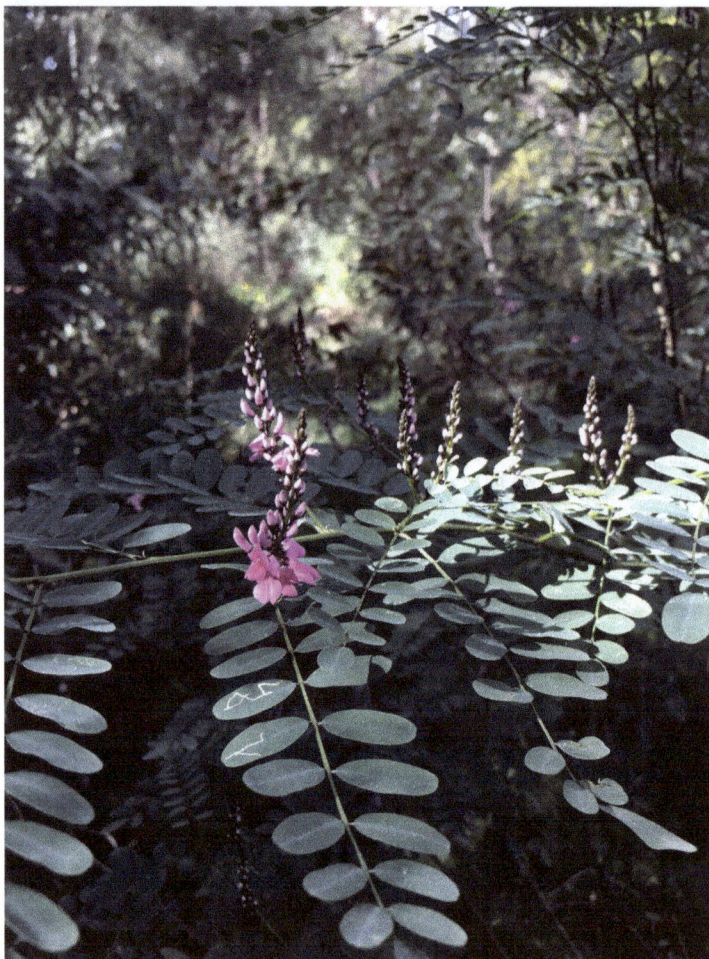

Shortly after photo was taken, this plant exploded into pink. Photo: H Malloy

Distribution: Variety of different habitats, mainly dry open woodland and eucalypt forest, but also in desert and in the margins of rainforest. Widespread in southern Australia from southeastern WA to northeastern Qld.

Other notes: Attracts butterflies.

Reasonably fast-growing and responds well to hard pruning after flowering to create a denser shape, but avoid pruning into very old wood. Can regrow and/or sucker from roots, e.g., after fire. Can be trained to grow in a prostrate form if planted at an angle to cascade down on a slope (this can happen naturally after loosening by storms).

Plants can be processed to yield a yellow or blue indigo dye, though not as strong as some other *Indigofera* species.

Widely available at native plant nurseries.

Jacksonia scoparia

Common name(s): Native Broom, Dogwood (from its strong odour when burnt)

Max. height, usually: 4 m

Max. width, usually: 4 m

Form: Leafless silvery grey-green shrub with softly weeping crown of tufted branchlets.

Soil: Any well-drained; very drought resistant; does not tolerate waterlogging.

Light: Full sun or light shade.

Flower season: Golden yellow pea-like flowers Oct-Nov followed by small pods holding one seed each.

Best features: Prolific flowers, interesting leafless rounded shrub.

Propagation: Seed, cuttings.

Native to: Sydney but not Scotland Island. Studies differ as to whether it is part of PWSGF[Ψ]. Nearest wild-collected records are from Newport, Bilgola Head, and Avalon Beach.

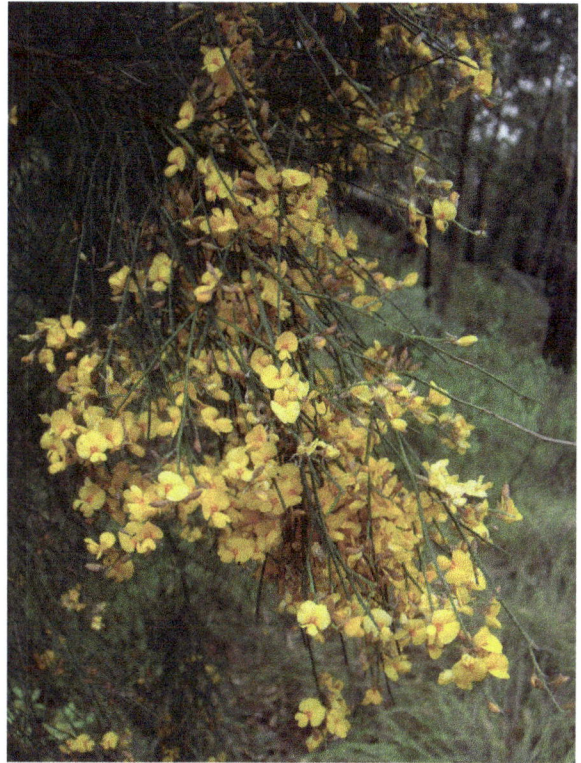

Photo: Alan Fairley https://resources.austplants.com.au/plant-database

Distribution: Widespread on low-nutrient gravelly soils associated with shales or clay, on hillsides and ridges; NSW, Qld.

Other notes: Hardy and adaptable. Naturally grows on shale and clay soils, but generally on hillsides, as it appears not to tolerate extended waterlogging. Fortunately, we are not short of hillside positions on Scotland Island. If a similar look is desired for wet or periodically inundated sites, consider *Viminaria juncea* (see profile) instead.

Photo: Gillian Gutridge, *Native Plants of the Northern Beaches, Sydney.* https://nbplantareas.com/

Appears leafless, though it does in fact have leaves; but they are reduced to the size of small scales. Young plants have normal-looking leaves. Makes a statement in a garden both in and out of flower.

As for most native shrubs, light pruning after flowering is recommended to encourage dense growth and strong flowering in following years.

Ψ   Bell & Stables 2012 don't report it. OEH 2016 reports it as an infrequent component of PSGF.

Juncus usitatus

Common name(s): Common Rush

Max. height, usually: 1 m

Max. width, usually: .5 to 1.5 m

Form: Rush with graceful arching stems.

Soil: Moist; tolerates some drought after establishment; prefers waterlogged, and does very well in clay-based soil. Salt-tolerant.

Light: Full sun to light shade.

Flower season: Pale brown flowers Nov to Feb.

Best features: Dramatic soft fountain form.

Propagation: Division; produces seeds but it is difficult to know when they are ripened. Self-seeded plants can be dug up and repositioned where needed. Seeds in the soil remain viable for at least five years or more.

Native to: Sydney but not Scotland Island. Not a component of PWSGF. Nearest wild-collected record is Bayview, 1948.

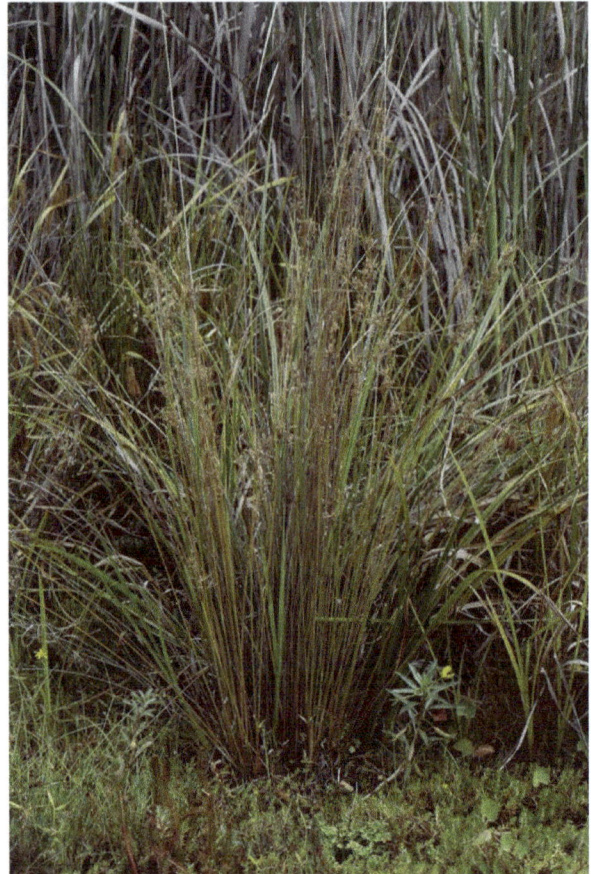

Photo: L. Vallee, Australian National Botanic Gardens

Distribution: Very common on stream banks and other moist places NSW, Qld, Vic.

Other notes: Requires moist conditions to establish by self-seeding, but doesn't need to remain constantly moist after plants are established.

Works well planted in groups around water features. Looks great planted in and around drainage channels, where it helps reduce erosion, cleans runoff water, and soaks up excess water.

Once you have planted a few, you will likely get volunteers coming up in places that remain damp for a few weeks after spring and summer rains.

If a tidier look is wanted, cut back to the ground every few years to get rid of the accumulation of dead stems, which can be unsightly.

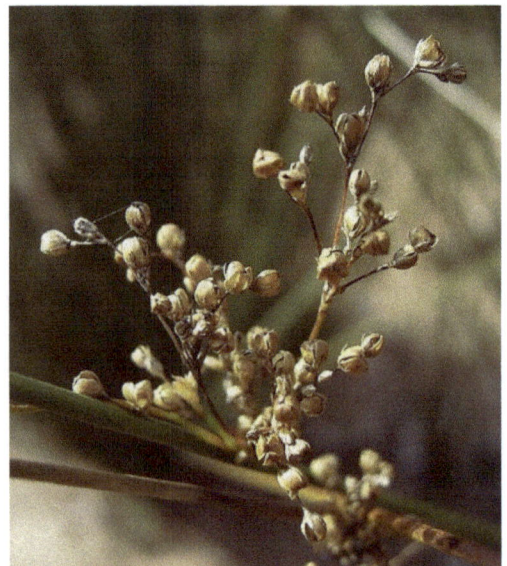

Photo: L. von Richter, The Royal Botanic Gardens & Domain Trust

Kennedia rubicunda

Common name(s): Dusky Coral Pea

Max. height, usually: Depends on what it climbs; stems up to 4 m long.

Max. width, usually: Depends on what it climbs; can cover large areas.

Form: Vigorous twiner.

Soil: Well-drained; drought resistant.

Light: Sun or partial shade.

Flower season: Mostly Sept to Dec, with some flowers at other times.

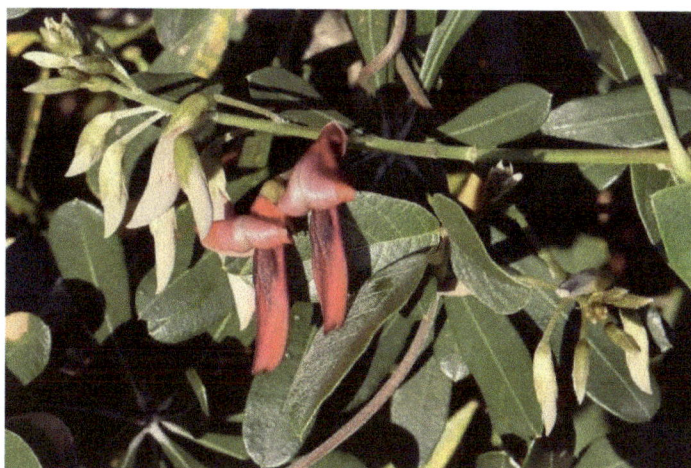

Photo: Gillian Gutridge, Native Plants of the Northern Beaches, Sydney. https://nbplantareas.com/

Best features: Brilliant dusty red flowers stand out well in contrast to the leaves and surrounding vegetation. Nitrogen-fixer; helps build up good soil.

Propagation: Seed; cuttings. The seed retains viability for many years.

Native to: Sydney and Scotland Island. Studies differ as to whether it is a component of PWSGF[Ω].

Distribution: Qld, NSW and Vic, in a variety of habitats from coast to mountains, usually in open forest and rainforest margins.

Other notes: Deep olivey-green three-segmented leaves are attractive year round. Lovely when allowed to climb on large shrubs where it won't become a problem. Greatly enhances what might otherwise be bare limbs. Very attractive when blooming amongst the purple blossoms of *Hardenbergia*, which flowers at the same time.

With *Hardenbergia*. Photo: Jenny aka Floydwafer, iNaturalist

It has somwhat of a reputation of becoming rampant in a garden situation. In my garden, the other natives seem able to keep it in check. Perhaps the rampant behaviour is from a cultivar that was bred as a groundcover, or this occurs where there isn't a diversity of other native plants, or in gardens that are moist with rich soil (mine isn't).

Can be used to cover embankments or structures; might need supplemental water and loamy soil to get good coverage, but beware of that tendancy toward rampant growth.

Ω   Bell & Stables 2012 don't report it. OEH 2016 report it as a typical component of PSGF.

Kunzea ambigua

Common name(s): Tick Bush, Butterfly Bush

Max. height, usually: 3 m

Max. width, usually: 3 m

Form: Stiff, spreading shrub, but quite variable, and some forms have more of a weeping habit.

Soil: Any well-drained soil; does not tolerate waterlogging. Very drought-resistant.

Light: Full sun to light shade.

Flower season: Honey-scented fluffy white flowers Sept to Nov, followed by small fruits which release numerous small seeds.

Photo: M Fagg https://www.anbg.gov.au/photo/image-collection.html

Best features: Attractive flowers, very hardy, low maintenance.

Propagation: Seed, cuttings.

Native to: Sydney but not Scotland Island. Not part of PWSGF. Nearest wild-collected records are from Bilgola, Avalon, and Newport.

Distribution: Heath and dry sclerophyll forest, chiefly south from the Sydney basin; NSW, Vic, Tas.

Other notes: Very hardy and reliable, and no maintenance is needed. Very tolerant of windy conditions. Good screener or informal hedge, though it is not especially fast-

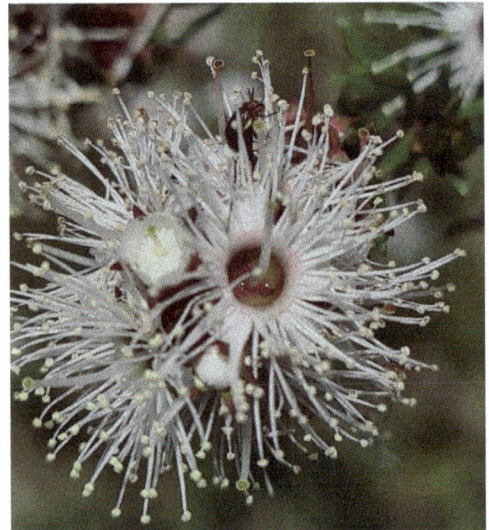

Photo: Jenny aka Floydwafer, iNaturalist

growing. Commonly used in bush regeneration and sand dune stabilisation, and widely available in native nurseries.

Branching tends to be a little eccentric, kind of like flames reaching out. Responds well to pruning if a more symmetrical look is desired, which can be done after flowering and again in autumn. Don't prune in winter as you may risk cutting off developing flower buds.

Attracts nectar-feeding birds, butterflies and colourful soldier beetles when in flower.

A pink form is available, which may have originated as a hybrid with *K. capitata*, a much smaller species. A prostrate form is also available, growing to .5 m high by 1.5 m wide. Other cultivars are available with a maximum height of around 2 m.

Lagenophora gracilis

Common name(s): Slender Bottle Daisy

Max. height, usually: 25 cm

Max. width, usually: 8 cm

Form: Tiny perennial herb with rosette of spoon-shaped leaves and tiny daisy-type flowers.

Soil: Moist well-drained; not very tolerant of drought, despite its tiny little fleshy roots.

Light: Full sun or semi-shade.

Flower season: Tiny white flowers Oct to Feb.

Best features: Very cute.

Propagation: Seed.

Native to: Sydney and Scotland Island. Not a component of PWSGF. Nearest wild-collected record is Bayview, 1941.

Distribution: Moist gullies and near water; chiefly in coastal districts in NSW, Qld, Vic, Tas, and SA

Other notes: Good along a semi-shaded path, but may be at its best in a container where its cuteness can be fully appreciated.

When its preferred growing conditions are met, it can become locally common (but never troublesome).

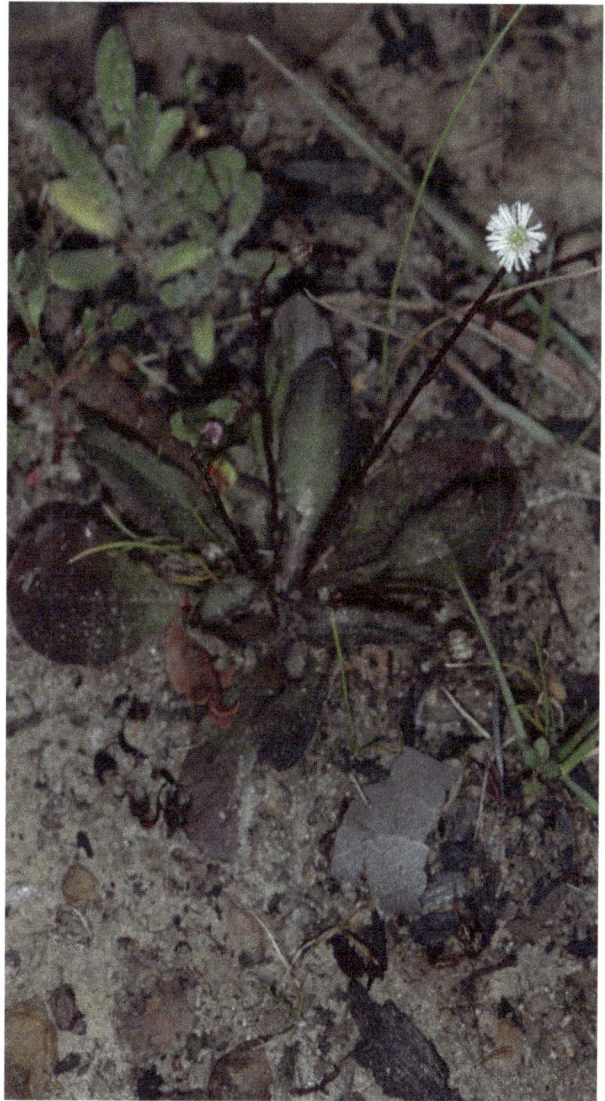

Photo: Chris Lindorff.
https://creativecommons.org/licenses/by/2.5/au/

Often functions as an annual, coming and going on its own schedule; one year there was a sizable patch alongside Scotland Island's north-most firetank, but the next year it was much reduced, and two years later it was hard to find any there.

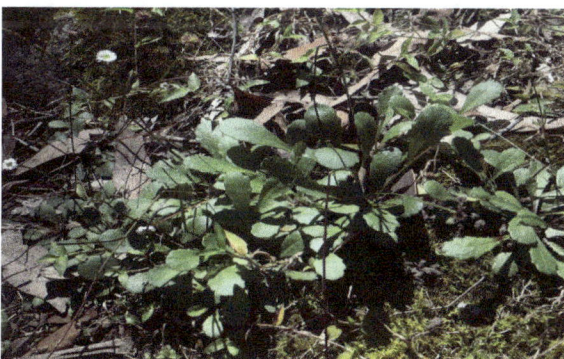

Photo: H Malloy

Leptospermum macrocarpum

Common name(s): Large-fruit Tea Tree

Max. height, usually: 1 m

Max. width, usually: 2 m

Form: Low, scrambling shrub.

Soil: Prefers well-drained moist sandy soil; tolerates heavy clay and poor drainage.

Light: Full sun to heavy shade.

Photo: M. Fagg https://www.anbg.gov.au/photo/image-collection.html

Flower season: Striking flowers with white, pale pink or dark red petals surrounding large shiny green centre; summer to autumn; followed by large, attractive shiny brown fruits.

Best features: Very large flowers (for a *Leptospermum*) of various shades of pink and green; flowers in summer when little else does.

Propagation: Seed, cuttings. Seedlings very small and hard to handle.

Native to: Not Sydney, unless you are talking about Sydney Basin, which includes the Blue Mountains. Not Scotland Island and not PWSGF. Nearest wild-collected record is Kurrajong.

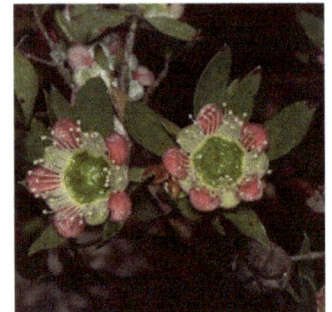

Photo: M. Fagg https://www.anbg.gov.au/photo/image-collection.html

Distribution: Endemic to the Blue Mountains, in poor sandstone soils on north-west slopes at the base of cliffs, in full sun or part shade; dry forest or heath on exposed rocky sandstone sites of Blue Mountains.

Other notes: A Sydney Basin native plant, but not native to the Northern Beaches area..

For such a striking flower, it is a relatively hardy, easy-to-grow plant, even though it is a sandstone-loving species. The various flower colours occur together within the small populations where the species grows in the wild. Therefore, to get a particular colour, you must grow it from cuttings taken from a parent with that colour, as it doesn't come true from seed.

An attractive hybrid between *L. macrocarpum* and two other species of *Leptospermum* is available in commercial nurseries under the cultivar name 'Mesmer Eyes', growing to 1.5 m high by 1 m wide, with even bigger flowers than *macrocarpum*. However, it flowers in spring, not summer.

Leptospermum polygalifolium[Ψ]

Common name(s): Tantoon, Jellybush, Lemon-scented Tea Tree (The lemon-scented leaves were used as a tea substitute in the early days of settlement.)

Max. height, usually: 2.5 m

Max. width, usually: 2 m

Form: Shrub or small tree, sometimes with weeping branches.

Soil: Sandy, clay, or loam; drought-tolerant. Does not like waterlogging.

Light: Full sun to part shade.

Flower season: White flowers Oct to Dec.

Best features: Profuse flowers, attractive shape; good screener.

Photos (above and below): Gillian Gutridge, *Native Plants of the Northern Beaches, Sydney.* https://nbplantareas.com/

Propagation: Seed, cuttings.

Native to: Sydney but not Scotland Island and not PWSGF. Can be seen on several local bushwalking trails – e.g., Cromer Heights, Deep Creek, Katandra Bushland Sanctuary[Ω].

Distribution: NSW and Qld; sandy soil or on sandstone, also on basalt derived soils.

Other notes: Hardy and reliable, it has been in cultivation for many years.

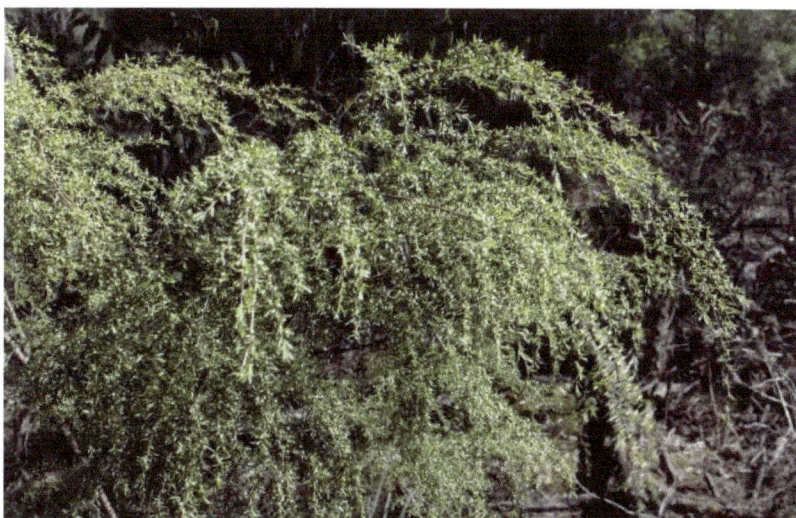

Can be pruned to create a denser plant. Watch for webbing caterpllars; remove by hand.

Often goes by an older name in nurseries, *Leptospermum flavescens.* There are many named cultivars, including "Cardwell" which flowers very well and has a weeping habit, from a subspecies that occurs in Qld. Other cultivars include "Pacific Beauty", "Copper Glow" and "Coastal Carpet".

Tantoon is also a parent species of several attractive hybrids, such as "Pink Cascade" and "Tickled Pink". "Pink Cascade" is said to be fairly resistant to webbing caterpillars.

[Ψ]   Full name: Leptospermum polygalifolium subsp. polygalifolium
[Ω]   Gillian Gutridge, *Native Plants of the Northern Beaches, Sydney.* https://nbplantareas.com/

Leucopogon juniperinus

Common name(s): Prickly Beard-heath

Max. height, usually: 1 m

Max. width, usually: 1 m

Form: Prickly, somewhat straggling shrub; the small leaves are sharply pointed.

Soil: Probably tolerates any well-drained soil including clay, as it grows on both shale- and sandstone-derived soils (shale-derived soil is generally clayey).

Light: Full sun to light shade; naturally grows in forest understorey, but also grows along roads, where it would get more direct sun.

Photo: Gillian Gutridge, *Native Plants of the Northern Beaches, Sydney.* https://nbplantareas.com/

Flower season: Tubular white flowers May-Oct, followed by yellow berries.

Best features: Prickly habitat and protection for small birds; lovely heath-type tubular flowers.

Propagation: No information available on internet for this species. Seed for other leucopogons may take up to three months to germinate[*]; cuttings unreliable[†].

Native to: Sydney and Scotland Island. Studies differ as to whether it is a part of PWSGF[Ψ]. Can be seen flowering for much of the year on the north side of Bangalley Headland[Ω].

Distribution: Dry and wet sclerophyll forest and woodland on various soils over shale or sandstone, west to Guyra and lower Blue Mountains; also Qld, Vic.

Other notes: I am not personally familiar with growing this species (yet). Not frequently cultivated except as part of specialist gardens for bird habitat; the prickly leaves help keep small birds safe.

Hard to find it in stock at native plant nurseries.

---

[*]   https://www.abc.net.au/gardening/how-to/leucopogons/9427462
[†]   https://anpsa.org.au/plant_profiles/leucopogon-lanceolatus/
[Ψ]   Bell & Stables 2012 don't report it. OEH 2016 reports it as typical PSGF.
[Ω]   Gillian Gutridge, *Native Plants of the Northern Beaches, Sydney.* https://nbplantareas.com/

Leucopogon lanceolatus (also known as L. affinis)[*]

Common name(s): White Beard; Lance-leaf Beard Heath

Max. height, usually: 3 m

Max. width, usually: 2 m

Form: Bushy shrub.

Soil: Moist, well-drained. May be tolerant of waterlogging, as it is found in moist gullies and swampy areas.

Light: Semi-shade.

Flower season: Usually spring, but can flower throughout the year except January. Bell-shaped white flowers followed by red berries said to be edible.

Photos (above and below): Gillian Gutridge, *Native Plants of the Northern Beaches, Sydney.* https://nbplantareas.com/

Best features: Attractive small bell-shaped flowers with interesting furry insides, dark green leaves and bushy form.

Propagation: Difficult. See propagation notes on profile for *L. juniperinus.*

Native to: Sydney and Scotland Island[Ψ]. Not part of PWSGF.

Distribution: Widespread in eucalypt forest and woodland on various substrates on coast and ranges; NSW, Qld, Tas, SA.

Other notes: Rarely seen in gardens. Said to be more successful in cultivation than most other species of *Leucopogon.* From what I gather, it is not prickly.

I am not personally familiar with this species (yet), and have never seen it in person as of this writing. As a result of reading about it, I have put it on my own 'must-buy' list.

Hard to find it in stock at native plant nurseries.

---

[*]   The subspecies that we have here on Scotland Island is known as *Leucopogon lanceolatus* var. *lanceolatus* in the Sydney Royal Botanic Gardens' PlantNET. However, the Australian Plant Census considers this name illegitimate and now refers to this species as *L. affinis.*

[Ψ]   Recorded by Brad Jones as occurring in Elizabeth Park. Also recorded as a wild-collected dried specimen on Scotland Island in 1922.

Lindsaea linearis

Common name(s): Screw Fern

Max. height, usually: 30 cm

Max. width, usually: Spreads indefinitely.

Form: Very small fern.

Soil: Moist, poorly drained clay, sandy, or loam soils.

Light: Full sun (if reliably moist) or lightly filtered sun.

Flower season: n/a

Best features: Pretty, delicate-looking fern; fronds are like a string of bow-ties or pie wedges.

Propagation: Difficult. Should not be removed from the wild, as it does not transplant well.

Native to: Sydney and Scotland Island. Not part of PWSGF.

Distribution: Widespread in moist areas, often amongst rocks in open forest or heath or near swamps; NSW, Qld, Vic, Tas, WA, SA. Also New Zealand.

Photo: H Malloy

Other notes: Best as drifts under trees, where the light is good but they are protected from overhead sun, and where the soil remains moist. Can be difficult to establish in a garden situation.

Resembles Necklace Fern (*Asplenium flabellifolium)* except Screw Fern has a dark stem, whereas Necklace Fern has a green stem. The location of the spore-cases also differs; in Screw Fern the spore cases are along the outer edge of the leaflet, like a Maidenhair Fern, whereas Necklace Fern has them in radiating lines parallel to the veins of the leaflet.

Not available commercially. Your best bet would be to find someone who has it in their garden and ask for some. Or enjoy it while you volunteer to weed in a bushland reserve near you.

Lobelia (formerly Pratia) purpurascens

Common name(s): Pratia, White Root

Max. height, usually: < 12 cm

Max. width, usually: Indefinite.

Form: Small mat-forming herb.

Soil: Moist well-drained.

Light: Part to full shade.

Flower season: White to pale mauve flowers Nov to May.

Best features: Tiny, tidy groundcover; dainty flowers.

Propagation: Division.

Native to: Sydney and Scotland Island. Typical component of Dry PWSGF.

Photos (above and below): H Malloy

Distribution: Widespread in shady, moist situations in woodland and grasslands in NSW, Qld, and Vic.

Other notes: Formerly known as *Pratia purpurascens*, and still referred to that way in older reference books.

Will grow in sunny locations if kept very moist. Popular for filling in between stepping stones or pavers.

Tolerates low amounts of foot traffic.

Stressed plants in sun seem to get a viral disease (?) which causes the stems and leaves to distort into a twisted pinkish mass, which is kind of pretty if you don't look too closely.

Milky sap can irritate the skin of some people.

The flowers are visited by butterflies – especially the Brown Ringlet (*Hypocysta metirius*).

Widely available at nurseries (both commercial and native).

Logania albiflora

Common name(s): Narrow-leaf Logania

Max. height, usually: 2 m

Max. width, usually: 1.5 m

Form: Dainty upright shrub with narrow leaves.

Soil: Prefers sandy, or sandy-loam, slightly acid soil.

Light: Semi-shade.

Flower season: Fragrant white flowers in spring.

Best features: Very fragrant and free-flowering; attractive shiny leaves year round.

Propagation: Seed, cuttings (slow to strike).

Native to: Sydney and Scotland Island[*]. Not part of PWSGF. Nearest wild-collected records are Cowan Creek and Terrey Hills. Can be seen on Deep Creek bushwalk trails[Σ].

Photos (above and below): Gillian Gutridge, *Native Plants of the Northern Beaches, Sydney*. https://nbplantareas.com/

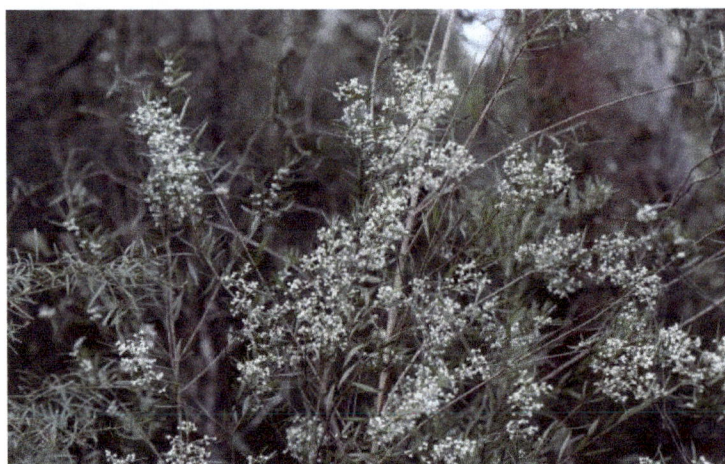

Distribution: Wet sclerophyll forest and woodland, widespread, but mostly uncommon, from coastal districts west to Condobolin district; NSW, Qld, Vic.

Other notes: Wrigley and Fagg note "worth growing for perfume alone". Sounds like it would do well wherever *Zieria smithii* (a close cousin and fellow Scotland Island native) thrives. As is also true for *Z. smithii* and related plants, the flower buds form up in early autumn, a promise of the show to come.

The genus *Logania* is in a family (Loganiaceae) that contains many species that are extremely poisonous, so take care that pets or children do not eat the plant.

I have only just made the acquaintenance of this species. I now have several plants settling in the ground near the living room windows, so that we can enjoy the fragrance when it flowers.

Most native plant nurseries carry it.

---

[*]   Recorded by Craig Burton and Brad Jones.

[Σ]   Gillian Gutridge, *Native Plants of the Northern Beaches, Sydney*. https://nbplantareas.com/

Lomatia myricoides

Common name(s): Long-leaf Lomatia, River Lomatia

Max. height, usually: 5 m

Max. width, usually: 3 m

Form: Medium shrub to small tree.

Soil: Most soils if reasonably drained; prefers loam or sand. Tolerates drought and occasional periods of waterlogging (e.g., by a rain-filled gully). Prefers regular watering.

Light: Semi-shaded.

Flower season: White, cream or rarely pink-tinged flowers in summer.

Photos (above and below): Gillian Gutridge, *Native Plants of the Northern Beaches, Sydney.* https://nbplantareas.com/

Best features: Attractive shade-loving shrub; flowers said to be perfumed; summer-flowering; attracts butterflies.

Propagation: Seed, cuttings.

Native to: Sydney but not Scotland Island. Not part of PWSGF. Nearest wild-collected records are Narrabeen, Berowra, and Oxford Falls Creek.

Distribution: Widespread, moist sheltered areas such as along watercourses or in sclerophyll forest on the coast and ranges; NSW, Vic.

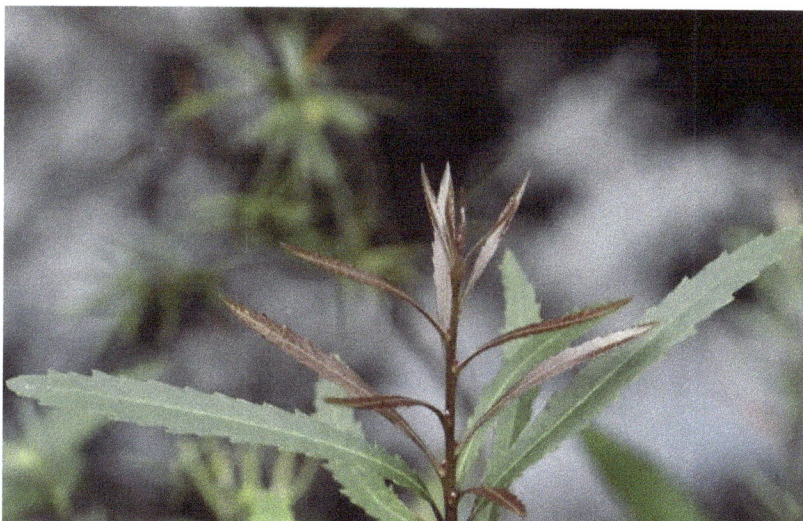

Other notes: Flowers are a little reminiscent of grevilleas, to which it is distantly related. Slow-growing. Not often seen in gardens and I am not very familiar with it yet.

I have planted one in a semi-shaded location alongside a road runoff diversion channel, where a *Callicoma* is thriving.

May work for gardens on south-facing slopes that do not receive any direct sun in winter, as long as they receive at least dappled sun in the spring and summer.

Most native plant nurseries carry it on their stocklists.

Lomatia silaifolia

Common name(s): Crinkle Bush, Parsley Fern and Wild Parsley

Max. height, usually: 1.5 m

Max. width, usually: 1 m

Form: Shrub.

Soil: Well-drained; tolerates clay. Tolerates drought but flowers better with regular water. Does not tolerate waterlogging.

Light: Part sun to heavy shade.

Flower season: White or cream flowers in summer, said to be scented.

Best features: Fast-growing; attractive fern-like leaves (like some grevilleas); flowers are held well up above foliage, making them a good cut flower.

Propagation: Said to be easy from seed, cuttings.

Native to: Sydney but not Scotland Island. Not part of PWSGF. Nearest wild-collected records are from KCNP ("on clayey sand"), Mona Vale and Careel Head.

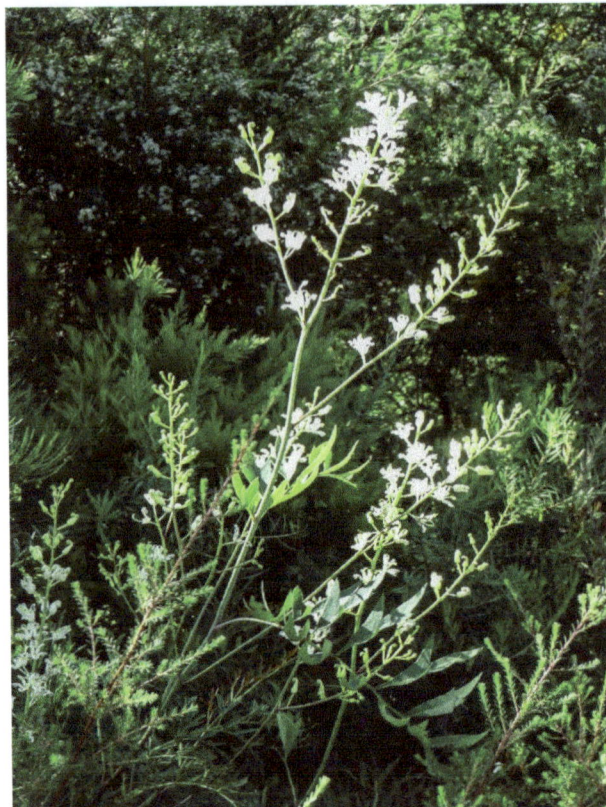

Photo: Jeff Howes https://resources.austplants.com.au/plant-database/

Distribution: Widespread in heath, sclerophyll forest and woodland, mainly on the coast and tablelands; NSW, Qld.

Other notes: Long-lived plant that regenerates after bushfire from a lignotuber (woody bulb-like swelling at base of plant).

Cut flowers are said to attract flies and kill them, which sounds like a useful feature. Take cut flowers for indoors or cut the old flowering branches back by two thirds after flowering, which will promote new growth from the lignotuber, making a bushier and more attractive plant.

Attracts bees and butterflies.

In the same family as grevilleas, and the leaves and flowers are very reminiscent of a grevillea.

Does not require supplemental watering but hardly flowers in drier years unless given regular watering.

Extremely variable in terms of leaf shape and colour, so you may find you like some better than others. Most native plant nurseries carry it on their stocklists.

SYDNEY LOCAL NATIVE

Maekawaea rhytidophylla (formerly Desmodium rhytidophyllum)[*]

Common name(s): Hairy Trefoil, Rusty Trefoil

Max. height, usually: Stems up to 1 m long.

Max. width, usually: 40 cm

Form: Scrambling or trailing herb or subshrub, with rusty, velvety leaves.

Soil: Well-drained, dry; sandy, stony or clay-based seem to be acceptable; very drought tolerant.

Light: Dappled or part shade.

Flower season: Small hot pink flowers Feb to Mar.

Best features: Attractive velvety trifoliate leaves; bright green new leaves contrast with darker old leaves; accepts dry positions without wilting; bright pink flowers are cheerful though tiny.

Propagation: Seed.

Native to: Sydney and Scotland Island. Typical of Dry PWSGF.

Distribution: Usually found on sandy or stony soils in dry sclerophyll forest in NSW, NT, Qld; also New Guinea.

Other notes: Easily overlooked when not in flower, as the leaves resemble those of *Kennedia rubicunda* (see profile).

No cultivation information generally available, and not often available from nurseries.

Looks good trailing down embankments, as it does along the fire trail near the peak of Scotland island.

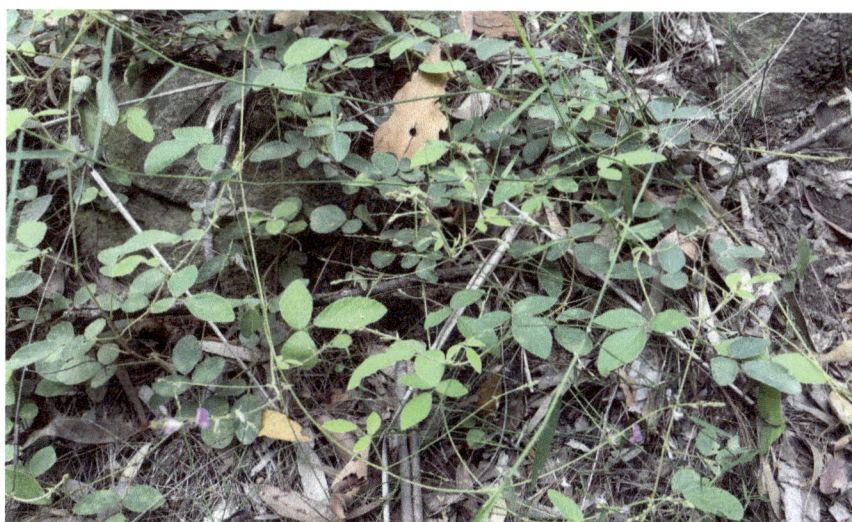

Along fire trail (road) in Elizabeth Park. Photo: H Malloy

As is the case for its smaller relative *Pullenia* (see profile), *Maekawaea* is a member of the legume family and is a nitrogen-fixer. Growing it helps to enrich the soil, and it grows happily alongside other groundcovers. Will climb or clamber if it encounters grasses or low shrubs, but it is not troublesome.

---

[*] The name change was made in 2020: H. Ohashi & K. Ohashi, *Journal of Japanese Botany* 95: 264.

Melaleuca nodosa

Common name(s): Prickly-leaf Paperbark

Max. height, usually: 1.5 to 3 m, up to 10 m in some cases.

Max. width, usually: 2 m

Form: Rounded shrub or (more usually) a small sparse tree with slightly drooping branches and narrow, sometimes needle-like leaves.

Soil: Clay- or shale-based or sandy; prefers well-drained. Tolerates both drought and waterlogging to a point, though it does best on well-drained soil. Tolerates salt spray.

Photo: Gillian Gutridge, *Native Plants of the Northern Beaches, Sydney.* https://nbplantareas.com/

Light: Flowers best in full sun but will tolerate shade, though with reduced flowering.

Flower season: Profuse spherical heads of honey-scented white to yellow flowers Sept to Nov.

Best features: Flowers like balls of white to yellow fluff. Prickly habit may provide shelter for birds. Attractive corky to papery bark. Nectar-bearing flowers are attractive to lorikeets as well as honeyeaters and flying foxes.

Propagation: Seed, cuttings. Seed is very, very small.

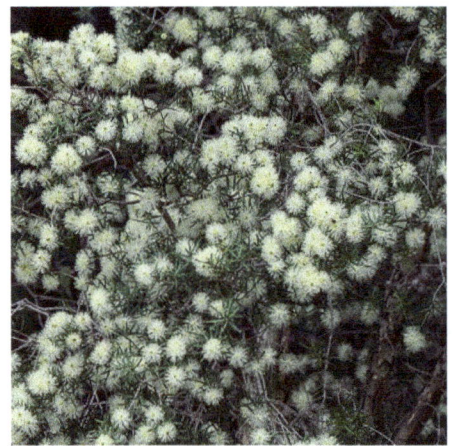
Photo: Heather Miles https://resources.austplants.com.au/plant-database/

Native to: Sydney but not Scotland Island. Not part of PWSGF. Nearest wild-collected records from Narrabeen and Dee Why.

Distribution: East coast of NSW and southern Qld and a disjunct occurrence in north Qld. Wide range of habitats, from alluvial and clay woodlands and forests in western Sydney to sandstone heathland, headland and shrubland, to tropical savannah woodlands.

Other notes: Unpredictable when grown from seed. Some grow narrow and upright like a small, graceful tree (see photo at right) and some grow as a rounded shrub. Ask at the nursery if they know which form their plants were propagated from.

Some specimens can withstand severe pruning, which stimulates coppice growth; so if it gets too tall you can start over, so to speak, by cutting it to the ground in early spring. Can be grown as a spiky hedge.

Most native plant nurseries carry it.

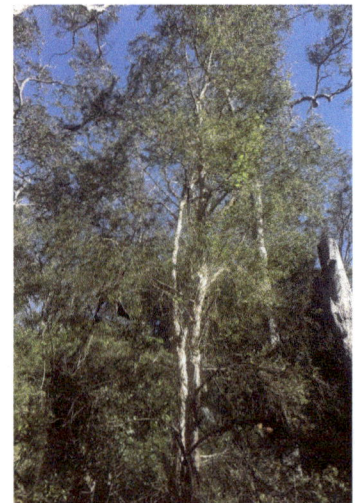
Photo: H Malloy

Microlaena stipoides

Common name(s): Weeping Grass, Weeping Rice Grass, Weeping Meadow Grass

Max. height, usually: 70 cm

Max. width, usually: Normally forms small, short tufts but can spread indefinitely if moisture is available.

Form: Graceful grass; tufted or spreading by rhizomes to form indefinitely large drifts.

Soil: Prefers moist, but tolerates drought.

Light: Dappled or light shade.

Flower season: Drooping stalks of spikelets Sept to Mar.

Photo: John Tann on Flickr.
https://creativecommons.org/licenses/by/2.0/

Best features: Stays fresh green and in active growth for most of the year.

Propagation: Seed, division. Unusually for a native grass, seeds do not have a dormancy period; fresh seed germinates readily.

Native to: Sydney and Scotland Island. Typical for both Dry and Moist PWSGF.

Distribution: Heathlands, woodlands, and forests in all Australian states as well as in NZ, PNG, Indonesia and the Philippines.

Photo: John Tann on Flickr.
https://creativecommons.org/licenses/by/2.0/

Other notes: Excellent lawn alternative, but can be invasive into garden beds. Tolerates mowing. Seeds tend to get in your socks and be an annoyance, so perhaps not too good along paths.

A cousin to rice, as well as to the invasive weed *Ehrharta erecta*. The grains are high in protein and research is underway to develop it as a commercial crop for human consumption.[*]

Highly variable regarding size and colour, although a particular drift or patch may be homogenous due to its all being descended from one genetic individual. Some individuals have a burgundy tint.

Makes a lovely groundcover on its own under flowering shrubs in a more formal native garden. However, as is also the case for Maidenhair Fern and Native Violets (both *V. banksii* and to a lesser extent, *V. hederacea*), when grown as a monoculture, *Microlaena* will colonise sunny areas during spring or other times of plentiful water, only to collapse in an unsightly mess when dry weather comes. Best to keep it in shaded areas only.

Available at native nurseries.

---

[*]   Davies, C. L., D. L. Waugh and E. C. Lefroy. Perennial Grain Crops for High Water Use - The case for *Microlaena stipoides*. A report for the Rural Industries Research and Development Corporation, RIRDC Publication No 05/024. February, 2005. Archived at: https://web.archive.org/web/20120302071643/https://rirdc.infoservices.com.au/downloads/05-024.pdf

Olearia tomentosa

Common name(s): Toothed Daisy-bush

Max. height, usually: 2 m

Max. width, usually: 2 m

Form: Small to medium shrub.

Soil: Well-drained loamy or sandy soil; moderately tolerant of salt spray.

Light: Full sun or part shade.

Flower season: White (sometimes mauve) daisy flowers Aug to May.

Best features: Grey-green toothed or scalloped leaves, conspicuously veined and a little bit furry.

Propagation: Seed (unreliable), cuttings.

Native to: Sydney but not Scotland Island and not PWSGF. Nearest wild-collected records are Morning Bay and Bayview. Can be seen on trails at Deep Creek and Katandra Bushland Sanctuary[Ω].

Distribution: NSW and Vic; dry sclerophyll forest, scrub and heath; widespread in coastal sites.

Photos (above and below): Gillian Gutridge, *Native Plants of the Northern Beaches, Sydney.* https://nbplantareas.com/

Other notes: Hardy, attractive mounding shrub not often seen in gardens.

Prune annually after flowering to keep it from getting leggy. Though it survives extended droughts, it will need supplemental water to look its best.

Available from some native nurseries. Also look in commercial nurseries for named selection "Mauve Magic" which has flowers that open up mauve and age to pure white.12

[Ω]   Gillian Gutridge, *Native Plants of the Northern Beaches, Sydney.* https://nbplantareas.com/

Oplismenus imbecilis

Common name(s): Slender Basket Grass

Max. height, usually: 30 cm

Max. width, usually: 1 m

Form: Freely branching, creeping grass.

Soil: Well-drained moist soil.

Light: Dappled to part shade.

Flower season: Small spikes most of the year.

Best features: Small nonaggressive groundcover.

Propagation: Division.

Native to: Sydney and Scotland Island.A typical component of Moist PWSGF.

Distribution: Shady forest in NSW, Qld, Vic, NT.

Other notes: Some plants have attractive reddish stems.

Photo: H Malloy

O. imbecilis is better behaved than its more aggressive sister species *O. aemulus,* which is more familiar to most gardeners. *O. aemulus* can easily be distinguished by its wider leaves, often conspicuously wavy. Both species can be mown to make an informal lawn. It is probably best not to encourage *O. aemulus* too much, as it self-seeds and spreads by runners at a galloping pace. Even worse, the flowers of *O. aemulus* turn ragged and unsightly towards the end of the summer; if you can mow it, the problem is not so bad.

O. imbecilis requires more shade than *O. aemulus,* and the stems are more upright-growing, with the leaves held at right angles to the stem (similar to *Entolasia*). The flowers of *O. imbecilis* stay tidy looking, in contrast to the ragged messes on top of *O. aemulus* towards the end of the summer.

Not available from local native nurseries. Best to ask someone who has it to give you some divisions of it; most gardeners would be glad to share.

Ozothamnus diosmifolius

Common name(s): Rice Flower, White Dogwood, Pill Flower and Sago Bush

Max. height, usually: 2 m

Max. width, usually: 1-2 m

Form: Multistemmed open shrub.

Soil: Well-drained; very drought tolerant.

Light: Full sun or light shade.

Flower season: White or pink "flowers" (composite flowers) in clusters of 20 to 100 at ends of branches most of the year, with a peak in spring and early summer.

Best features: Fast growing; long flowering period; profuse flowers; long lasting cut flower, and complements other, more flamboyant flowers.

Propagation: Seed; cuttings.

Native to: Sydney and Scotland Island. Not a component of PWSGF.

Distribution: Heath and rainforest margins, often on ridges; widespread locations on the coast, tablelands and western slopes of NSW and Qld north from Eden to Wide Bay.

Other notes: Tends to grow erratically and can become straggly after three seasons or so if left unpruned, but still a knockout when in flower.

Pink forms are available, e.g., "Just Blush", "Royal Flush" and "Red Gingham"; also cultivars with a more compact habit.

If you have trouble remembering the scientific name, you could try my husband's pronunciation of the name: "oh-so-famous".

Photo: H Malloy

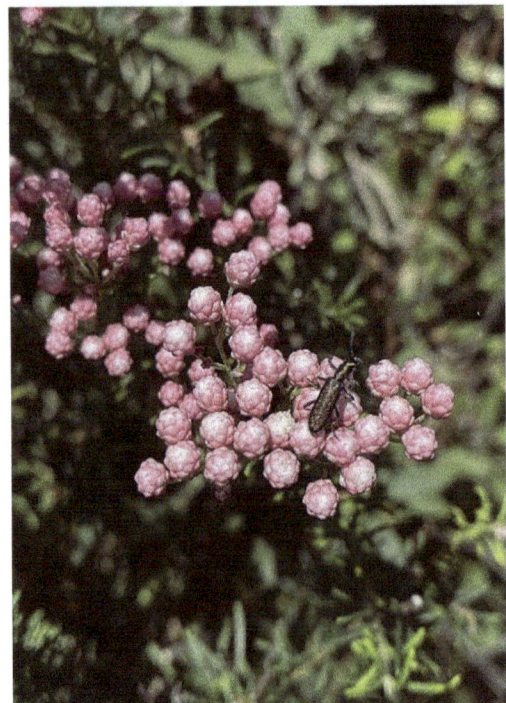

Photo: Allthingsnative
https://commons.wikimedia.org/wiki/File:Ozothamnus_diosmifolius_(closeup_of_buds).jpg
https://creativecommons.org/licenses/by-sa/4.0/deed.en

Panicum simile

Common name(s): Two Colour Panic Grass

Max. height, usually: 70 cm

Max. width, usually: 40 cm

Form: Delicate clumping grass.

Soil: Sandstone; seems to like it very dry.

Light: Full sun.

Flower season: Summer.

Best features: Pink tinge to the developing seedheads; tidy form.

Propagation: Seed, division.

Native to: Sydney and Scotland Island[*]. Typical for Dry PWSGF.

Distribution: Low nutrient soils in woodland or scrub in NSW, Qld, Vic, NT.

Other notes: Produces copious seeds. In poor conditions, e.g., on very dry sites, it may function as an annual.

Might be best in a mass planting so that the pink tinge and tidy form can be appreciated.

Every part of the branched flowering stems seems to be pitched at the same angle, creating a soothing subtle fractal pattern.[†]

Panicum is the old Latin name for millet (now known as *Setaria italica*). Other members of the genus are grown for food, e.g. proso millet *(P. miliaceum)*, which is extensively cultivated.

I haven't personally observed this yet, but I would imagine that cockatoos and other birds would relish the seeds.

Several local native plant nurseries carry it.

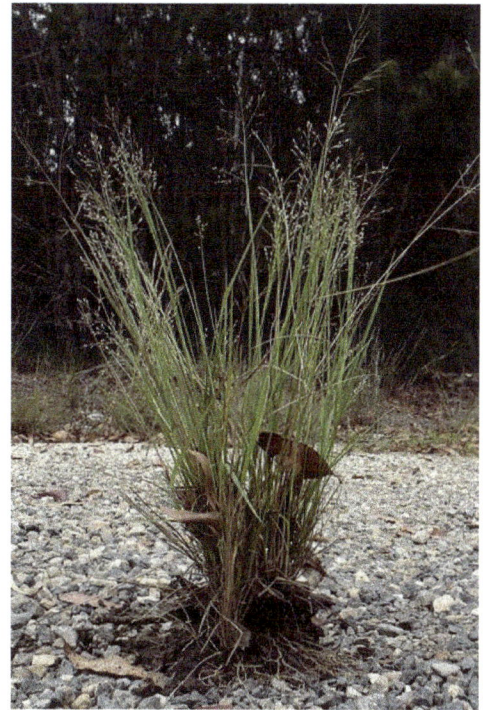

Photo: Harry Rose
https://commons.wikimedia.org/wiki/File:Panicum_simile_plant6_(8247732849).jpg
https://creativecommons.org/licenses/by/2.0/deed.en

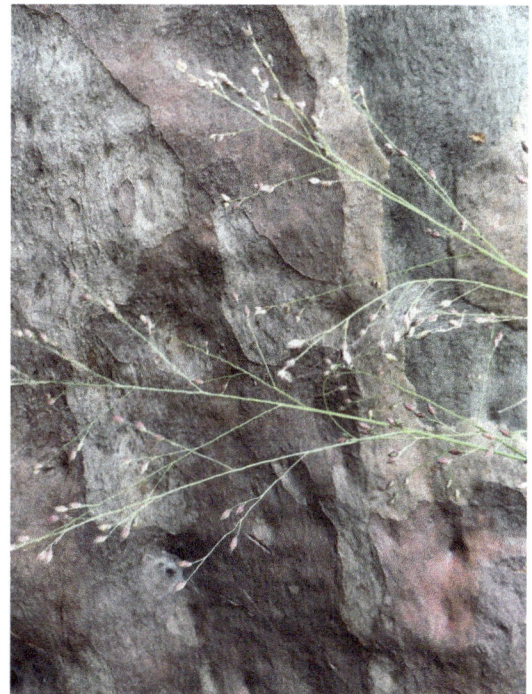

Pink seedheads against a pink spotted gum trunk. Photo: H Malloy

---

* Currently found in several places in Elizabeth Park. Not recorded as occurring on Scotland Island by previous vegetation surveys.

† https://www.theatlantic.com/science/archive/2017/01/why-fractals-are-so-soothing/514520/

Patersonia glabrata

Common name(s): Leafy Purple Flag, Native Iris

Max. height, usually: 80 cm

Max. width, usually: 30 cm

Form: Large clump of flowering stems clothed in linear, grass-like leaves.

Soil: Sandy or clay loam soils; well-drained or poorly drained; prefers moist soils.

Light: Full sun or semi-shade.

Flower season: Purple flowers Sept to Nov.

Best features: Vivid flowers; attractive foliage year round.

Propagation: Seed (said to be easy), division.

Native to: Sydney but not Scotland Island and not PWSGF. See it on many local bushwalking trails, e.g., Bangalley Head, Chiltern North[Ω]. Also in KCNP on Waratah Trail.

Distribution: In woodland, dry sclerophyll forest and coastal heath on coast and tablelands; Vic, NSW and Qld.

Other notes: Resembles *P. sericea*, and both species may grow together in the same location. Easily distinguished because the leaves of *P. glabrata* emerge along the flowering stems, whereas the leaves of *P. sericea* emerge directly from the ground (like irises).

The colourful "petals" are botanically speaking sepals, with the true petals much reduced.

Reliable plant for rockeries or mass planting, but may need supplemental watering to look good.

Photo: Gillian Gutridge, *Native Plants of the Northern Beaches, Sydney.* https://nbplantareas.com/

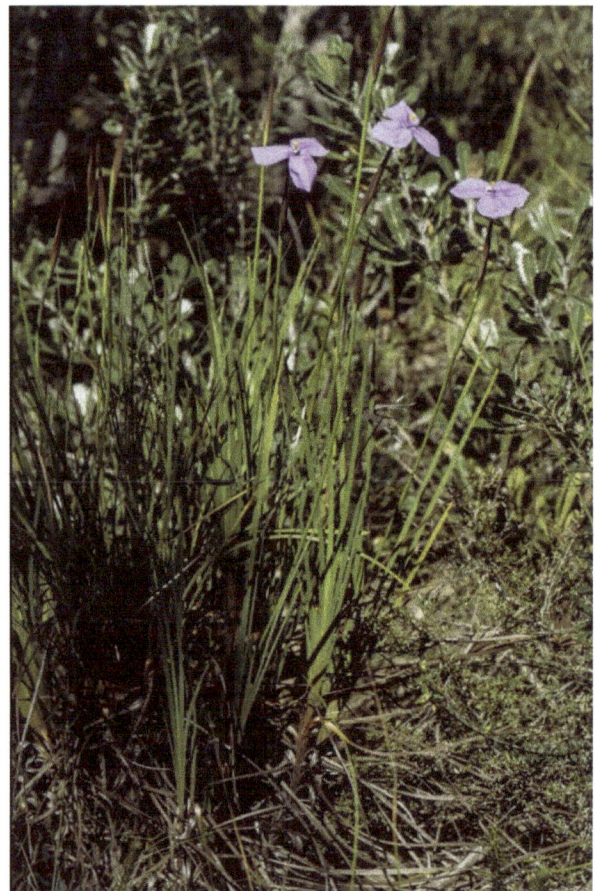

Photo: Alan Fairley https://resources.austplants.com.au/plant-database

Needs more watering than *P. sericea*. If you have a hot dry garden on sandy soil, try *P. sericea* instead (see next profile).

Both species are available from some native plant nurseries.

Ω   Gillian Gutridge, *Native Plants of the Northern Beaches, Sydney*. https://nbplantareas.com/

Patersonia sericea

Common name(s): Silky Purple Flag, Native Iris

Max. height, usually: 60 cm

Max. width, usually: 40 cm

Form: Densely tufted grass-like plant.

Soil: Well-drained sandy soil; drought-tolerant.

Light: Full sun to filtered shade.

Flower season: Purple flowers July to Dec (peak in Sept), opening one per day.

Best features: Vivid colour stands out dramatically against dark grey-green leaves.

Propagation: Seed (difficult), division.

Native to: Sydney but not Scotland Island and not PWSGF. See it on many local bushwalking trails, e.g., Bangalley Head, Chiltern North, Chiltern[Ω].

Distribution: NSW and Vic in dry sclerophyll forest and heath on sandy soil.

Other notes: Blue like an iris, and in the iris family as well.

Each flower only lasts a day, but there is a seemingly endless procession of flowers emerging from a pair of silky-hairy black or olive-coloured bracts at the end of a leafless stalk. The flowering shoots begin emerging from the ground just past the winter solstice.

Slow-growing but long-lived.

Reliable in sandy gardens for hot dry positions, but will need some watering to look its best.

Grows well in a pot.

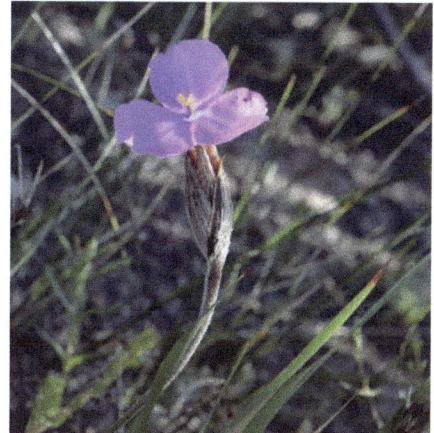

Photos (above and below): Gillian Gutridge, *Native Plants of the Northern Beaches, Sydney.* https://nbplantareas.com/

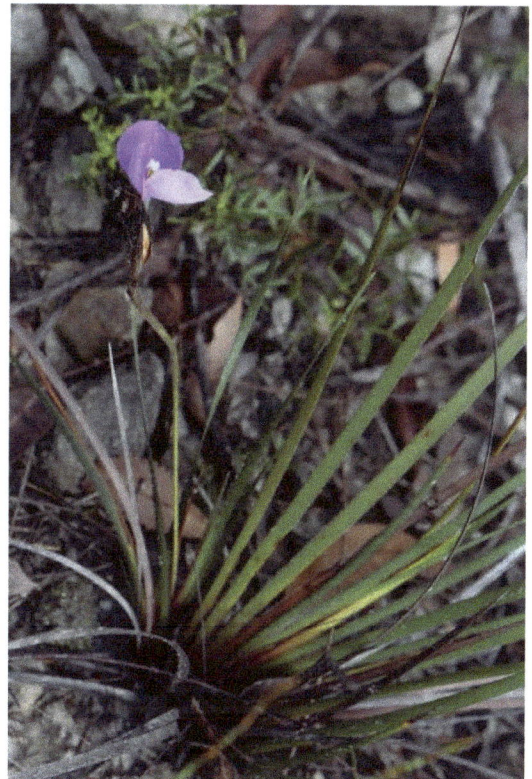

If you have clay soil or poor drainage, try *P. glabrata* instead, which is also locally native but clay-tolerant. Both species are available from some native plant nurseries.

Ω   Gillian Gutridge, *Native Plants of the Northern Beaches, Sydney.* https://nbplantareas.com/

Pelargonium australe

Common name(s): Wild Geranium, Native Storksbill

Max. height, usually: 50 cm

Max. width, usually: 1 m, but can spread to fill a larger space via self-seeding.

Form: Soft fuzzy scalloped leaves on short stems.

Soil: Well-drained; drought tolerant; tolerant of salt spray.

Light: Full sun or dappled shade.

Flower season: Pink or white flowers Oct to Mar.

Best features: Fast-growing groundcover; long flowering period; attractive fuzzy leaves.

Propagation: Seeds, cuttings. May self-seed.

Native to: Sydney and Scotland Island[*]. Not a component of PWSGF. Nearest wild-collected record is Narrabeen, 1913.

Distribution: Sand dunes, coastal cliffs and rocky outcrops and further inland in semi-arid areas, in all Australian states except NT.

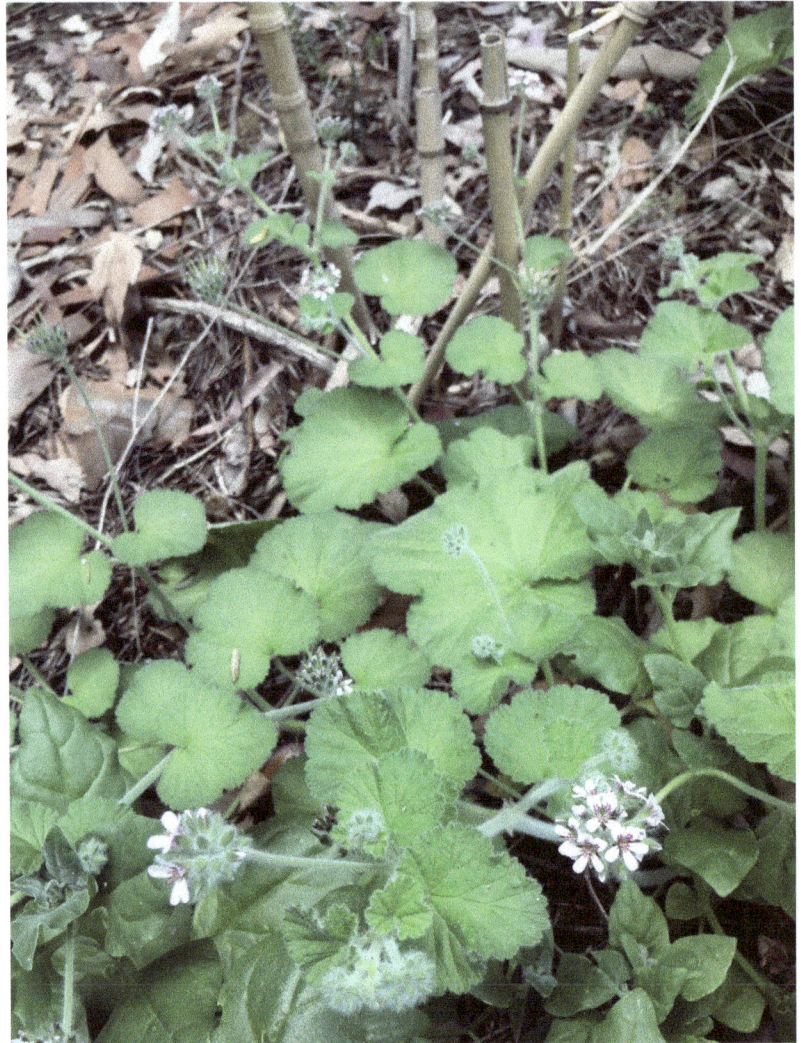
Photos (above and below: H Malloy)

Other notes: Provides shelter to small animals such as skinks, small animals and insects – especially valuable in areas where there is no overhead tree canopy.

Border or rockery plant. Tolerates salt spray.

Attracts pollinators when planted around a veggie patch.

Large leaves provide a strong accent in a garden.

Good candidate for dry spots under trees.

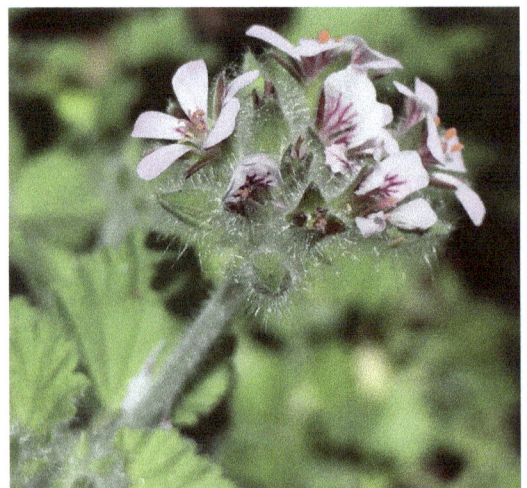

There is an attractive hybrid available under the name "Applause" between *P. australe* and a larger-flowered species, *P. rodneyanum.* It retains many of the qualities of *P. australe*, but with bigger, darker pink flowers, and does not self-seed.

---

[*]   Recorded in Elizabeth Park by Brad Jones 2009.

Pellaea falcata

Common name(s): Sickle Fern

Max. height, usually: 60 cm

Max. width, usually: Spreads indefinitely.

Form: Small fern.

Soil: Moist, well-drained soil; mulch or provide a few rocks to cool the roots and conserve moisture.

Light: Likes some sun; semi-shade to dappled shade.

Flower season: n/a

Best features: Fresh-looking, shiny bright green fronds.

Propagation: Spores, division.

Native to: Sydney but not Scotland Island. Not part of PWSGF. Nearest wild-collected record is from Bayview, where it was growing in forest amongst rocks.

Distribution: NSW, Qld, Vic, Tas; widespread on the coast and ranges in moist, shady or rocky places in sclerophyll forest and rainforest.

Photo: Marita Macrae

Other notes: Hardy attractive fern which at first glance resembles the common fishbone fern *Nephrolepis cordifolia* (an invasive weed not native in the Central Coast region). Sickle Fern has smooth bright green fronds and shiny dark brown wiry stems, vs. the dull green fronds and scaly stems of Fishbone Fern.

Too much sun makes it unattractively yellow, and can be avoided by moving the fern to a shadier spot. Yellow colour can also come from iron deficiency, which is common in ferns in a garden situation and can be treated by applying iron chelates and feeding with fish emulsion.

Very popular as both a garden plant and an indoor plant, and widely available at commercial nurseries.

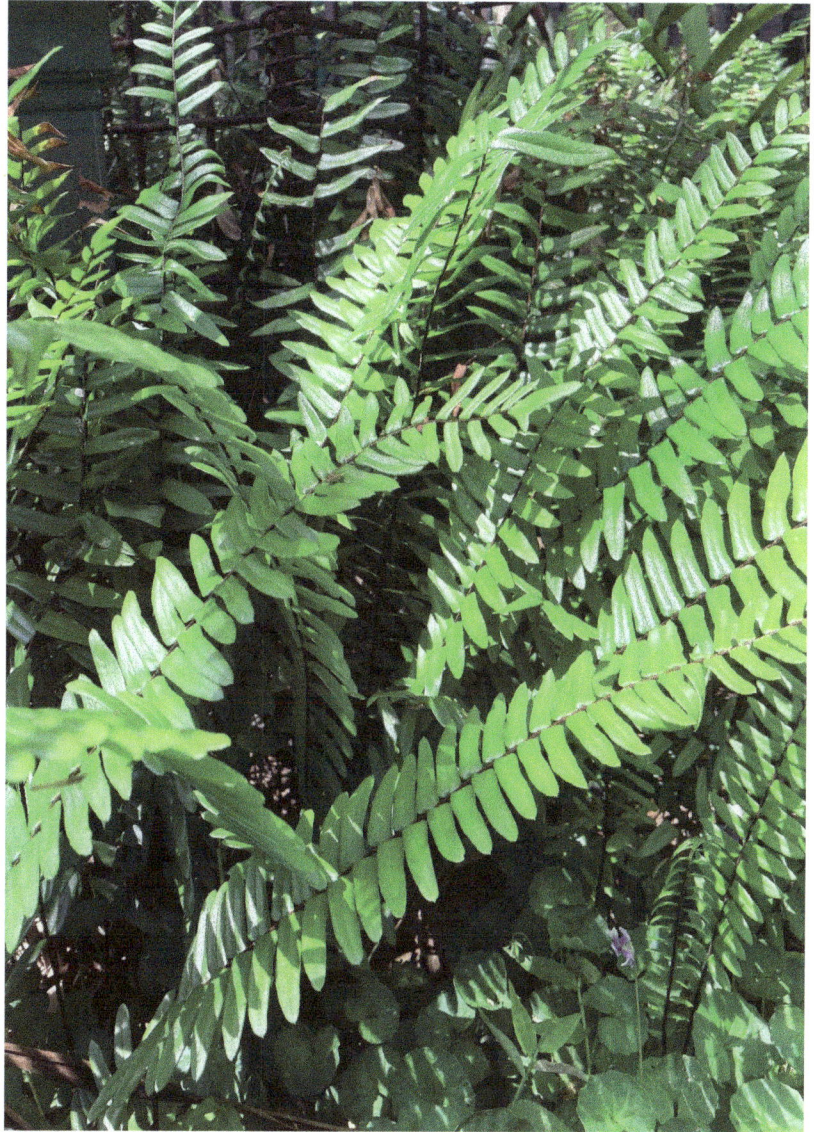

Persoonia levis

Common name(s): Broad-leaf Geebung

Max. height, usually: 5 m

Max. width, usually: 3 m

Form: Shrub or small tree.

Soil: Well-drained sandy soil; drought-tolerant.

Light: Full sun to dappled sun.

Flower season: Yellow flowers in summer and autumn (Dec to Apr), sometimes with flowers at other times too, followed by edible fleshy green fruit widely known to Australian children as snottygobbles.

Best features: Very bright green leaves held vertically stand out against the usual grey-green of bushland; dark papery bark peels off in patches to reveal blood-red colour beneath.

Propagation: Seed (difficult), cuttings.

Native to: Sydney and Scotland Island; typical of Dry PWSGF.

Distribution: Heath to dry sclerophyll forest, in NSW and Vic.

Other notes: Striking shrub at all times of the year. Looks like it was drawn by a child. Best garden use is probably as contrast for other more conventially pretty plants, or perhaps as a specimen planting in a bush-themed garden.

The fruits fall before they are ripe, and they complete their ripening on the ground, where they are eaten by possums, currawongs, and people. The skin and seeds are inedible.

Photo: H Malloy

Photo: Dan Clarke https://resources.austplants.com.au/plant-database/

Persoonia species are notoriously hard to propagate, but they are becoming more common in nurseries. Available at some native plant nurseries.

Occasionally hybridises with *P. linearis,* which is also found on Scotland Island. The hybrid is referred to as *Persoonia x lucida* or Shiny Geebung and is also sometimes cultivated.

Persoonia linearis

Common name(s): Narrow-leaf Geebung

Max. height, usually: 5 m

Max. width, usually: 2 m

Form: Upright shrub.

Soil: Sandy or clay free-draining soil.

Light: Prefers dappled sun or part shade; tolerates full sun. Somewhat drought-tolerant.

Flower season: Yellow flowers Dec to May near the ends of branches, which then continue growing outwards. Fruits have purplish blotches when ripe.

Best features: Attractive soft linear leaves, fresh green colour; flaky black and red bark; cute flowers.

Propagation: Seed, which is difficult; cuttings, which are difficult.

Native to: Sydney and Scotland Island. Typical part of Dry PWSGF.

Distribution: NSW and Vic, in sclerophyll forest or woodland on various soils.

Other notes: Superficially similar to the showier *P. pinifolia* which is more widely grown in gardens, and is also native to the Northern Beaches. *P. pinifolia* has long, tapering racemes of yellow flowers at the ends of branches in late winter to summer (in contrast to *P. linearis* which flowers in summer). Why not have both?

As with most members of the genus, finding it in a nursery can be a challenge. You could try calling local native plant nurseries and placing an order – see list of nurseries for phone numbers.

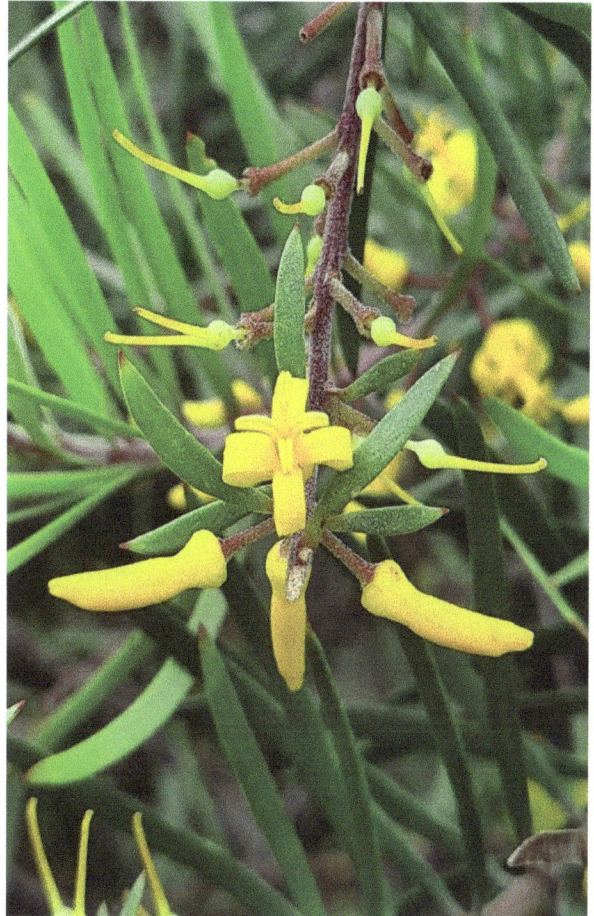

Photos (above and below): Jenny aka Floydwafer, iNaturalist

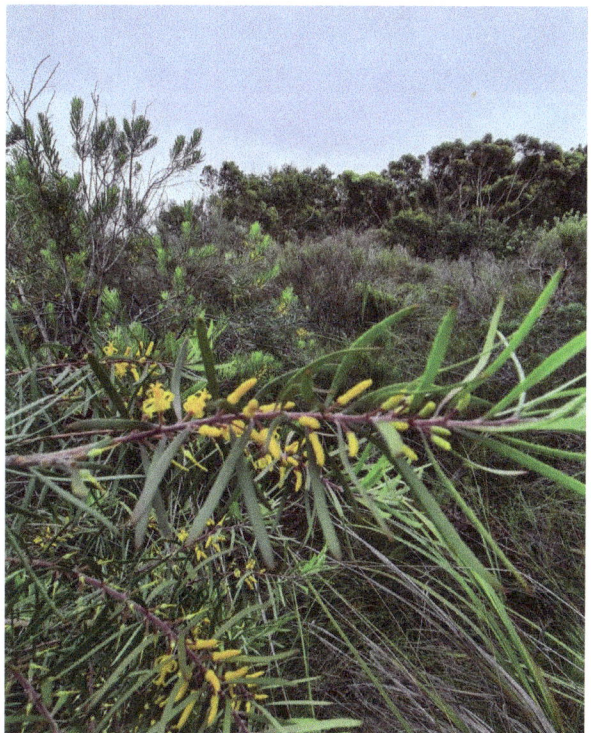

Phebalium squamulosum[Ω]

Common name(s): Forest Phebalium

Max. height, usually: 2 m

Max. width, usually: 2 m

Form: Spreading shrub or small erect tree.

Soil: Well-drained soil; tolerates dryness once established.

Light: Filtered to part sun.

Flower season: Profuse flowers in the cream to bright yellow range in early spring.

Best features: Charming and showy flowers; flower buds are decorative also and begin to be formed months in advance; tidy rounded shape.

Photos (above and below): Gillian Gutridge, *Native Plants of the Northern Beaches, Sydney*. https://nbplantareas.com/

Propagation: Cuttings.

Native to: Sydney but not Scotland Island, and not part of PWSGF. Can be seen in KCNP on Chiltern trail. Also other local bushwalks: Cromer Heights, Deep Creek, and West Head[Σ].

Distribution: Sclerophyll forest, widespread on sandstone, in NSW, Qld, Vic.

Other notes: Reliable and tough once established. Mulch annually and prune lightly after flowering to keep them compact and promote better flowering next season.

A gardener with clay subsoil reports that in some spots in his garden they don't establish well, though in other spots they seem to do fine; his plants receive little additional water after the first year or so[Ψ].

Makes a delightful combination with Pink Spider Flower (*Grevillea sericea;* see profile*)*, which enjoys the same lightly shaded conditions.

Another garden use is under trees with thirsty roots, where other plants wither away from dryness.

Most native plant nurseries carry it.

[Ω]   Full name: Phebalium squamulosum subsp. squamulosum – i.e., the normal form and in this case also the most common one.

[Σ]   Gillian Gutridge, *Native Plants of the Northern Beaches, Sydney*. https://nbplantareas.com/

[Ψ]   Jeff Howes, Australian Plant Society NSW, https://austplants.com.au/Phebalium-squamulosum-ssp-squamulosum-Scaly-Phebalium

Phebalium squamulosum subsp. argenteum

Common name(s): Silvery Phebalium

Max. height, usually: 1.5 m

Max. width, usually: 1.5 m

Form: Small spreading shrub.

Soil: Well-drained clay, loam or sand; tolerates salt spray and wind.

Light: Part shade.

Flower season: White or cream flowers in early spring.

Best features: Profuse flowers as for the normal form of the species; attractive silvery stems, flower buds and new growth; tidy shape.

Propagation: Cuttings.

Native to: Sydney but not Scotland Island and not PWSGF. Nearest wild-collected record is from Cronulla, but Northern Beaches is within its range, which is from Port Stephens south to Vic border.

Photo: Will Cornwell, iNaturalist. http://creativecommons.org/licenses/by/4.0

Distribution: Heath on sandstone, chiefly on the coast from Port Stephens south to Vic border.

Other notes: Tidy and eye-catching all year. Adapted to cliff tops, it is tougher than the normal form and with more compact growth. Has a silvery sheen on the stems and new growth, including the flower buds.

Grows well in pots, as it is smaller than the normal form, so it looks a like a bonsai (but with no work). We had one in a pot for around 15 years but sadly I neglected it during a house move and it died, though it had been a trooper for so long previously, through three other house moves. It just got better and better.

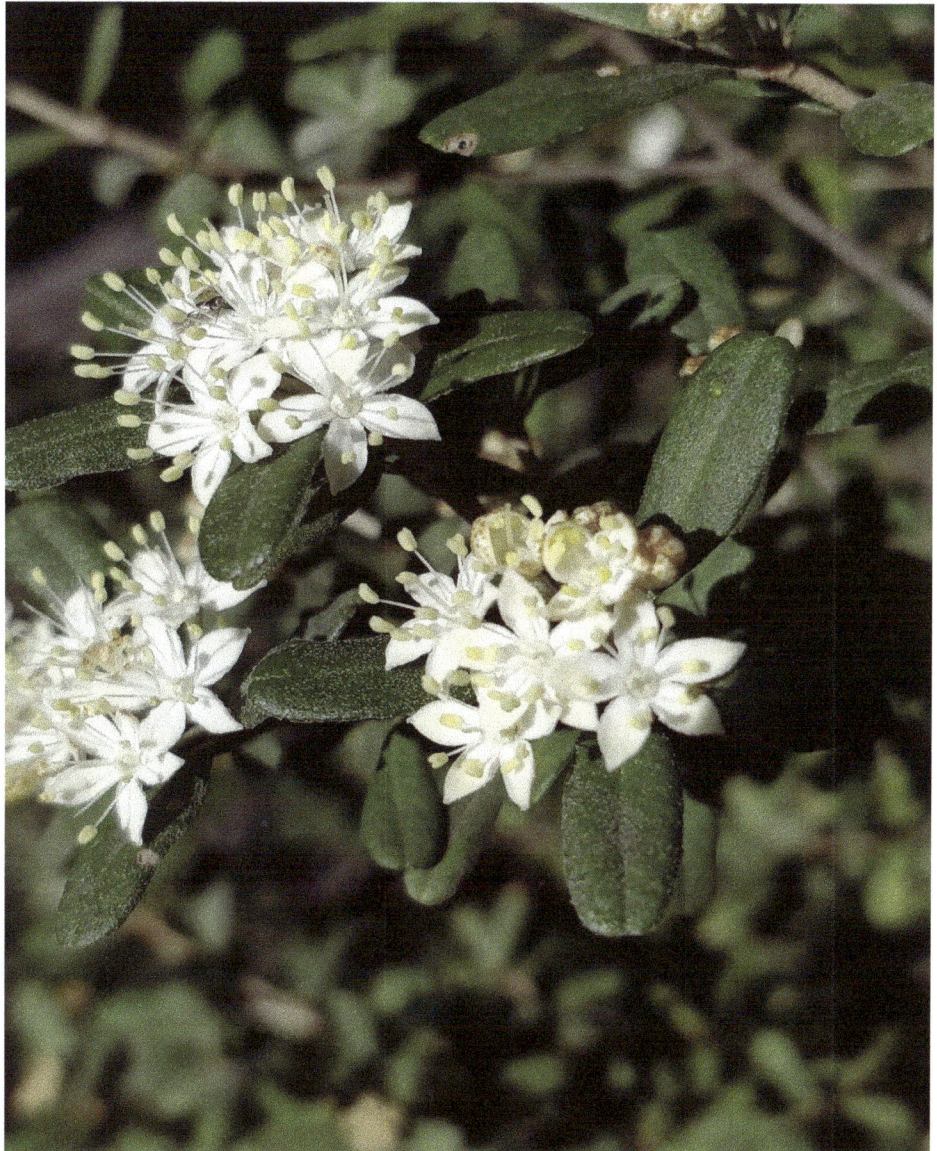

Philotheca (formerly Eriostemon) myoporoides

Common name(s): Gin and Tonic Plant, Long-leaf Wax Flower

Max. height, usually: 2 m

Max. width, usually: 1-2 m

Form: Dense shrub.

Soil: Well-drained; tolerates drought; does not tolerate waterlogging; best on a slope.

Light: Prefers light or dappled shade; tolerates full sun if kept moist.

Flower season: Profuse white flowers from pinkish buds, mainly spring and autumn, with peak Sept to Nov.

Best features: Stunning when in flower.

Propagation: Cuttings; slow to take root.

Native to: Sydney but not Scotland Island. Not a component of PWSGF. Nearest wild-collected records are St Ives and Brooklyn. Can be seen on Katandra bushwalks[Σ].

Distribution: Dry sclerophyll woodland and forest as well as heath, usually on sandy to loam soils, often in sheltered moister areas. Widespread in NSW, Qld, Vic.

Other notes: Aroma is pleasantly citrusy (or gin-and-tonic-y).

A real knockout when in flower, and the fleshy, slightly bubbly-textured leaves are interesting the rest of the year as well.

Good screening plant; growth is dense down to the ground. Low-maintenance, as it is self-rounding. Good in large pots.

Food plant for caterpillars of the beautiful Orchard Swallowtail Butterfly.

Very popular and many cultivars available.

Photo: Jeff Howes https://resources.austplants.com.au/plant-database/

Female Orchard Swallowtail Butterfly. Photo: Garry Sankowsky

Photo: Jeff Howes https://resources.austplants.com.au/plant-database/

Σ   Gillian Gutridge, *Native Plants of the Northern Beaches, Sydney.* https://nbplantareas.com/

Philydrum lanuginosum

Common name(s): Woolly Waterlily, Frogsmouth

Max. height, usually: 1.2 m

Max. width, usually: .5 m

Form: Aquatic perennial tufted herb.

Soil: Sandy, clay or loam; periodically inundated, or in or alongside a watercourse.

Light: Full sun or part-shade.

Flower season: Yellow flowers on spikes in summer.

Best features: Flowers open on successive days as the spike grows, with a bract folding back to support each new flower's two delicate petals (said to resemble a frog's mouth); leaves and bracts are woolly-hairy.

Propagation: Seed; self-seeds in suitable conditions.

Native to: Sydney but not Scotland Island and not PWSGF. Nearest wild-collected record is from Mona Vale in 1931, where it was growing "in water course, base of stem submerged."[Σ]

Distribution: In swamps, along margins of streams and dams; widespread in NSW, Qld, Vic, WA, NT.

Other notes: Ideal for a pond or along streams or gullies to help stabilise soil. Can be planted alongside or in shallow water. Useful in artificially created wetlands to clean urban storm runoff, for example in Annandale's Whites Creek wetland[Φ], which turned 20 years old in 2022.

As this is a summer-flowering species, it would be worth trying for those on south-facing slopes where little sun reaches in winter, and the ground stays fairly moist, especially if planted in or close alongside rain runoff channels.

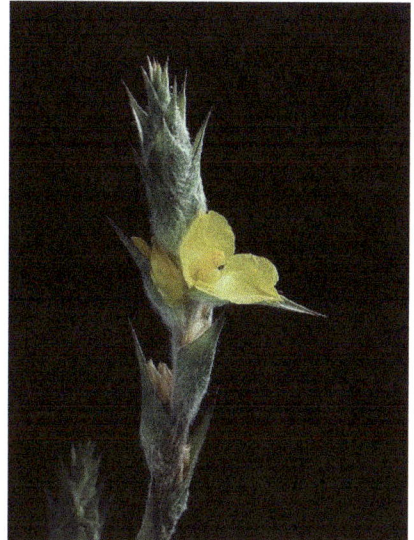

Photo: D Hardin, The Royal Botanic Gardens & Domain Trust

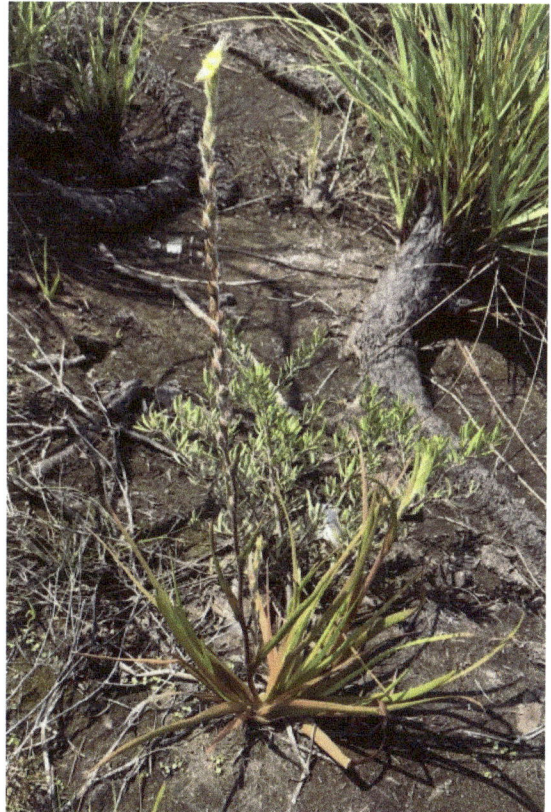

Photo: Gillian Gutridge, *Native Plants of the Northern Beaches, Sydney.* https://nbplantareas.com/

Hard to find in local native nurseries. You might find it in nurseries specialising in water plants.

Σ   Preserved specimen in Australian National Herbarium of *Philydrum lanuginosum* Banks ex Gaertn. recorded on 1931-12-25. Record is viewable on *The Australasian Virtual Herbarium* website at https://avh.ala.org.au/occurrences/a8dda9be-1b8e-4a85-8e9e-8a74581c1f6b.

Φ   https://www.innerwest.nsw.gov.au/ArticleDocuments/1126/Whites%20Creek%20background%20information.pdf.aspx

Pimelea linifolia

Common name(s): Slender Rice Flower

Max. height, usually: 1.5 m

Max. width, usually: 1m

Form: Small shrub.

Soil: Well-drained sandy, clay or loamy soil, protected from wind.

Light: Dappled or full sun.

Flower season: White (sometimes pink) flowers in spring; sporadically year round.

Best features: Sweet small plant with eye-catching heads of up to 70 flowers opening from the outside inwards; leaves are in opposite pairs at right angles to each other (decussate) – an interesting visual texture.

Propagation: Cuttings. Seeds are difficult.

Native to: Sydney but not Scotland Island and not PWSGF. See it on nearly all local bushwalk trails, e.g., Bangalley Head, etc.

Distribution: Widespread in NSW, Qld, Vic, Tas, SA, in heathland, shrubland, and dry sclerophyll woodlands.

Other notes: Very common in eastern Australia and a familiar sight for bushwalkers.

Plant in groups to make a bigger impact in the garden, or as a specimen in a rockery.

Prune after flowering to keep compact and increase flowers for the next time.

There is a prostrate form that grows in ACT. A low, mounding form is available as "White Jewel", which may be hardier than the normal form.

Attracts bees and butterflies. Host plant for caterpillars of the Yellow-spot Blue Butterfly (*Candalides xanthospilos*).

Carried by most native plant nurseries. Some also carry "White Jewel".

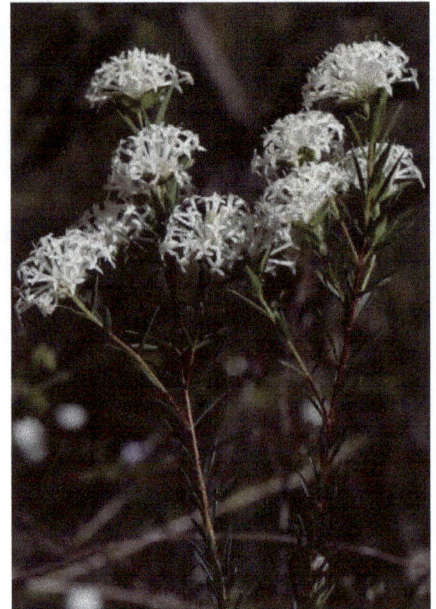

Photos (above and below): Gillian Gutridge, *Native Plants of the Northern Beaches, Sydney.* https://nbplantareas.com/

Photo: Kerri-Lee Harris, www.southernforestlife.net

Platysace lanceolata

Common name(s): Shrubby Platysace, Native Parsnip

Max. height, usually: 1.5 m

Max. width, usually: 1 m

Form: Small shrub.

Soil: Well-drained clay or gravelly soils; tolerates drought.

Light: Dappled sun to half shade.

Flower season: White flowers densely packed in rounded heads (compound terminal umbels), Dec to Feb.

Best features: Pleasing cottage-garden type flowers in the middle of summer; undemanding plant.

Propagation: Little information is available other than that *Platysace* species are difficult to propagate from seed[Ψ].

Photos (above and below): H Malloy

Native to: Sydney and Scotland Island, but not PWSGF. See it on many local bushwalking trails: Bangalley Head, Chiltern, Deep Creek, etc.[Ω]

Distribution: Widespread in NSW, Qld, Vic in woodland and heath, often on sandy soil.

Other notes: Foliage smells like carrots when bruised. Butterflies love the flowers. Some forms have pink flowerbuds opening to white flowers.

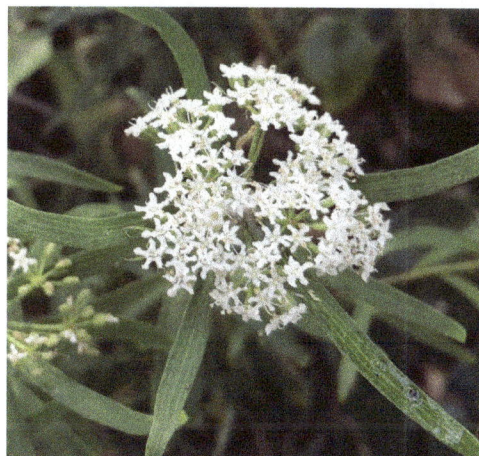

There are two forms: the narrow-leaved one and a form with broad, nearly heart-shaped leaves (not shown). The form on Scotland Island is the narrow-leaved form, which is available from some local native plant nurseries.

There is a dwarf selection of the heart-shaped leaf variety called "Edna Walling Flower Girl", and it is charming, but as a rule, local types will be more likely to thrive in your conditions.

Ψ   https://academic.oup.com/biolinnean/article/130/1/61/5814167?login=false
Ω   Gillian Gutridge, *Native Plants of the Northern Beaches, Sydney*. https://nbplantareas.com/

Plectranthus parviflorus

Common name(s): Cockspur Flower

Max. height, usually: 50 cm

Max. width, usually: 40 cm

Form: Herbaceous subshrub growing from a small tuberous rootstock.

Soil: Loam, sand, or clay; moderate to well-drained soil; somewhat drought tolerant.

Light: Dappled to part shade with protection from afternoon sun.

Flower season: Blue and white flowers in spring and throughout the year given sufficient moisture.

Best features: Fast-growing and generally undemanding; flowers are small but plentiful and are held up above foliage.

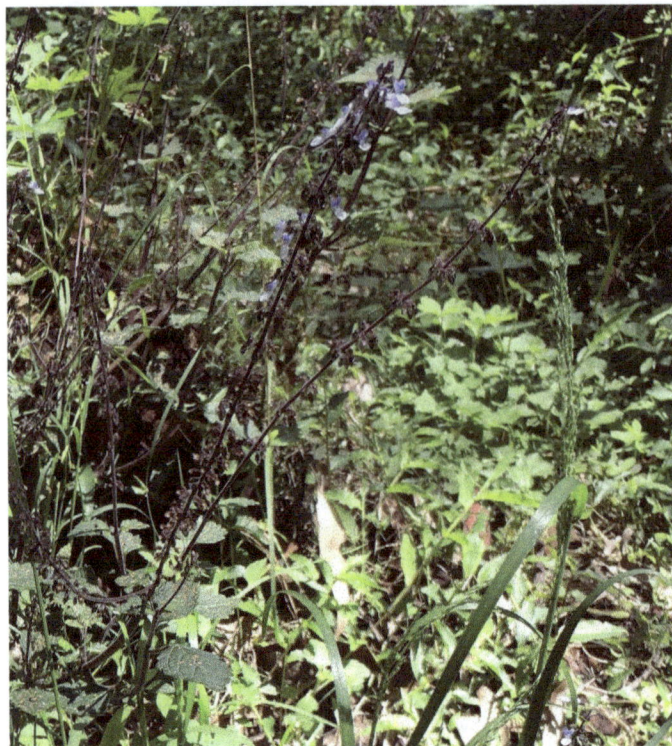

Photo: H Malloy

Propagation: Seeds, cuttings. Produces prolific seeds; seedlings can often be found right where they are wanted.

Native to: Sydney but not Scotland Island[Ω] and not PWSGF. Nearest wild-collected record is from Bayview.

Distribution: Widespread in NSW, frequently in rocky areas and associated with creeks and rivers; also Qld, Vic, E. Asia and Pacific Islands.

Other notes: Variable species; intergrades with some other native species of *Plectranthus* (*P. graveolens* and *P. suaveolens*). Prone to flea beetle attack, which disfigures the leaves. Tubers are edible when cooked; said to be like potatoes with commercial potential.

There is a variegated cultivar which is said not to suffer from flea beetle damage, called "Blue Spires". In addition to being variegated and flea-beetle-resistant, "Blue Spires" also has slightly larger flowers than the normal form, in a clear blue. Widely available from commercial nurseries.

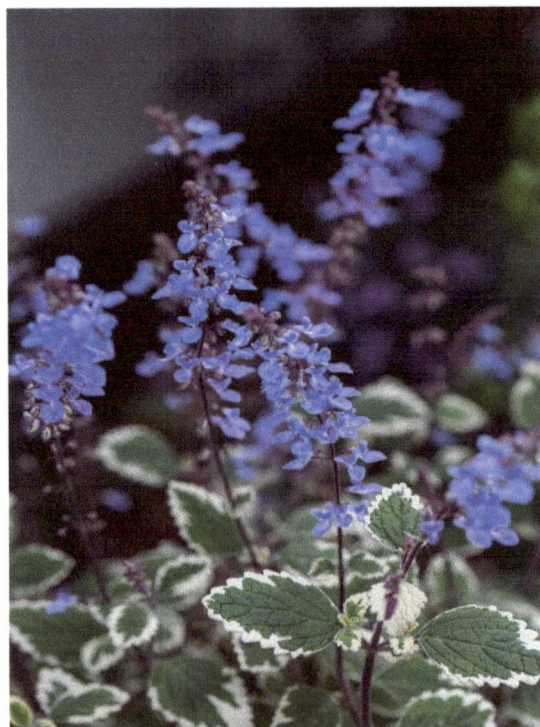

"Blue Spires" cultivar. Photo: Rae Basset, thebotanicalplanet.com.au

---

[Ω] Plants were given to many residents by Northern Beaches Council for several years and occasionally these seed into Elizabeth Park, but there are no records of it being there prior to approx. 2017.

Poa affinis

Common name(s): none; you could call it "Forest Tussock Grass".

Max. height, usually: 40-120 cm, depending on nutrient and light levels, and age of plant.

Max. width, usually: 20 cm

Form: Small clumping grass.

Soil: Well-drained. Prefers clay-based soil. Tolerates sandy soil if moist. Does not tolerate drought.

Light: Prefers dappled shade or part shade. Suffers in full sun. Tolerates deep shade but does not grow or flower as much.

Flower season: Dancing open panicles of dangly flowers on flexible stems Nov to Dec. Plants in shade flower a few weeks later than plants in more open situations.

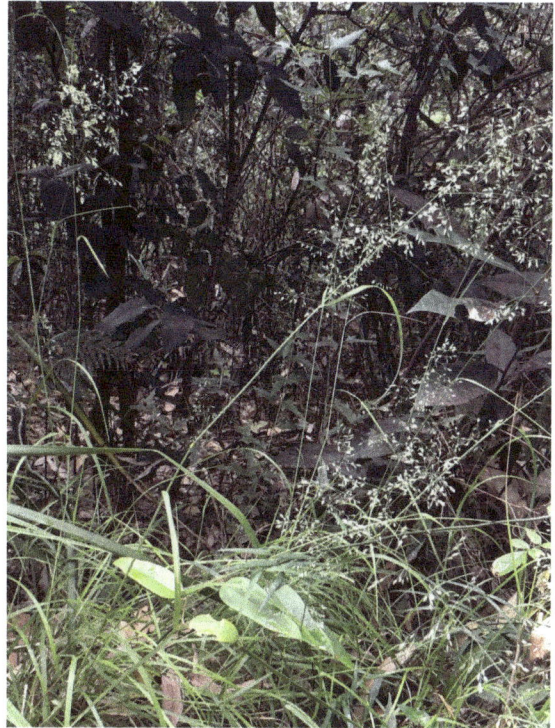
Along path in Elizabeth Park. Photo: H Malloy

Best features: Soft, dense tussocks; lush appearance; dainty flowerheads.

Propagation: Seed, division.

Native to: Sydney and Scotland Island. An uncommon component of Dry PWSGF$^{\Omega}$ or a typical component of PSGF$^{\Psi}$, depending on which study you consult.

Distribution: Common where it occurs; sporadic in dryish woodland on clay soils, or moist sandstone soils in valleys or shaded hillsides; coastal in NSW and Vic.

Other notes: Looks great in a meadow under tall trees. Combines well with other shade-loving grasses such as *Entolasia marginata* and *Echinopogon ovatus* (see profiles for those species).

May self-seed, but plants are shallow-rooted and easily pulled up to restrict its spread. Old flowerstalks lie down and take root along the nodes to form new plants; cut off the old flowerstalks to prevent this if desired.

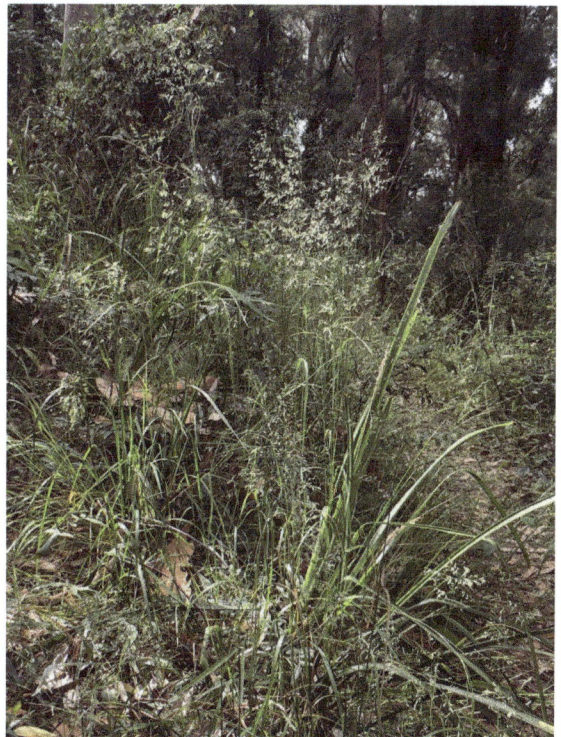
Path in Elizabeth Park. Photo: H Malloy

Some local native plant nurseries carry it.

Ω   Bell & Stables 2012
Ψ   OEH 2016

Poa labillardierei

Common name(s): Tussock Grass

Max. height, usually: 1.2 m

Max. width, usually: 40 cm

Form: Tufted grass.

Soil: Well-drained sand, clay or loam. Drought tolerant.

Light: Full sun to part shade.

Flower season: Most of the year.

Best features: Lush fountains of foliage; fast-growing; low maintenance.

Propagation: Seed, division.

Native to: Sydney but not Scotland Island or PWSGF, or Northern Beaches. Nearest wild-collected record is Homebush.

Distribution: River flats and moist situations, and in forests, extending up open sheltered slopes; NSW, Qld, Vic, Tas, SA.

Other notes: Though not native to Pittwater, it is a component of several Spotted Gum ecological communities found in the Lake Macquarie district that have strong similarities to PWSGF[Σ].

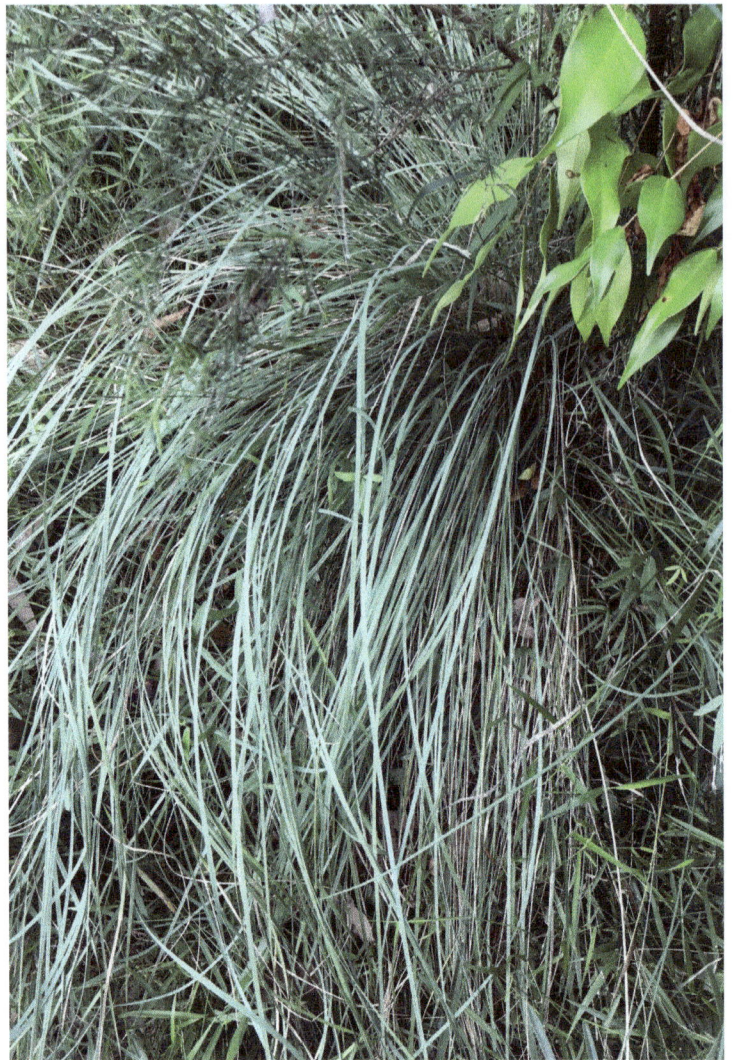

Photo: H Malloy

Has been used extensively in large landscaping projects such as golf course edges and roundabouts, where the tussocks work as a repetitive element. It is also useful in the garden as a contrast element. An easy way to diversify your garden and add habitat for lizards, rails and many insects.

Larger and hardier than *P. affinis*. Use it in places where the sun would be too much for *P. affinis*, or where a stronger sculptural statement is needed. Though it needs moister conditions than *P. affinis* in order to self-seed, that is not a drawback in a garden situation where self-seeding is not always wanted. After establishment, it is drought-tolerant and fast-growing, and it is easily divided to make more clumps. Cut back after good rains in autumn or winter if a tidier clump is desired.

Available from most native plant nurseries. A blue-green cultivar named "Eskdale" is widely available.

Σ   Bell, S.A.J. (2016) Volume 2: Vegetation Community Profiles, Lake Macquarie Local Government Area. Working Draft v2. Unpublished Report to Lake Macquarie City Council. March 2016. Eastcoast Flora Survey.

Podolobium (formerly Oxylobium) ilicifolium

Common name(s): Prickly Shaggy-pea, Native Holly, Holly-leaf Pea, Bacon and Eggs, Bushwalkers Bane

Max. height, usually: 3 m

Max. width, usually: 1 m

Form: Upright shrub; leaves have sharp prickly points like holly.

Soil: Well-drained; tolerates drought; can grow in very shallow soils.

Light: Full sun or light shade.

Flower season: Yellow or orange pea-like flowers with red markings, spring to early summer.

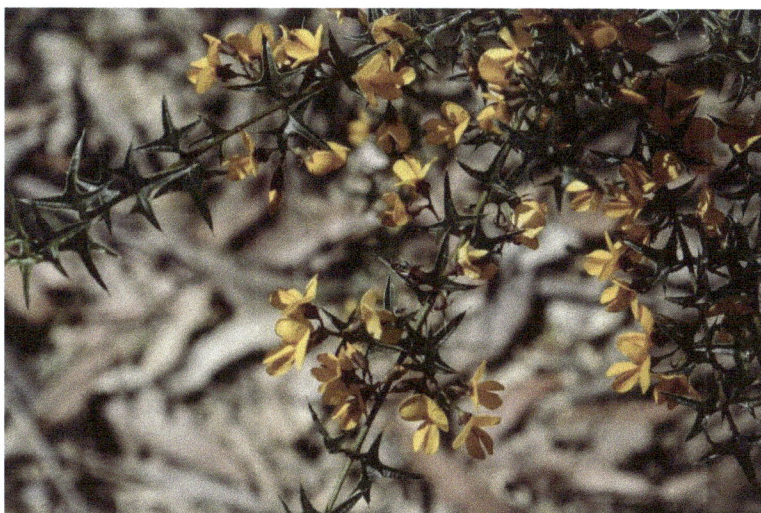
Photo: Alan Fairley https://resources.austplants.com.au/plant-database/

Best features: Brilliant gold and red flowers contrast well with olive-blue-green leaves; prickles (for bird habitat); tasty nibble (pods).

Propagation: Seed; cuttings. Seed retains viability for many years.

Native to: Sydney and Scotland Island. An uncommon component of Dry PWSGF$^\Omega$ or a typical component of PSGF$^\Psi$, depending on which study you consult.

Distribution: Widespread in dry or moist sclerophyll forest, on clay or sandstone, coastal and subcoastal parts of NSW, Qld, Vic.

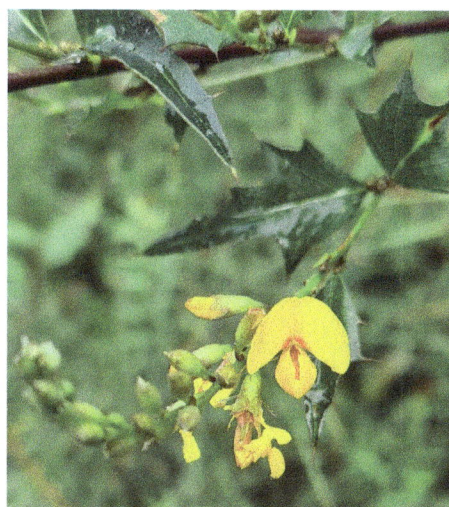
Photo: Jenny aka Floydwafer, iNaturalist

Other notes: Fruit are reported to be tasty when green, like tiny snow peas or green beans.[*]

Not common in cultivation.

Very eye-catching when in full flower in woodland.

A grouping would be good for small bird habitat (due to prickles).

The specimens in Elizabeth Park on Scotland Island are on the small side for the species (up to ~2 m), so perhaps in the home garden they would benefit from a little supplemental water.

Ω   Bell & Stables 2012

Ψ   OEH 2016

*   Per member "Corin" who says he has eaten a lot of them, and "Howling Dingo" who says they are rather tasty https://bushcraftoz.com/threads/podolobium-ilicifolium-native-holly.174/

Pomaderris intermedia

Common name(s): Lemon Dogwood, Lemon Hazel ("Hazel" was an old common name for the genus – from the resemblance of their leaves. These days it is generally restricted to *P. apetala.*)

Max. height, usually: 3 m

Max. width, usually: 2 m

Form: Large shrub or small tree with open branching.

Soil: Prefers well-drained acidic soil; plant on a slope to avoid drainage issues. Tolerates drought.

Light: Full sun to semi-shade.

Flower season: Bright yellow flowers in large flower heads Sept to Oct.

Best features: Bright flowers, large dark green leaves with woolly white undersides, relatively fast-growing.

Propagation: Seed; cuttings.

Native to: Sydney but not Scotland Island and not PWSGF. Nearest wild-collected records are from Palm Beach, Terrey Hills, and Belrose.

Distribution: Open sclerophyll forest on the coast and ranges; NSW, Vic, Tas.

Photo: M Fagg. https://www.anbg.gov.au/photo/image-collection.html

Photo: M Fagg. https://www.anbg.gov.au/photo/image-collection.html

Photo: CSIRO. https://www.scienceimage.csiro.au/

Other notes: Good screener if pruned lightly after flowering from an early age, to promote dense growth.

A host plant for the very beautiful but rarely seen Yellow-spot Jewel butterfly (*Hypochrysops byzos*).

Pomaderris mediora

Common name(s): Headland Pomaderris, Headland Hazel

Max. height, usually: 1-3 m

Max. width, usually: 1-3 m

Form: Low-lying or erect shrub.

Soil: Well-drained sandy or clay soil; probably drought resistant; probably does not tolerate waterlogging.

Light: Full sun to light shade.

Flower season: Cream flowers Sept to Oct.

Best features: Showy display of profuse starry flowers made fluffy-looking by long anthers; attractive small, tidy velvety leaves.

Propagation: Seed; cuttings.

Native to: Sydney but not Scotland Island or PWSGF. Can be seen on walking trail at Turimetta Headland.

Distribution: Heath and stunted scrub on ridges and headlands, chiefly Central Coast region, from the Hawkesbury River to Bulli.

Growing at Turimetta Headland. Photos (above and below): Gillian Gutridge, https://nbplantareas.com

Other notes: Not well known in cultivation, so I have extrapolated the details of its requirements from other species of *Pomaderris* such as *P. intermedia* (see previous profile).

In the wild, individuals vary from 1 m to 3 m. This wide relative range in heights could be explained either by the harsh headland habitat, or by genetic differences; I am assuming the reason is the environment, but that is only a guess.

I have been growing it for a few months in a sun-drenched area of my garden, and I think it will be beautiful whether it turns out to grow tall or stays short. If you want a plant with the headland look that can be relied on to stay small, consider *Commersonia hermanniifolia* and *Zieria prostrata* (see profiles for those species; *Z. prostrata* is from Coffs Harbour so not a Sydney local native).

Available from some native plant nurseries.

Poranthera microphylla

Common name(s): Small Poranthera

Max. height, usually: 10 cm

Max. width, usually: 5 cm

Form: Tiny soft annual herb, usually found in groups or drifts.

Soil: Well-drained sandy, clay or loamy soil; very drought tolerant. Does not tolerate waterlogging.

Light: Part shade to dappled shade.

Flower season: Tiny white flowers spring to autumn.

Best features: Cute and self-seeds well, but not in a weedy way.

Propagation: Seed; self-seeds when happy.

Native to: Sydney and Scotland Island. Not a component of PWSGF.

Distribution: Widespread in forest and woodland; NSW, Qld, Vic, Tas, WA, NT.

Other notes: Can sometimes be found growing along paths or roadsides in shaded forest, such as Fitzpatrick Trail on Scotland Island.

I include this cute little plant not because I am imagining a lot of people would bother to seek it out,

Growing with *Pseuderanthemum variabile*. Photo: H Malloy

but rather to reassure anyone who already has this growing as a volunteer in their garden that it is neither an introduced weed, nor objectionable in any way.

Can form enchanting large drifts in forest in spring after a few dry years. It can escape severe weather in the form of seeds, and then return after conditions improve.

This is another plant that requires perfectly weed-free conditions in order for its charms to be seen.

It is not available in any nursery that I know of. Best way to obtain it if you don't already have it is to ask someone who does have it for a few plants.

Prostanthera denticulata

Common name(s): Rough Mint-bush

Max. height, usually: 1 m

Max. width, usually: 2 m

Form: Straggling shrub, forming mounds over time.

Soil: Well-drained sandy, loamy or gravelly sois; tolerates clay soil; drought tolerant once established.

Light: Morning sun and afternoon shade.

Flower season: Profuse purple or mauve flowers spring to early summer.

Photos (above and below): Gillian Gutridge, https://nbplantareas.com

Best features: Spectacular when in flower; hardier than most other species of *Prostanthera;* tolerates clay; tiny dark green leaves are attractive year round.

Propagation: Cuttings.

Native to: Sydney and Scotland Island. Studies differ as to its place in PWSGF$^{\Omega}$.

Distribution: Damp areas in forest and woodland, usually near the coast, in sandy loamy soils, overlying sandstone; confined to Sydney district. NSW Flora Online considers that specimens from central NSW and from Vic are more properly part of a different taxon, as yet undescribed. If that is correct – as seems likely – that would make this a Sydney endemic.

Other notes: Leaves and stems are rough to the touch but it is not prickly. Good along paths where the minty fragrance is released by brushing past it. Also good mass-planted as groundcover.

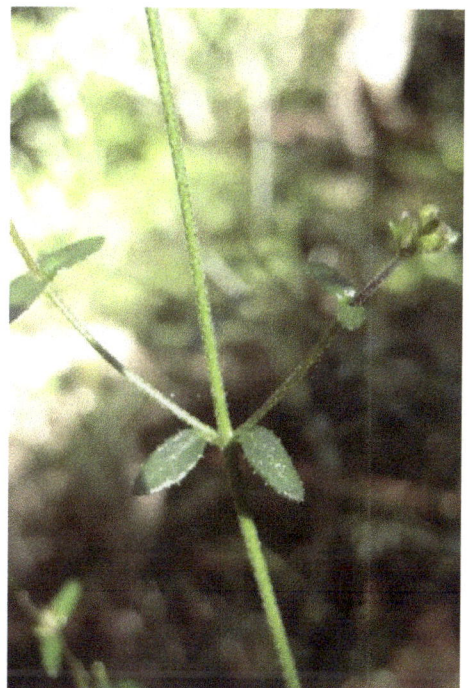

If it has a flaw, it is that the internodes are rather long (see photo), though this is made up for by exuberant growth, which eventually creates density. There is a compact form available, which is dense from early growth, sold in commercial nurseries as "Purple Haze".

Available at most local native plant nurseries.

Ω Bell & Stables 2012 don't report it. OEH 2016 reports it as an uncommon component of PSGF.

Prostanthera incisa

Common name(s): Cut-leaf Mint Bush, Native Thyme

Max. height, usually: 3 m

Max. width, usually: 1 m

Form: Strongly aromatic erect, openly branched shrub.

Soil: Well-drained acidic soils; prefers sandy soil on a slope. Does not tolerate waterlogging or drought. Appreciates enrichment from organic matter and mulch.

Light: Dappled shade.

Flower season: Purple to mauve flowers in spring.

Photo: Ros and Ben Walcott, www.walcottgarden.com

Best features: Fast-growing; spectacular when in flower; good screen plant; hedgeable.

Propagation: Seed; cuttings (very easy).

Native to: Sydney but not Scotland Island. Not a component of PWSGF. Nearest wild-collected record is Epping.

Distribution: Sheltered sites in rainforest margins or wet sclerophyll forest along NSW coastland from Qld border all the way to Vic, as well as Central Tablelands in NSW, and in scrub along watercourses.

Other notes: Widely grown in cultivation, and for good reason as it is a knockout when in flower. Does well on Scotland Island, but may need supplemental water in drought (mine generally wilt on dry hot days). Best planted close to the house and on paths where it is easier to keep it watered and where you can enjoy the stunning flowers (in spring) and pleasant minty fragrance (all year round).

Prefers sites sheltered from wind.

Reshoots readily when pruned back annually after flowering to a height of 50 cm, and this is a way to ensure a specimen's longevity; can be short-lived otherwise (2-3 years).

Leaves can reportedly be used in any dish to replace thyme, e.g., in breads. Use leaves or the tender branch tips whole; both leaf and stem can be used[*]. Can also make an herbal tisane from the flowers and leaves.

A pink-flowered form is available.

---

[*]   https://tuckerbush.com.au/native-thyme-prostanthera-incisa/

Prostanthera scutellarioides

Common name(s): Skullcap-leaf Mint Bush

Max. height, usually: 1.5 m

Max. width, usually: 1.5 m

Form: Erect or spreading shrub.

Soil: Well-drained sandy or clay soil.

Light: Dappled sun with protection from afternoon sun, or up to three-quarters shade.

Flower season: Covered with purple flowers for well over a month during the spring peak, and sporadic flowers the rest of the year.

Photo: Ros and Ben Walcott, www.walcottgarden.com

Best features: The purple flowers contrast well with the dark green leaves; it is very hardy and it flowers in the second year after planting; good screener and good cut flower.

Propagation: Easy from cuttings.

Native to: Sydney but not Scotland Island, nor PWSGF, nor Northern Beaches. Nearest wild-collected records are from Upper Lane Cove River, Wisemans Ferry, and Parramatta.

Distribution: Dry sclerophyll forest and woodland on alluvial, poor lateritic sands and heavy clay soils, mostly on the tablelands of NSW and Qld.

Other notes: Unlike most mint bushes, the foliage of this species has only the subtlest minty aroma. Another difference from most mint bushes is that this species is less prone to wilting during dry spells, and it naturally grows on heavy clay as well as sandy soils.

Grows very well in up to three-quarters shade. Choose a site where it will get dappled shade in summer, and afternoon shade. On the east side of your house is a good choice, if there is also overhead tree shade there to protect it from midsummer noonday sun. This species would be well worth trying for gardens on south-facing slopes that are entirely shaded in winter. It probably won't have a good flowering at the usual spring time, but it may make up for it a bit later on.

Naturally grows along creeks, and accordingly, it requires supplemental water in dry periods in order to look its best. Copes well with dryness, and although it may drop its leaves during prolonged drought, it quickly recovers and puts out new leaves when watered again.

Prune to remove about 1/3 of last season's growth after the peak of flowering is over to keep them compact and strong, and to promote better flowering next year.

Pseuderanthemum variabile

Common name(s): Pastel Flower, Love Flower, Saintpaulia Weed

Max. height, usually: 30 cm

Max. width, usually: Spreads up to 1 m

Form: Creeping herb with highly variable appearance, varying in leaf shape and colour as well as flower colour.

Soil: Well-drained. Prefers well-composted soil. Drought tolerant, though it prefers moist conditions. Flower colour is more intense in moister conditions.

Light: Prefers dappled or light shade.

Flower season: Lilac, purple, blue, pink or white flowers, often spotted, Dec to Mar.

Best features: Beautiful flowers as well as leaves, in bewildering variety, when little else is in flower.

Propagation: Seed; cuttings. Self-seeds from large seed capsules, and also grows readily from cuttings.

Native to: Sydney and Scotland Island. Typical of Dry PWSGF.

Distribution: Rainforest and wet sclerophyll forest, woodlands, open forest and vine thickets in NSW, Qld. Also New Guinea and New Caledonia.

Other notes: Ideal groundcover for a shaded area under small- to medium-sized trees where little else will grow; not bothered if the soil is somewhat dry on account of the tree's roots.

Photo: H Malloy

Photo: Garry Sankowsky, www.rainforestmagic.com.au

Food plant for butterflies in the family Nymphalidae, such as the stunning Blue Pansy or Argus[*] (which sadly does not get much south of Brisbane).

A form with tuberous roots is a nuisance weed in orchid-growing greenhouses, where it is known as Saintpaulia Weed.[ψ] It is not weedy in a garden situation, however.

---

[*] https://www.nhm.ac.uk/our-science/data/hostplants/search/list.dsml?
searchPageURL=index.dsml&Familyqtype=starts+with&Family=&PFamilyqtype=starts+with&PFamily=&Genusqtype=starts
+with&Genus=&PGenusqtype=equals&PGenus=Pseuderanthemum&Speciesqtype=starts+with&Species=&PSpeciesqtype=eq
uals&PSpecies=variabile&Country=&sort=Family

[ψ] https://www.australianorchids.com.au/blogs/blog/75807237-pseuderanthemum-variabile-love-flower-pastel-flower-what-a-pest-
of-a-weed-in-orchid-collections?page=3

Pullenia (formerly Desmodium) gunnii

Common name(s): Slender Tick-trefoil

Max. height, usually: 25 cm

Max. width, usually: Indefinite.

Form: Prostrate mat-forming or sprawling perennial.

Soil: Prefers moist well-drained soil.

Light: Dappled or part shade.

Flower season: Tiny magenta flowers late summer to autumn.

Best features: Soil-enriching small ground-cover; attractive clover-like leaves; tiny cute pink flowers and cute seed pods.

Propagation: Seed; division.

Happily growing with several other groundcovers. Photo: H Malloy

Native to: Sydney and Scotland Island*. An uncommon component of Dry PWSGF$^\Psi$ or typical of PSGF$^\Omega$ depending on which study you consult.

Distribution: Common in coastal sclerophyll forest, usually in shady conditions; in NSW, Qld, Vic, and Tas.

Other notes: Overlooked unless in flower; small and grows among other groundcovers.

Very hardy even in positions receiving full sun, as long as it can get shade from other groundcovers or small shrubs. Tends to grow under other plants rather than scrambling over them, except for the tips of the stems which bear the flowers.

As it is in the legume family, it is a nitrogen-fixer and can help build good soil in your garden.

The pods are scalloped, each scallop enclosing one seed. Instead of opening along the long side like a pea, the pod breaks between the scallops, and the hairy segments stick to animals for dispersal.

Superficially similar to *Grona* (formerly *Desmodium) varians*, which generally has oblong leaflets (not rounded or clover-like), paler pink or white flowers and is more widespread though never common.

Very decorative when grown in a small container allowing it to spill over the sides. Otherwise it is too small to create much visual impact in a garden setting, but it is a great addition from the point of view of biodiversity and soil health.

---

*   Not recorded in any previous vegetation survey of Scotland Island but apparently naturally present in at least four places in Elizabeth Park, mostly in shady places. Possibly plants identified in previous surveys as *Desmodium varians* were this species, as I have not personally seen *D. varians* on the island.

Ψ Bell & Stables 2012

Ω OEH 2016

Pultenaea daphnoides

Common name(s): Large-leaf Bush-pea

Max. height, usually: 3 m

Max. width, usually: 1 m

Form: Upright shrub.

Soil: Prefers well-drained sandy or loamy soil; tolerates clay soil – plant on a slope to ensure drainage. Tolerates drought as long as it has overhead shade; best with afternoon shade as well. Not wind tolerant.

Light: Prefers dappled shade under established trees.

Flower season: Deep yellow flowers with red markings ("eggs and bacon") in late winter to spring (Aug to Nov).

Best features: Beautiful large flowers in dense heads; attractive wedge-shaped leaves with a little slightly prickly point.

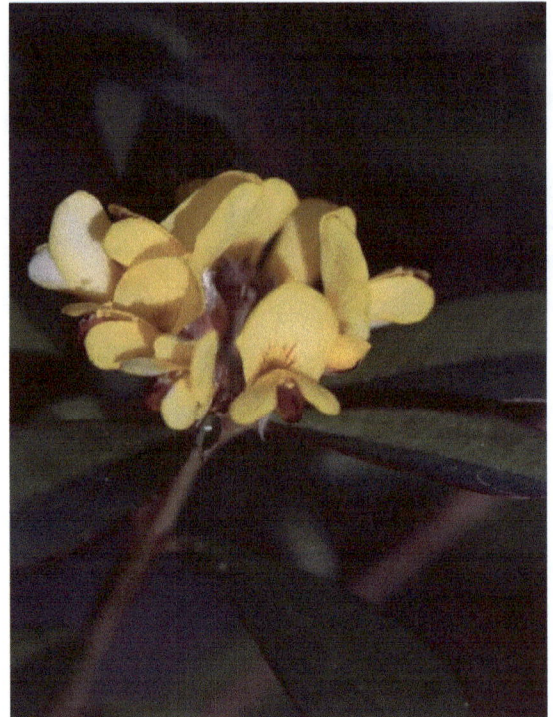

Photo: Gillian Gutridge, *Native Plants of the Northern Beaches, Sydney.* https://nbplantareas.com/

Propagation: Seed, cuttings. A lot of seed gets destroyed by insects, so germination rate is low.

Native to: Sydney but not Scotland Island and not PWSGF. Can be seen on many local bushwalks including Bangalley Head, Chiltern North, Cromer Heights, and Deep Creek[Ω].

Distribution: Heath to wet sclerophyll forest on sandy soils, mainly in coastal areas, in NSW, Qld, Vic, Tas, SA.

Other notes: Branching is quite open, which can make the plant look sparse, especially when young. It is a good idea to plant three or more in a grouping 20 cm or so apart, which will give the appearance of a single plant or a thicket, as they might grow in the wild. In addition, because members of this genus can be a little difficult to establish, you may lose a third of the tubestock you plant. It seems some individuals

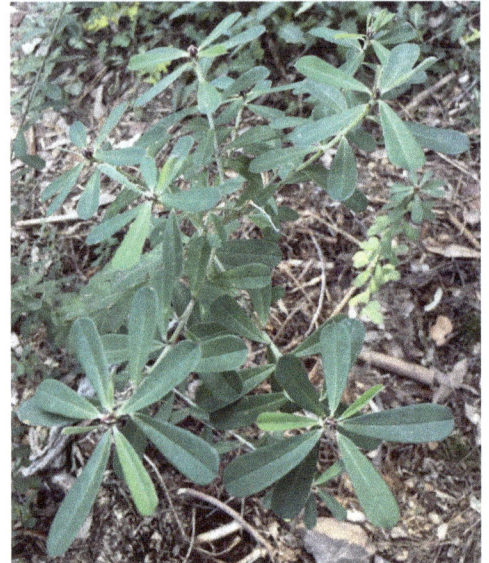

Photo: H Malloy

just fail to thrive, and eventually die off during some extra stress such as a sudden hot day, or prolonged rain. Of course, you can always plant additional ones later on, e.g., next to one that seems to be in a particularly good spot. But even in a particularly good spot, where two are going like the clappers, a third one might just sulk. That's just how they are; it's probably not you!

Available at most native plant nurseries.

Ω   Gillian Gutridge, *Native Plants of the Northern Beaches, Sydney.* https://nbplantareas.com/

Pultenea flexilis

Common name(s): Graceful Bush-pea

Max. height, usually: 3 m

Max. width, usually: 1.5 m

Form: Large shrub or small rounded tree.

Soil: Prefers moderate- to well-drained sandy soil; drought tolerant.

Light: Dappled or semi-shaded.

Flower season: Flowers are yellow to orange, sometimes with red markings; winter to spring (Aug to Oct).

Best features: Spectacular in flower; graceful shape.

Propagation: Seed, cuttings.

Native to: Sydney but not Scotland Island. Typical of Dry PWSGF. See it on bushwalk tracks such as Deep Creek[Ψ]. Wild-collected records include Palm Beach isthmus, Mona Vale and Narrabeen.

Distribution: Dry sclerophyll forest on coast and tableslands, on acid, well-drained soils, NSW and Qld.

Photos (above and below): Gillian Guttridge, *Native Plants of the Northern Beaches, Sydney*. https://nbplantareas.com/

Other notes: Good as a background shrub in a large garden, or feature specimen in any kind of garden. Looks best in a group as foliage is sparse. Prune lightly after flowering.

Plant a grouping of two or three in each position where you want it. Very likely, one or two in each grouping will fail to establish well, and will eventually die, but the rest will more than reward your effort.

Available at most native plant nurseries.

Ψ Gillian Guttridge, *Native Plants of the Northern Beaches, Sydney*. https://nbplantareas.com/

Pultenea villosa

Common name(s): Eggs and Bacon (catchall term for many genera and species), Bronze Bush-pea, Hairy Bush-pea, Kerosene Bush

Max. height, usually: 2 m

Max. width, usually: 3 m

Form: Prostrate to erect shrub with arching branches.

Soil: Prefers moist clay soil with average drainage; said to tolerate moister soils than many other pea-flowers; tolerates sandy soil; moderately drought tolerant.

Photo: Dan Clarke https://resources.austplants.com.au/plant-database/

Light: Prefers a sunny spot with light, overhead protection from full sun for at least half the day; gets spindly in heavier shade.

Flower season: Bright yellow flowers in spring.

Best features: Extremely profuse flowers; graceful arching branches; attractive tiny, fuzzy leaves.

Propagation: Seed, cuttings.

Native to: Sydney but not Scotland Island and not PWSGF. Nearest wild-collected records are from Cabarita, Beecroft, Kurringai and Terrigal.

Distribution: Dry sclerophyll forest to heath or grassland, on a variety of substrates but generally dry clay soils, on Cumberland Plain in NSW; also Qld, Vic.

Other notes: In cultivation for many years, and one of the easier species of *Pultenaea*. In general, they are known for being a little difficult to establish in a garden. Plant a grouping of two or three in each position where you want it, in case some of them don't survive their first year or two.

So spectacular when in flower that its best use may be as a specimen plant. Could also make an informal hedge. Tolerates light pruning very well, although it generally doesn't need pruning in order to stay good-looking and healthy for years.

Available at most native plant nurseries.

Rhododendron viriosum[*]

Common name(s): Native Azalea

Max. height, usually: 1-2 m

Max. width, usually: 1-2 m

Form: Open branched shrub with thick leathery leaves.

Soil: Well-drained. Prefers moist, acidic soil with high organic content; probably does not tolerate waterlogging but seems to like daily watering.

Light: Prefers dappled morning sun and afternoon shade. Tolerates direct sun for a few hours per day if well-watered.

Photo: H Malloy

Flower season: Red trumpets Feb to Mar.

Best features: Profuse and showy flowers in the dead of summer; shiny green leaves; stems of new growth are a muted shade of the same red as the flowers.

Propagation: Seed (difficult); cuttings (slow).

Native to: Not native to Sydney and not Scotland Island. Endemic to North Qld. Not a component of PWSGF.

Distribution: North Qld, on seven tropical mountain tops. Considered rare but not threatened.

Other notes: Purists desiring to plant only local Sydney natives may want to avoid this plant.

Requires daily watering in hot weather. When not in flower, the thick, shiny dark green leaves make this worth growing for that reason alone. When in flower, it is a showstopper.

Does well in a pot, as it is slow-growing. Ours was in a pot for 15 years before I planted it.

Probably best planted on a slope, to prevent waterlogging. We've seen the best flowering on ours from feedings of worm casting tea. Commercial rhododendron food, by contrast, seems to inhibit flowering, possibly due to too much nitrogen, which promotes leaf growth at the expense of flowering. Best wait until after flowering has finished for the year to fertilise if you are using high-nitrogen fertiliser.

The species has been in cultivation for a long time, and most plants available for sale probably derive from cuttings of plants in only a few lineages, so there is little variability among them.

---

[*]   Formerly known as *R. lochiae*, a name which is now given to a similar species having a curved flower tube.

Schelhammera undulata

Common name(s): Lilac Lily

Max. height, usually: 20 cm

Max. width, usually: 10 cm

Form: Small herbaceous plant.

Soil: Prefers moist, well-drained soil; somewhat drought tolerant.

Light: Dappled shade.

Flower season: Pink flowers, sometimes with darker streaks, mainly Oct to Nov, but with some flowers at all times of the year.

Best features: Delicate, tidy plant and attractive tiny flowers.

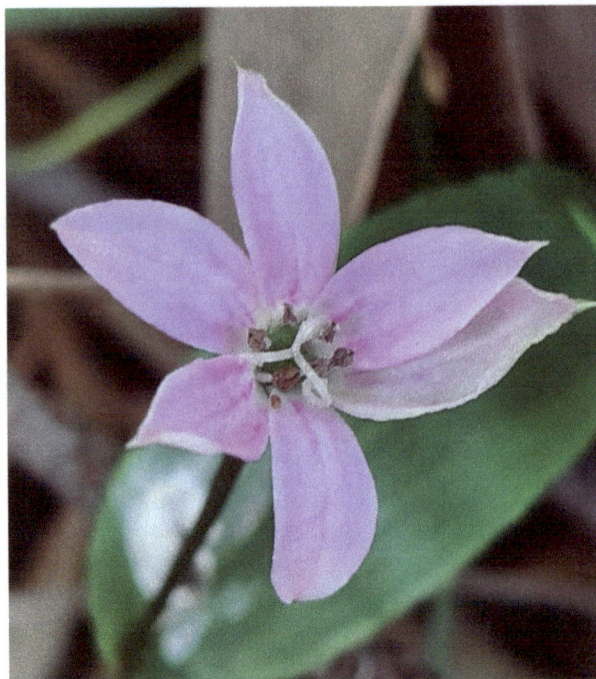

Photo: Jenny aka Floydwafer, iNaturalist

Propagation: Seed, which germinates readily when fresh. New plants flower the following spring if conditions are right. Seed is ripe beginning mid-Dec when the hot weather begins.

Native to: Sydney and Scotland Island. An uncommon component of Dry PWSGF$^\Omega$ or a typical component of PSGF$^\Psi$, depending on which study you consult.

Distribution: Widespread, but not common; grows in moist shady locations in dry sclerophyll forest; NSW andVic.

Other notes: Little pink treasures in shade reward those with good eyesight.

When not in flower, it is easily confused with a common weed, *Tradescantia fluminensis*.

With *Viola hederacea* and Weeping Grass (*Microlaena stipoides*).
Photo: H Malloy

Unfortunately, Bush Turkeys (*Alectura lathami*) seem to find Lilac Lily rhizomes or corms very tasty. If you live in turkey territory, you will need to include some large rocks in your design to stop them uprooting and eating the corms, or surround that area of your garden with a low fence (keeping in mind that though bush turkeys can fly, they don't do it often). Turkeys can all but eradicate Lilac Lily from an area very quickly, leaving behind scratched-out craters and wilted, severed above-ground parts as evidence of their feasting.

Ω Bell & Stables 2012
Ψ OEH 2016

Smilax glyciphylla

Common name(s): Sweet Sarsaparilla

Max. height, usually: 5 m long when supported.

Max. width, usually: 3 m when unsupported.

Form: Vine climbing by means of tendrils; no prickles.

Soil: Moist, well-drained; drought-tolerant.

Light: Dappled shade.

Flower season: Cream and green flowers in late spring to summer, followed by black fruits.

Best features: Attractive vine; tasty tea.

Propagation: Seed, cuttings.

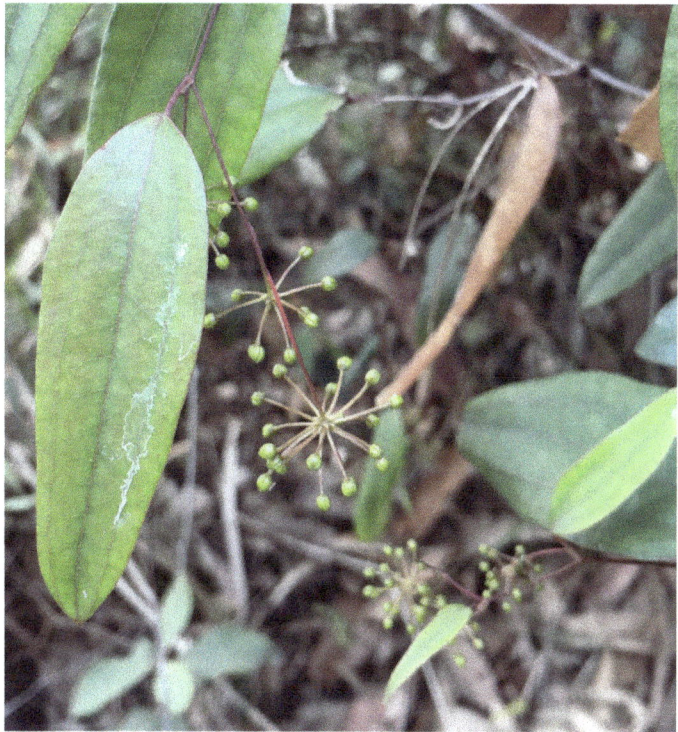

Photos (above and below): H Malloy

Native to: Sydney and Scotland Island. Typical component of both Dry and Moist PWSGF.

Distribution: Widespread in rainforest, sclerophyll forest and woodland; chiefly in coastal districts; NSW, Qld.

Other notes: Attractive foliage makes it a good candidate for a trellis, or you might allow it to climb up a small tree that is looking a little plain. Not a smotherer.

You must have several vines if you want fruit, as male and female flowers are on separate plants.

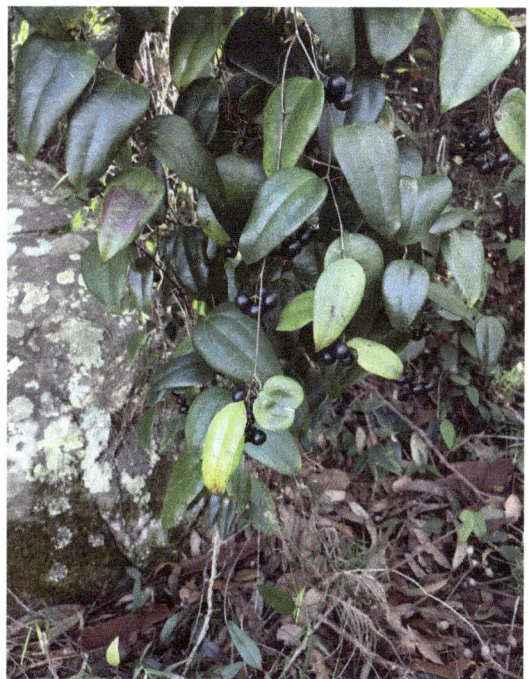

The leaves can be used to make a sweet herbal tea with a licorice-like taste; simply scrunch up a leaf or two in a cup and steep in boiled water. In colonial days, it was used in this way to combat scurvy (vitamin C deficiency); it also happens to be a pleasant tea, with both sweet and bitter notes. Alternatively, a new leaf can simply be chewed for the pleasant, refreshing taste; it is also said to ease a sore throat. In 2005, the leaves and tea were shown to have antioxidant activity, though that doesn't necessarily translate to a health benefit in humans[Ψ].

Ψ   Sean D Cox, K Chamila Jayasinghe, Julie L Markham, Antioxidant activity in Australian native sarsaparilla (Smilax glyciphylla), *Journal of Ethnopharmacology*, 101:103, 3 Oct 2005, pp. 162-168. Extract available for free online on ScienceDirect website.

Solanum prinophyllum

Common name(s): Forest Nightshade

Max. height, usually: 50 cm

Max. width, usually: 2 m

Form: Sprawling short-lived herb, often annual.

Soil: Well-drained sandy, clay or loamy soil; prefers moist.

Light: Dappled.

Flower season: Lilac flowers throughout the year.

Best features: Interesting and incredibly prickly annual plant; enriches the soil where it has grown; food source for a species of lady bug.

Propagation: Seed.

Native to: Sydney and Scotland Island. Studies differ as to whether it is part of PWSGF[Ψ].

Distribution: Sclerophyll forest and on margins, and in disturbed rainforest; coast and adjacent ranges; NSW, Qld, Vic.

Other notes: Despite the common name (Forest Nightshade), the plant is unlikely to be highly toxic, as it is not closely related to the infamous Deadly Nightshade (*Atropa belladonna*), though it is in the same family. The nightshade family has nearly one hundred genera and around 2,700 species. *Solanum* is the largest genus in the family, with around 1,500 species, and includes three important food crops: potato, tomato, and eggplant. The *Solanum* genus has its own bitter-tasting toxin, which is well known to anyone who has eaten green potatoes.

Photo: TM Tame, The Royal Botanic Gardens & Domain Trust

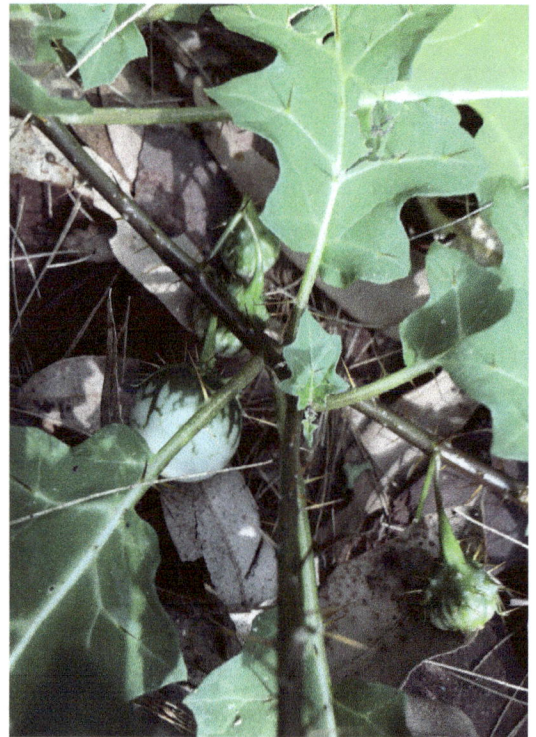

Photo: H Malloy

Judging by the way it pops up here and there, it appears to be efficiently dispersed by some animal which finds the tomato-like fruits palatable – possums?

Probably not available for sale commercially, given that most people would not want such a prickly plant.

Ψ   Bell & Stables 2012 don't report it. OEH 2016 reports it as diagnostic of PSGF.

Syncarpia glomulifera

Common name(s): Turpentine, Yanderra

Max. height in gardens, usually: 25 m; taller in forests, and shorter on poor soil.

Max. width in gardens, usually: 6 m; narrower in forests when single-trunked.

Form: Stately single-trunked tall tree, or a dramatic grouping of four or five arching trunks.

Soil: Sandy, loamy or clay soils, but prefers moist clay or shale soils; prefers a sheltered location such as a group of trees; drought-tolerant.

Light: Prefers light shade; tolerates full sun.

Flower season: White flowers in large, fused globular groups, Aug to Dec, with a peak in Sept.

Best features: Dramatic fibrous bark, with deep vertical furrows; thick dark green leaves in pseudo-worls of four provide dense canopy; large white flower clusters of up to seven flowers; children love the woody "space ship" fruits.

Propagation: Seed.

Native to: Sydney and Scotland Island; studies differ as to whether it is a component of PWSGF[Ω].

Distribution: Widespread in coastal districts and lower ranges; in NSW, Qld.

Other notes: Attractive stately form from a young age. Hardy and adaptable for large gardens. Provides good shade with its large, thick leaves. In PWSGF, it is a large understorey tree, staying just under the light shade of the Spotted Gums. Very long-lived, possibly to as long as 500 years.

Photo: H Malloy

Photo: Neil Murphy, Eatons Hill, Qld

Photo: Gillian Gutridge, Native Plants of the Northern Beaches, Sydney. https://nbplantareas.com/

The dramatic moody-looking multi-trunked specimens in Elizabeth Park on Scotland Island likely grew at the same time from the same multi-seeded aggregate fruit (see first photo above). The normally ramrod-straight trunks arch torturously away from each other, as far as they can given where their roots are.

Available at most native plant nurseries.

Ω   Bell & Stables 2012 don't report it. OEH 2016 reports it as diagnostic of PSGF.

Synoum glandulosum

Common name(s): Scentless Rosewood

Max. height, usually: 8 m

Max. width, usually: 3 m

Form: Large shrub to small tree; dense foliage.

Soil: Well-drained sandy, clay or loam; prefers soil enriched with humus or well-aged compost, with extra water in dry times. Somewhat drought tolerant.

Light: Part-shade to dappled shade.

Flower season: Attractive large white or cream flowers in late Feb.

Best features: Sweetly scented white flowers; large colourful red fruits opening to reveal large red seeds; dense shade tree.

Propagation: Grows easily from fresh seed.

Native to: Sydney and Scotland Island, and typical of Moist PWSGF.

Distribution: Widespread in warmer rainforest; in NSW, Qld.

Other notes: This is one of those cross-over species that is found in rainforest as well as moist Spotted Gum forest. In a rainforest, it can grow to 20 m, but in the Spotted Gum forest on Scotland Island, as well as in a garden situation, it remains a small, attractive tree.

Photo: H Malloy

Photo: Gillian Gutridge, *Native Plants of the Northern Beaches, Sydney.* https://nbplantareas.com/

Useful wherever a small tree providing dense shade is wanted. Unlike the superficially similar Cheese Tree (*Glochidion ferdinandi;* see profile*)*, which tends to look scruffy unless kept very moist, it tolerates hot, dry locations comparatively well. Frequently self-seeds thanks to birds.

Male and female flowers are on separate trees, so if you want to get fruit, you have to plant two or three. A member of the mahogany family, and the wood can be used for many useful things.

Most native plant nurseries carry it.

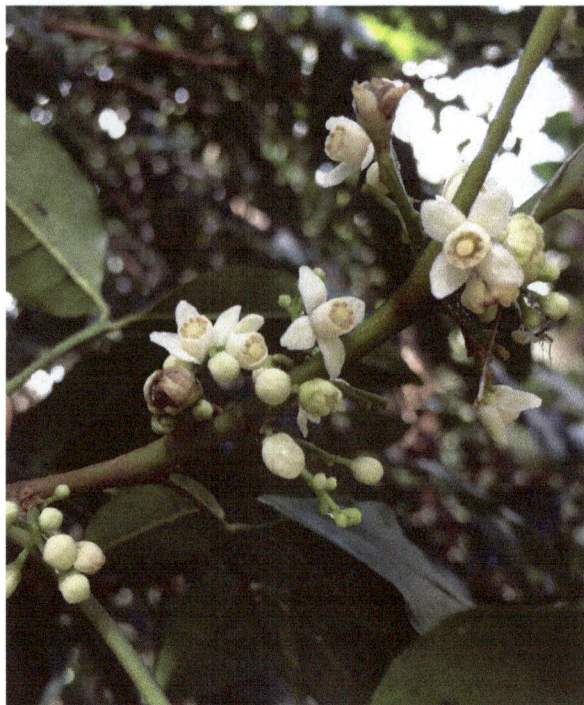

Syzigium paniculatum

Common name(s): Daguba (Cadigal), Magenta Lilly Pilly, Magenta Cherry

Max. height, usually: 10 m in garden situation.

Max. width, usually: 5 m in garden situation.

Form: Attractive shrub or small tree.

Soil: Prefers humus-rich well-drained sandy, clay or loamy soils and assured moisture; drought resistant. Does not tolerate waterlogging.

Light: Full sun to part shade.

Flower season: Showy clusters of fluffy white flowers in spring, followed by edible magenta fruits.

Photo: TM Tame, The Royal Botanic Gardens & Garden Trust

Best features: Fast-growing; fruits are an attractive purple to magenta, and can be used to make jam; new leaves are an attractive reddish colour.

Propagation: Seed, cuttings.

Native to: Sydney and Scotland Island, though the plants now on Scotland Island may be descended from garden specimens, as it has been known to naturalise in other areas. Nearest wild-collected record is from North Avoca, in a private reserve of Blackbutt open forest, dated 1991.

Distribution: Endemic to NSW; subtropical and littoral rainforest on sandy soils or stabilized dunes, often near the sea.

Other notes: Endangered in the wild, largely due to habitat loss by clearing and agricultural use. Presently only occurs in the wild in five broad areas, including Jervis Bay, Coalcliff, Botany Bay, Central Coast and Seal Rocks.

In cultivation for a long time and very popular, especially for hedges. Mulch and fertilise annually, with watering during dry periods, for best growth.

Susceptible to attacks by psyllid insects, which causes leaves to be disfigured with distorted growth and heavy pimple-like wounds. There are other species also known as "lilly pilly" which are not similarly affected by psyllids, and may be a better choice if that is a concern; *Acmena smithii* is one example.

Numerous cultivars are available, such as "Backyard Bliss", which grows to 5 m x 2 m. "Lillyput" is a cultivar that grows to 2 m x 2 m. The cultivars are also susceptible to psyllid damage. If this is a concern, it would be unwise to purchase from a large nursery where psyllid outbreaks are likely; such nurseries are likely to spray regularly but not completely eradicate the pests.

Themeda triandra (formerly T. australis)

Common name(s): Kangaroo Grass

Max. height, usually: 1.5 m

Max. width, usually: .5 m

Form: Clumping or spreading grass; clumping is the usual form.

Soil: Well-drained moist sandy soils to heavy clays. Drought tolerant. Does not tolerate waterlogging.

Light: Full sun to light shade.

Flower season: Sept to Feb.

Best features: Attractive fountain foliage and large interesting seed heads with long twisted black awns.

Propagation: Seed; division of clumps. Ripe seed begins to be available Dec. onwards, but approx. 2/3 of ripe-looking seeds are incompletely developed and infertile.

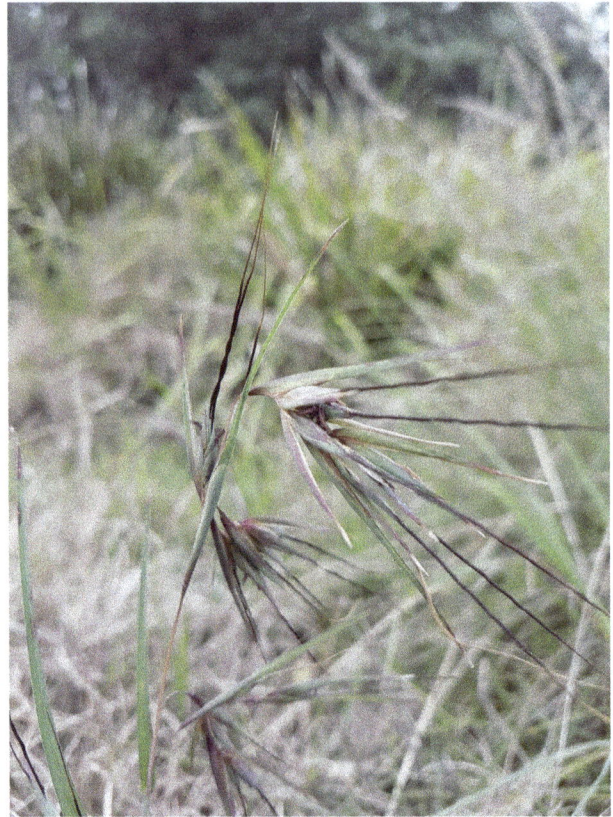

Photo: Jenny aka Floydwafer, iNaturalist

As with most native grasses, there is an inhibition system that prevents most of the ripe seed from germinating for one to two months, so it is best to store seed for planting the following spring.

Native to: Sydney and Scotland Island. Typical of Dry PWSGF.

Distribution: All Australian states; also New Guinea, Asia and Africa. In Australia, it is most common where grazing disturbance is low, moisture collects, and periodic fires occur.

Other notes: Long-lived with a deep root system once established. Does not tolerate mowing or heavy grazing. Clumps can be cut back in early spring to encourage new green growth. Grows most actively in the warm season (C4 grass), and dormant in winter. Leaf colour varies, with colours varying from blue-green to grey green, with red-tinged leaf base.

Kangaroo Grass was a staple grain food for Indigenous Australians, who ground the seeds into flour and porridge.

Try to get a form that corresponds to the light conditions of your garden; some forms are more shade-tolerant than others and more appropriate for lightly shaded woodland-type gardens.

There is a cultivar available with a spreading (not clumping) habit, "Mingo". As for any cultivar, beware that cultivars may derive from a geographically remote and/or very different environment, and may not prosper as well as stock locally sourced.

Trochocarpa laurina

Common name(s): Tree Heath, Axebreaker, Sandberry, Wheel-fruit, Waddy Wood

Max. height, usually: 10 m, in dappled shade.

Max. width, usually: 3 m

Form: Compact shrub to crooked tree.

Soil: Well-drained humus-rich clay, sandy or loam soil.

Light: Dappled shade.

Flower season: Small white flowers in summer.

Best features: Attractive dark green shiny leaves with 5+ parallel veins; new leaves hang straight down and are often pinkish; dense foliage; dainty little flowers.

Propagation: Seeds: slow and difficult.

Native to: Sydney and Scotland Island. Studies differ regarding its place in PWSGF[Ω]. Nearest wild-collected records are from Church Point, 1952 and Careel Bay, 1930.

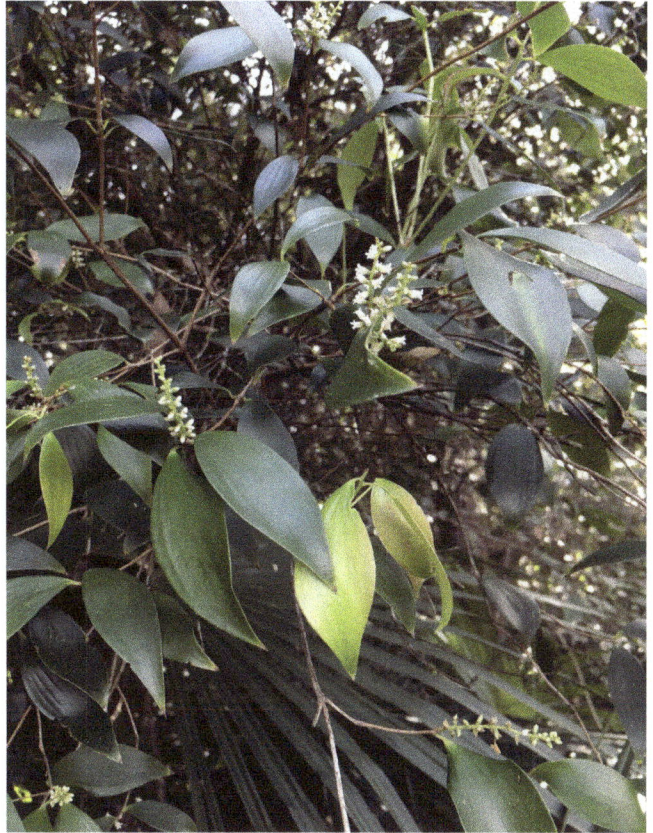

Photos (above and below): H Malloy

Distribution: Wet sclerophyll forest, rainforest; NSW, Qld.

Other notes: Fruits are eaten by Pied Currawongs. As with many bird-dispersed rainforest plants, plants spring up in all sorts of places, some of which are not ideal, such as in full sun or in poor soil. Such plants show the toughness of this species. In dry years they get to the brink of death, and yet bounce back once rains return. Somehow even when in these exposed situations, they look good, but stunted.

If you have one of these poorly placed self-sown Tree Heaths, you can give it a extra water during dry times, or (better) plant a wattle to its north.

The dense shade of Tree Heath provides daytime roosts for owls (can you find the Australian Boobook in the photo?).

Available from many native plant nurseries.

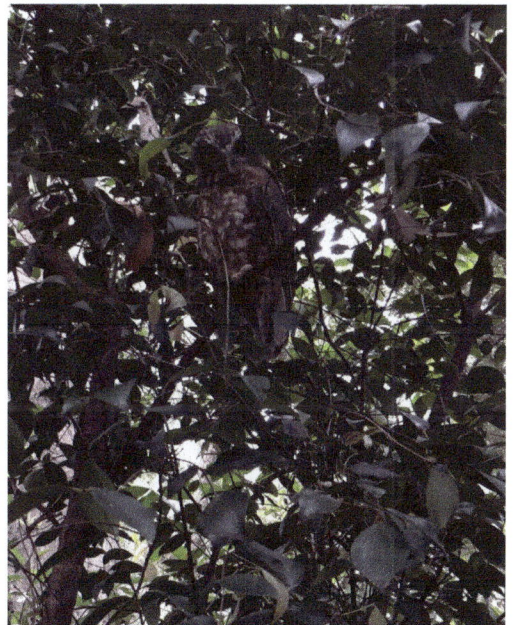

Ω   Bell & Stables 2012 don't report it. OEH 2016 reports it as an uncommon component of PSGF.

Veronica plebeia

Common name(s): Creeping or Trailing Speedwell

Max. height, usually: 10 cm

Max. width, usually: Stolons can reach 1 m in length and can cover indefinite areas.

Form: Matting herb, rooting at leaf nodes.

Soil: Moist, well-drained.

Light: Full sun to full shade.

Flower season: Tiny lilac to blue flowers Sept to Jun.

Best features: Tiny, delicate flowers contrast well with intricately detailed leaves.

Propagation: Seed; division.

Native to: Sydney and Scotland Island. Not a component of PWSGF.

Distribution: Eucalypt forest, grassland, on rainforest margins and as a weed in lawns and gardens; widespread in coastal districts; all Australian states and territories apart from NT.

Other notes: May die off during dry weather, but regenerates very well from seeds stored in the soil, which remain viable five years or more.

Looks pretty in a container when allowed to spill over the edges.

Best viewed up close to appreciate it fully, but the trailing form is also attractive when viewed at a distance.

Non-vigorous and although it can form a mat, it does not generally overwhelm other small plants.

Available at some native plant nurseries.

Photo: L von Richter, The Royal Botanic Gardens & Domain Trust

Photo: H Malloy

Viminaria juncea

Common name(s): Golden spray, Native Broom

Max. height, usually: 5 m

Max. width, usually: 2.5 m

Form: Shrub with sprays of pendant leafless branches.

Soil: Almost any soil; prefers swamps and waterlogged situations; tolerates merely moist soils if watered in summer. Tolerates salt and lime.

Light: Prefers full sun; tolerates part shade.

Flower season: Profuse sprays of red-marked yellow clover-scented flowers Nov to Dec.

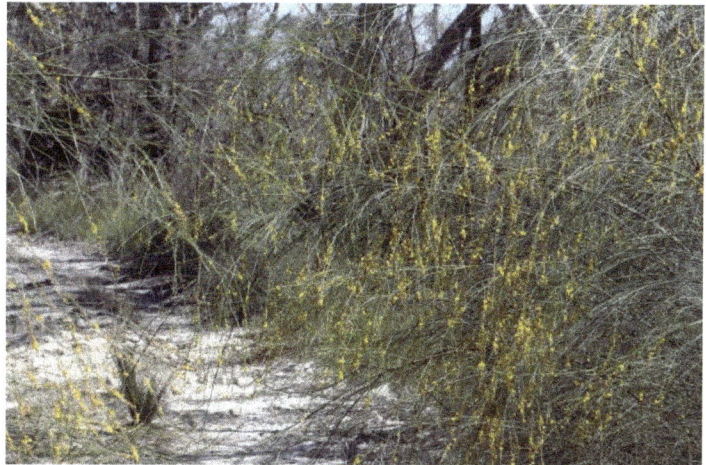

Photos (above and below): Gillian Gutridge, *Native Plants of the Northern Beaches, Sydney*. https://nbplantareas.com/

Best features: Fast-growing; long flower season, which can last six weeks in cool springs.

Propagation: Seed, which is produced in generous amounts.

Native to: Sydney but not Scotland Island and not PWSGF. Can be seen on local bushwalks including the Chiltern, Manly Dam, and Terrey Hills trails.

Distribution: Widespread, in swampy situations on the coast; NSW, Qld, Vic, WA, SA.

Other notes: Long-lived plant. Branches are extremely pliant and the plant withstands storms very well. Adaptable to drier conditions if it receives summer watering, but will be nearly maintenance free if planted in naturally moist or wet areas. If a similar plant is wanted for a dry spot, consider *Jacksonia scoparia* (which is also sometimes known as Native Broom) instead.

Can be grown as a shrub, and trimmed when young with that in mind. Alternatively, can be allowed to grow as a single trunk to a height of 6 m or so; the slender dark trunk contrasts well with the foliage, which is a waving mass of slender pendulous branches. Good in a massed group or as a single specimen for contrast with other shrubs.

Weeping form enhances ponds or other water features. Can be planted in or adjacent to drainage channels, where it would help prevent erosion.

Available at most local native plant nurseries.

Viola betonicifolia

Common name(s): Arrowhead Violet, Mountain Violet, Showy Violet, Betony-Leaved Violet

Max. height, usually: 15 cm

Max. width, usually: 30 cm

Form: Rosette-forming herb.

Soil: Prefers well-drained clay-based or loamy soil; tolerates sandy soil as long as it is kept moist.

Light: Half to full shade.

Flower season: Violet flowers in spring and again in autumn; flowering season is longer in cool, shaded conditions.

Best features: Interesting leaf shape; lovely flowers.

Propagation: Seed; division. Self-seeds in good conditions.

Photo: Australian National Botanic Gardens
http://www.anbg.gov.au/photo

Native to: Sydney but not Scotland Island. Not a component of PWSGF. Nearest wild-collected record is Hornsby.

Distribution: Shaded habitat in forests and creek banks; throughout coastal eastern Australia and Tasmania. Also India, Pakistan and southern Asia.

Other notes: Easy to grow as long as it gets sufficient modest moisture and at least 50% shade.

Pollinated by the Common Grass Yellow Butterfly. Photo: Garry Sankowsky

Good in a pot where it can be more easily seen, or in small drifts in a shaded moist area.

Continues to flower during the warmer summer months, but with small green flowers that self-fertilise and do not open their petals (cleistogamous). In the autumn after the heat of the summer has passed, it resumes flowering with normal-sized violet flowers that open in the usual way.

Food plant for the endangered Australian Fritillary Butterfly (formerly found from Bellingen north).

Food plant for the Australian Fritillary. Photo: Garry Sankowsky

Viola hederacea

Common name(s): Native Violet, Australian Violet

Max. height, usually: 10 cm

Max. width, usually: Forms patches 1 m or more.

Form: Matting herb spreading by stolons.

Soil: Prefers loamy soil; tolerates any well-drained.

Light: Prefers light to heavy shade; with too much sun they will die back when hot weather hits. In full shade they flower less or not at all.

Flower season: Flowers white with mauve centers, Oct to Feb.

Best features: Pretty flowers; spreads nicely but not aggressively.

Propagation: Seed; division of stolons

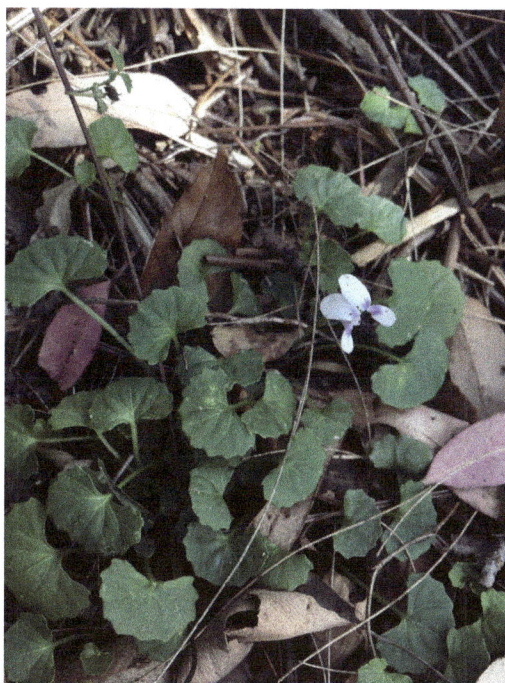
Photo: H Malloy

Native to: Sydney and Scotland Island. Studies differ as to whether it is a component of PWSGF$^\Psi$.

Distribution: Sheltered moist places NSW, Qld, Tas, SA.

Other notes: Most ornamental cultivars labelled as *Viola hederacea* are actually *Viola banksii*, which until 2003 was included within *V. hederacea*.[*] The type of violet that is native to Scotland Island is *V. hederacea*, not *banksii*. *V. hederacea* is a smaller plant, with mauve/white flowers, compared to the larger *banksii* with vivid deep purple/white flowers. The leaf shape also differs; *banksii* leaves are nearly round, whereas *hederacea* leaves are closer to a quarter moon.

Much of the advice and information online purportedly relating to *V. hederacea* actually relates to *V. banksii*.

V. banksii has a tendency to grow vigorously in the winter and spring and cover a large area, including sunny places, and then collapse en masse when the drier weather begins in Nov or Dec. In contrast, though *V. hederacea* also spreads, it is not so aggressive about it, so that it doesn't find itself trying to grow in such inappropriate places. *V. hederacea* also does not smother other small plants the way *V. banksii* does.

It is perhaps best to restrict both species to shaded areas only, to avoid the eyesore of large expanses of collapsed plants in hot weather.

Commercial nurseries are likely to mislabel *V. banksii* as *V. hederacea*. It is safer to shop at native plant nurseries.

Ψ Bell & Stables 2012 don't report it. OEH 2016 report it as an uncommon component of PSGF.
*   https://en.wikipedia.org/wiki/Viola_hederacea

Wahlenbergia gracilis

Common name(s): Australian Bluebell, Sprawling Bluebell

Max. height, usually: 20 cm

Max. width, usually: 10 cm

Form: Perennial herb.

Soil: Moist well-drained; does not tolerate waterlogging.

Light: Prefers semi-shade; tolerates full sun.

Flower season: Tiny blue flowers Sept to Nov.

Best features: Dainty tiny herb which will seed freely in some gardens.

Propagation: Seeds, which are profuse and fine like dust.

Native to: Sydney and Scotland Island. Not a component of PWSGF.

Distribution: Widespread in many situations, including lawns, gardens, and even urban pavement cracks[*]; chiefly on the coast, tablelands and slopes; NSW, Qld, Vic, Tas, SA, NT; also western Pacific Ocean islands.

Other notes: Grows well in a pot or planter if kept moist.

If growing in very dry, constrained circumstances it is inclined to look weedy.

In my garden it is charming in spring along path edges on a west-facing slope, but when hot dry weather comes, it gets powdery mildew and collapses. Renews afresh from roots when rains return, but in some years it dies off and renews from seed the following spring.

Available at some native plant nurseries.

Photo: L. von Richter, The Royal Botanic Gardens & Domain Trust

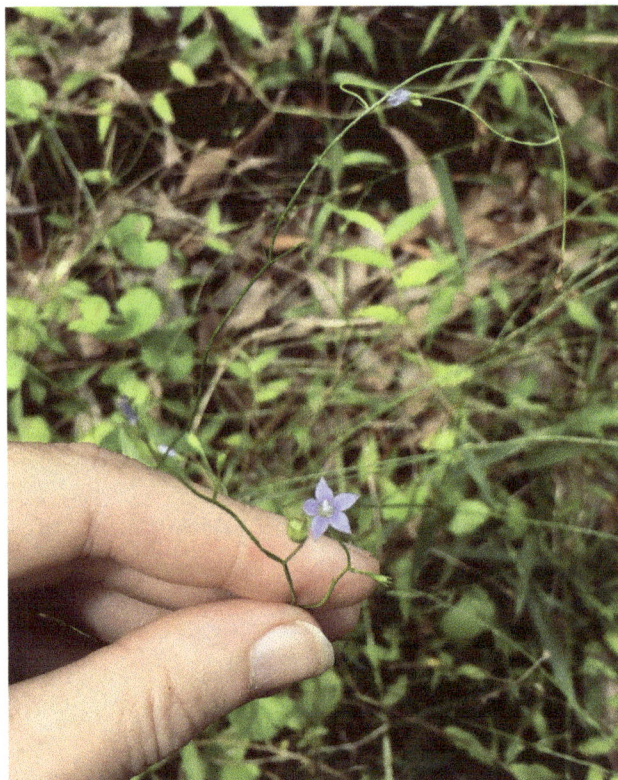

Photo: H Malloy

---

[*]   https://weedsofmelbourne.org/sprawling-bluebell-wahlenbergia-gracilis

Westringia fruticosa

Common name(s): Coastal Rosemary

Max. height, usually: 2 m

Max. width, usually: 4 m

Form: Stiff, bushy shrub.

Soil: Any; withstands wind and salt spray; drought tolerant.

Light: Full sun to light shade.

Flower season: White flowers most of the year, peaking Nov.

Best features: Self-rounding shape (usually); no maintenance required.

Propagation: Easy from cuttings.

Native to: Sydney but not Scotland Island. Not a component of PWSGF. Nearest wild-collected records are Mona Vale, Newport, and Warriewood.

Distribution: NSW, near the sea and harbour foreshores, often on exposed cliffs in skeletal soils.

Other notes: Good cut flower in arrangements.

Photo: Danielle Langlois
https://commons.wikimedia.org/wiki/File:Westringia_fruticosa_01.jpg
https://creativecommons.org/licenses/by-sa/3.0/deed.en

When planting, allow room for its full size, so that you will not need to prune it. But if necessary, it can be pruned to size or even hedged.

Many cultivars available in commercial nurseries, including an attractive grey-green one called "Smokey".

Photo: Georgios Liakopoulos
https://commons.wikimedia.org/wiki/File:Westringia_Fruticosa_(203360961).jpeg
https://creativecommons.org/licenses/by-sa/3.0/deed.en

Westringia longifolia

Common name(s): Long-leaf Westringia

Max. height, usually: 3 m

Max. width, usually: 3 m

Form: Open, bushy shrub.

Soil: Well-drained; very drought tolerant; salt tolerant.

Light: Prefers light shade; tolerates full sun.

Flower season: White or mauve flowers mostly July to Dec; often flowers again Feb to Mar.

Best features: Prolific spring flowers followed by second modest flowering in mid-summer; flowers in the mauve form contrast well with leaves; fast growing.

Propagation: Easy from cuttings.

Native to: Sydney but not Scotland Island. Not a component of PWSGF. Nearest wild-collected records are Five Dock and Burwood.

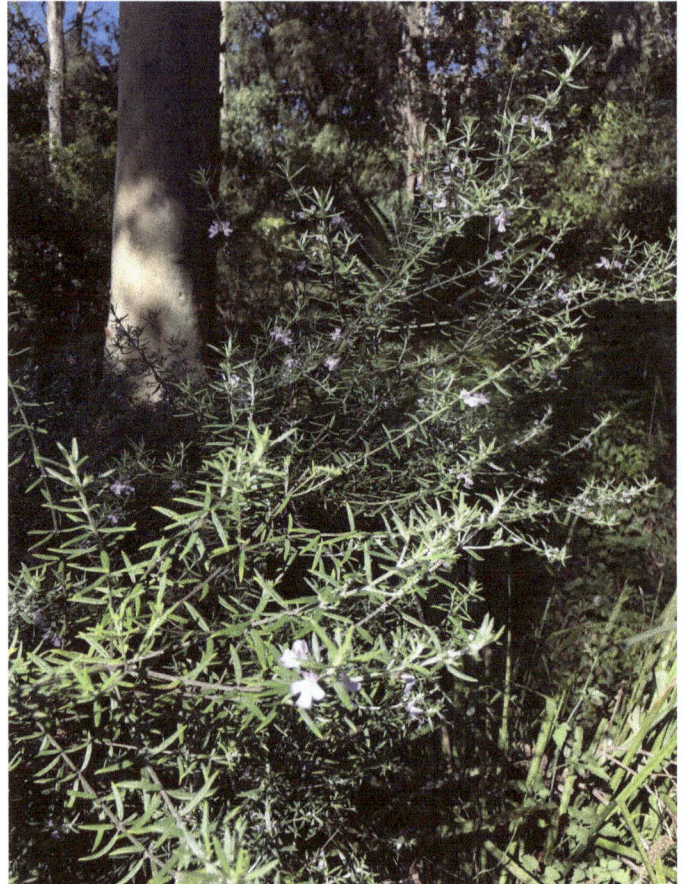

This is the second, sparser flowering; early February. Photo: H Malloy

Distribution: Shrubland, often in rocky areas, in sandy or loamy soils, often associated with creeks and rivers; usually inland; NSW and Qld.

Other notes: Tough and long lived. Salt tolerant.

Although it is roughly self-rounding, tip pruning after the main flowering period will help keep it symmetrical and bring it back into flower faster. Can also be pruned to keep it smaller, as its full size is rather large.

Good for hedging or screening, or background for a large garden.

Photo: H Malloy

Xanthorrhoea arborea

Common name(s): Broad-leaf Grass Tree

Max. height, usually: 1.5 m; flower spike adds 2 m to onto that.

Max. width, usually: 2 m

Form: Grass tree with trunk up to 2 m tall, but usually much shorter.

Soil: Well-drained sandy or sandstone-based soil; drought-tolerant but prefers moist soil; tolerates clay if on a slope.

Light: Prefers light shade; leaves can be burned by sudden increase in sun or temperature.

Flower season: Jan to Apr, but infrequent; flowering enhanced by bush fires.

Best features: Dramatic fountain form and flowering spike; some develop a trunk.

Propagation: Easy from seed, but slow.

Photo: H Malloy

Native to: Sydney and Scotland Island. Studies differ as to whether it is part of PWSGF[Σ]. Common as an understory shrub along the western foreshore of Pittwater.

Distribution: Sclerophyll forest, usually in sheltered sites, in sand or on sandstone; NSW in or near Sydney basin.

Other notes: Hard to find in nurseries. Some native plant nurseries carry a smaller species that is a Sydney local native, *X. resinosa*, found in heath or low woodland in NSW and Vic, which would likely be a better choice in very sunny locations, but not good in heavily shaded sites.

X. arborea, with its wide leaves, is well adapted to dappled shade, and conversely it may burn in too much sun or sudden hot weather, especially if already stressed.

When planted as mature specimens, Grass Trees generally die within two to three years, when the reserves they have built up are gone. Your best bet is to ask someone who has the species you want on their property to let you collect a few of the very plentiful seeds, and grow them yourself. Instructions are available on several websites[Ω]. Even when larger plants are available at nurseries, seedlings would be a better choice as survival is better for Grass Trees grown from small seedlings.

Growth in the first few years is slow; you will need to put a ring of rocks or stakes around the seedlings after you plant them out. Otherwise, they can get smothered by vegetation, or stepped on.

Σ   Bell and Stables 2012 don't report it. OEH 2016 report it as a component of PSGF.
Ω   https://ecobits.net.au/how-to-grow-grass-trees-from-seed-xanthorrhoea/
     https://www.davidbedford.info/growing-xanthorrhoeas.html

Xanthorrhoea macronema

Common name(s): Bottlebrush Grass Tree

Max. height, usually: 1 m

Max. width, usually: 1.5 m

Form: Trunkless grass tree with bottle-brush-like white flowers.

Soil: Well-drained; prefers sandy soil. Drought tolerant.

Light: Prefers lightly filtered to dappled shade; tolerates full sun. They survive but don't flower in heavy shade.

Flower season: Cream or yellow flower spike July to Jan; a given plant may not flower every year.

Best features: Spectacular flower spike like a bottle-brush; flowers open from the bottom upwards.

Propagation: Seed; easy but very slow-growing[Ω].

Native to: Sydney and Scotland Island. Studies differ as to whether it is part of PWSGF[Φ].

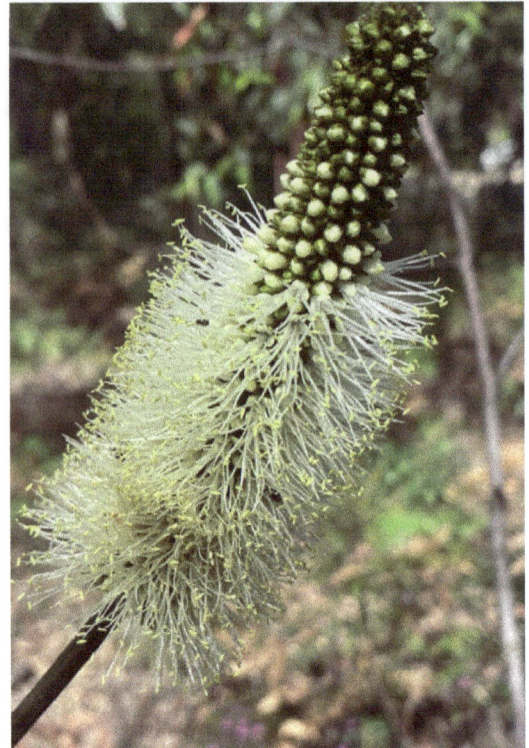

Photos (above and below): Mark Abell, Australian Plants Society NSW

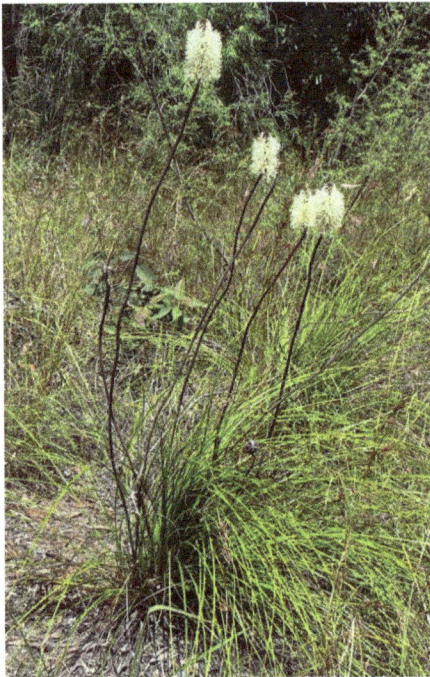

Distribution: Sclerophyll forest on coastal sands and ranges; in NSW north from the Sydney region; also Qld.

Other notes: Looks best in groups, so that at least one plant flowers per group each year. In a garden situation, pamper them with filtered sun, generous watering in dry weather, and well-aged compost or mulch, topped up annually. If grown in full sun, will need more water. Looks good on a mound or hill, so that the flamboyant inflorescences are raised up closer to eye level. This also allows the possibility of growing it on clay soil, if you can obtain enough sandy soil to make a mound.

Slow growing; needs protection for five or more years so that you don't forget it is there and step on it, or forget to weed it. A ring of bamboo stakes or rocks placed around it works well.

Hard to find in local native plant nurseries, but it may be available online or in more distant nurseries.

Ω   https://ecobits.net.au/how-to-grow-grass-trees-from-seed-xanthorrhoea/

Φ   Bell & Stables 2012 don't report it. OEH 2016 reports it as typical of PSGF. The OEH results can be stated more strongly, as it was the only plant species in the study that was not found in any plant community other than PSGF.

Zieria prostrata

Common name(s): Headland Zieria, Carpet Star (marketing name used by commercial nurseries)

Max. height, usually: 50 cm

Max. width, usually: 1 m

Form: Prostrate shrub.

Soil: Well-drained clay, sandy, or loamy soil; somewhat drought tolerant. Tolerates salt spray.

Light: Prefers dappled sun; tolerates full sun.

Flower season: White or pink four-petalled flowers in spring.

Photos (above and below): M. Fagg
https://www.anbg.gov.au/photo/image-collection.html

Best features: Attractive flowers which contrast well with the fresh green three-part leaves; neat mounding or cascading habit.

Propagation: Cuttings. Growing from seed is difficult, but seedlings are often found around plants. Capsules explode when ripe, scattering seeds.

Native to: **Not native to Sydney** and not Scotland Island and not PWSGF.

Distribution: Endangered and endemic to NSW; restricted to low coastal heaths on four headlands in Moonee Beach Nature Reserve, near Coffs Harbour.

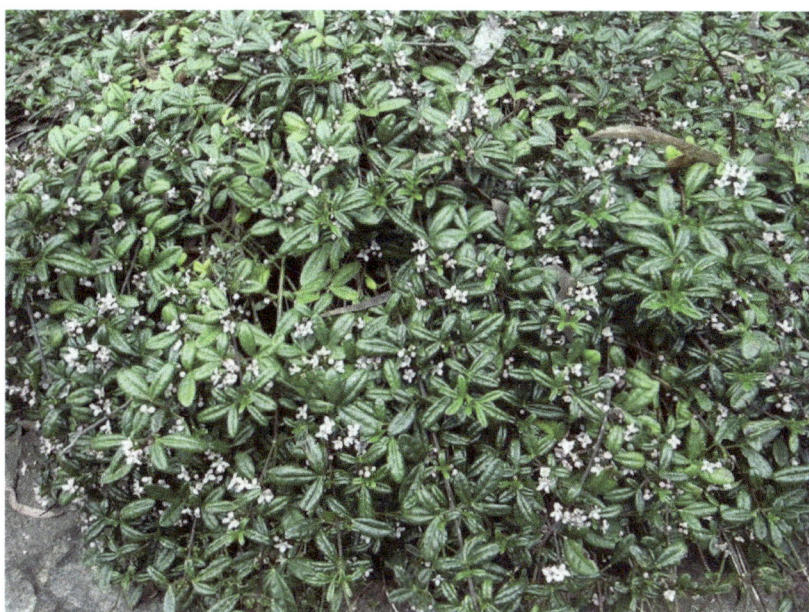

Other notes: Performs best with light afternoon shade and protection from wind. Does not tolerate foot traffic. Doesn't need pruning, and when grown in the ground, doesn't need fertilising. Just weed around it, basically. Allow it to cascade over rocks or embankments, or grow in a wide, low pot where it can cascade over the edges.

Somewhat resembles an attractive low-growing local native, *Zieria pilosa*, which sadly is not available to buy anywhere that I can find, but anyway its looks don't hold a candle to the "Carpet Star", which is truly a stellar plant. But it is not a Sydney local native, so purists should avoid it.

Widely available at many native plant nurseries. Also sold at commercial nurseries, usually with the marketing name "Carpet Star". Most cultivated plants descend from samples taken on Dammerels Head (one of the four headlands where it is endemic).

Zieria smithii

Common name(s): Sandfly Zieria, Lanoline Bush

Max. height, usually: 2 m

Max. width, usually: 1 m

Form: Upright shrub; robust, rounded shape on moist sites, but spindly and low on drier sites.

Soil: Well-drained; prefers light sandy soil with regular watering, and a position sheltered from wind.

Light: Dappled to part shade.

Flower season: White or pale pink flowers Aug to Oct.

Best features: Charming four-petaled flowers are small but numerous; shiny leaves with three leaflets make the plant attractive even when not in flower.

Propagation: Seed; cuttings. Will self-seed.

Native to: Sydney and Scotland Island. Studies differ as to whether it is a component of PWSGF[Ω].

Distribution: Widespread on the coast and ranges; NSW, Qld, Vic.

Other notes: Plant is strongly odorous when crushed and not to everyone's taste. Reputed to repel insects.

Prune lightly after flowering and keep watered.

King Parrots love to eat the seeds.

Host plant for several butterfly species.

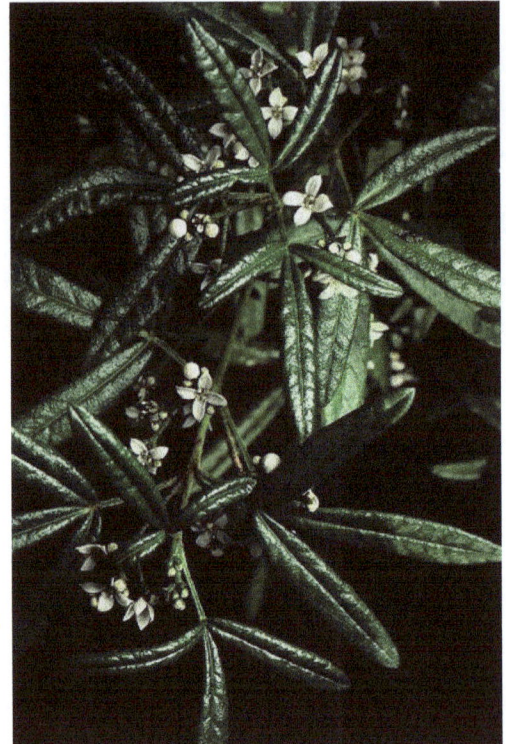

Photo: J. Plaza, The Royal Botanic Gardens & Domain Trust

Zieria with *Crinum*. Photo: Jeff Howe Photo: Jeff Howes
https://resources.austplants.com.au/plant-database/

Male Orchard Butterfly. Photo: Fir0002/Flagstaffotos
https://commons.wikimedia.org/wiki/File:Orchard_Butter
fly_-_melbourne_zoo.jpg
https://www.gnu.org/licenses/old-licenses/fdl-1.2.html

Ω   Bell & Stables 2012 don't report it. OEH 2016 report it as typical of PSGF.

Index of all species

Index by growth type and other categories

Orchids

Ferns

Grasses and grasslike plants

Large tufted plants (not grasslike)

Creeping groundcovers

Vines and climbers

Herbs and shrubs up to 1.5 m

Shrubs and trees up to 3 m

Trees up to 10 m

Trees over 10 m

Trees over 15 m

Species that are endemic to the Sydney Basin (or nearly so)

Species that are not native to the Sydney Basin

PWSGF (Pittwater Spotted Gum Forest)

Clay lovers (or at least tolerate clay)

Plants that tolerate waterlogging

Plants that tolerate drought

History of vegetation surveys of Scotland Island

1978 – Craig Burton

Unpublished report, including species lists and map showing vegetation communities of Scotland Island.

1990 – Polly Thompson

Unpublished list of plant species of Elizabeth Park.

1992 – Sally Fischer

Unpublished list of plant species of Scotland Island.

1994-2011 – Brad Jones

Very thorough unpublished list of Elizabeth Park species by Brad Jones, incorporating the lists of Craig Burton, Sally Fisher and Polly Thompson where Brad could independently corroborate sightings. Brad developed this list while completing his bushcare certification and afterwards as a contractor working for Pittwater Council (which has now been subsumed into Northern Beaches Council).

2018-present – this author

I have added to Brad's excellent list as follows:

- Plant species identified by myself, Peter Juniper (Northern Beaches Council Botanist) and others in the years since Brad stopped working on his list.

- A few species from Craig Burton's list, which Brad had omitted from his list because at the time he was actively working on his list they were no longer to be found in Elizabeth Park; but in the years since then have reappeared (e.g., *Acacia decurrens*, *Cassinia aculeata*). They could have grown from soil-stored seed, or from new dispersal onto the island from birds or human influence .

Scan the QR code with your phone or download from my Scotland Island bushcare blog at: https://bushcareblog.wordpress.com/lists/

History of surveys and reports on PSGF and PWSGF

1998 – NSW Scientific Committee lists PSGF (Pittwater Spotted Gum Forest) as endangered

This definition of PSGF is superseded by the Committee's 2013 report (see below).

Webpage includes a list of "characteristic species".

Scan the QR code on your phone or download at:

```
https://www.environment.nsw.gov.au/Topics/Animals-and-plants/Threatened-
species/NSW-Threatened-Species-Scientific-Committee/Determinations/Final-
determinations/1996-1999/Pittwater-Spotted-Gum-Forest-endangered-ecological-
community-listing
```

2011 – Unpublished vegetation mapping study commissioned by what was then known as Pittwater Council

Reportedly, this unpublished study proposed a vegetation association similar to what is now called PWSGF, which they called ***Coastal Dry Spotted Gum Forest*** and ***Coastal Moist Spotted Gum Forest***. The study was the joint effort of two botanical consulting firms, Bangalay Ecological and Bushfire (Claire deLacey and Steve Chamberlain) and Eastcoast Flora Survey (Stephen Bell).

2012 – Bell and Stables study

In 2012 Stephen Bell (with Mark Stables) published a portion of the 2011 study for Pittwater Council proposing that Wagstaffe Spotted Gum Forest (found north of the Hawkesbury River) and PSGF (Pittwater Spotted Gum Forest) are both variations on the same ecological community. Bell's analysis showed that there are two distinct forms of the community, which he termed ***Dry PSGF*** and ***Moist PSGF***.

From a gardener's point of view it is important to consider Bell's species lists separately, as the majority of the species listed are found only in the Dry or the Moist form, but not both. Of the 99 species mentioned in the study, only twelve species were shared across both groups. Bell's lists are reproduced in the section titled "Dry PWSGF and Moist PWSGF".

Full-text PDF available for free on the web. Scan the QR code on your phone or download at:

2013 – NSW Scientific Committee replaces PSGF concept listing with Bell's PWSGF concept (Pittwater and Wagstaffe Spotted Gum Forest)

This supercedes the 1998 determination and redefines PSGF to be part of the larger PWSGF (Pittwater and Wagstaffe Spotted Gum Forest), which is also endangered under Threatened Species Conservation Act 1995. Contains a new list of "characteristic species" which is similar but not identical to the species in the 1998, so I found it worthwhile to look at both when I was searching for garden candidates for Scotland Island.

The PWSGF concept is based on Bell and Stable's 2012 study and agreed that there are two forms of the community: dry and mesic (i.e., moderately moist). However, the Scientific Committee didn't break out separate lists for the two forms, although Bell and Stables had suggested that this might be desirable.

The other Northern Beaches areas (besides Scotland Island) identified as including some PWSGF include :

- Ku-ring-gai Chase National Park, on western shore of Pittwater.

- Stapleton Park in Avalon, on the ridge and slopes of Riviera Avenue.

- McKay Reserve in Palm Beach, on a ridge on Barrenjoey Peninsula overlooking western Pittwater.

- Crown of Newport Bushland Reserve, Howell Close, Newport.

- Angophora Reserve in the suburbs of Avalon and Clareville, 58 Palmgrove Road, Avalon.

The downloadable pdf contains a list of "characteristic species" as well as a list of common weeds, and some miscellaneous ecological and other background information. Scan the QR code on your phone or download at:

2016 – NSW OEH – The Native Vegetation of the Sydney Metropolitan Area

This is a large study published Nov 2016 by NSW Office of Environment and Heritage. The authors used statistical analysis to identify what species (or group of species) are "diagnostic" in determining whether a particular patch of bushland you are looking at is a particular plant community type or not.

Some species are uninformative because they are common everywhere, and some are so uncommon that not all patches of that community type have them.

For each community type, a sample site (400 sq meters) is expected to contain *at least 25 positive diagnostic species* provided the *total number of native species in the site is 42 or greater.*

The overall Sydney-wide study included data from 2200 floristic sites. There were 22 sites representing PWSGF, including the PSGF areas listed above as well as locations in the Wagstaffe (Bouddi Peninsula) area.

Scan the QR code on your phone or download at:

```
https://datasets.seed.nsw.gov.au/dataset/the-native-vegetation-of-the-sydney-
metropolitan-area-oeh-2016-vis-id-4489
```

Dry PWSGF and Moist PWSGF

Below are the 99 species listed in the Bell and Stables 2012 study (see "History of surveys" section). I have rearranged the lists to display the information of interest to gardeners, which is basically "what conditions do the plants prefer, and what do they dislike?"

There are two separate lists: one for "Dry PWSGF" and one for "Moist PWSGF". Names in **bold** appeared in both groups. *For these species, we can be very confident that the plant accepts a wide range of water-related conditions.*

Names preceded by an "A" or a "B" appeared in the upper 90% of diversity for the group they appear under, i.e. they are the most abundant within their group. *For these species that were abundant within a group, we can be very confident the plant will do well if our conditions are similar to that group.*

The lists are sorted alphabetically, so that the entries for the abundant species (the ones with an "A" or "B") sort in a clump together. The abundant species are then followed by the rare or not-so-common species for each group – these ones do not have an "A" or "B" before the name. *For these rare or uncommon species, we can be moderately confident the plant will do well if our conditions are similar to that group.*

Note that the unbolded names represent species that only occurred in one group; they did not occur at all in the other group. The unbolded names with an "A" or a "B" represent species that were abundant for their group and did not occur in the other group. *For the species, we can say with some confidence that they like the conditions of their own group, and dislike the conditions of the other group in some regard.*

For the unbolded names with no "A" or "B" – which are the rare or uncommon species for their group and which also did not appear in the other group – we can't draw any firm conclusions. *It is likely these plants have a water-related preference, but maybe they are overall so rare that it was just chance they didn't appear in the other group as well.*

Note that many of the Moist PWSGF species are also found in rainforest plant communities.

Group A: Dry PWSGF

A Acacia implexa
A Acacia ulicifolia
A Allocasuarina littoralis
A Allocasuarina torulosa
A Billardiera scandens
A Breynia oblongifolia
A Caesia parviflora
A Cassytha pubescens
A Corymbia maculata
A Desmodium rhytidophyllum
A Dianella caerulea

A Digitaria parviflora
A Elaeocarpus reticulatus
A Entolasia marginata
A Entolasia stricta
A Eucalyptus paniculata subsp. paniculata
A Eucalyptus umbra
A Eustrephus latifolius
A Geitonoplesium cymosum
A Glochidion ferdinandi var. ferdinandi
A Glycine clandestina
A Hardenbergia violacea

A Imperata cylindrica var. major
A Lomandra confertifolia subsp. pallida
A Lomandra filiformis subsp. filiformis
A Lomandra longifolia
A Lomandra multiflora subsp. multiflora
A Macrozamia communis
A Microlaena stipoides var. stipoides
A Myrsine variabilis
A Notelaea longifolia forma longifolia
A Pandorea pandorana
A Panicum simile
A Persoonia levis
A Persoonia linearis
A Phyllanthus hirtellus
A Pittosporum undulatum
A Pomax umbellata
A Pratia purpurascens
A Pseuderanthemum variabile
A Pteridium esculentum
A Pultenaea flexilis
A Smilax glyciphylla
A Themeda australis
Acrotriche divaricata
Adiantum aethiopicum
Angophora costata
Aristida vagans
Brachychiton acerifolius
Brachyscome angustifolium var. angustifolium
Calochlaena dubia
Cayratia clematidea
Cissus hypoglauca
Commelina cyanea
Corymbia gummifera
Cymbopogon refractus
Desmodium gunnii
Echinopogon caespitosus
Gymnostachys anceps
Hakea sericea
Hibbertia aspera subsp. aspera
Hibbertia dentata
Hibbertia diffusa
Hybanthus monopetalus
Livistona australis
Morinda jasminoides
Oplismenus aemulus
Oplismenus imbecillus
Passiflora herbertiana var. herbertiana
Pittosporum revolutum
Poa affinis
Podolobium ilicifolium
Polyscias sambuccifolia
Sarcopetalum harveyanum
Schelhammera undulata

Stephania japonica var. discolor
Wikstroemia indica
Wilkea huegeliana

Group B: Moist PWSGF
B Adiantum aethiopicum
B Brachychiton acerifolius
B Calochlaena dubia
B Cayratia clematidea
B Cissus hypoglauca
B Commelina cyanea
B Corymbia maculata
B Eucalyptus paniculata subsp. paniculata
B Eustrephus latifolius
B Ficus coronata
B Geitonoplesium cymosum
B Glochidion ferdinandi var. ferdinandi
B Gymnostachys anceps
B Livistona australis
B Lomandra longifolia
B Macrozamia communis
B Microlaena stipoides var. stipoides
B Morinda jasminoides
B Notelaea longifolia forma longifolia
B Oplismenus imbecillus
B Pandorea pandorana
B Passiflora herbertiana var. herbertiana
B Pittosporum revolutum
B Pittosporum undulatum
B Sarcopetalum harveyanum
B Smilax glyciphylla
B Stephania japonica var. discolor
B Synoum glandulosum subsp. glandulosum
B Wilkea huegeliana
Acmena smithii
Allocasuarina torulosa
Breynia oblongifolia
Carex longebrachiata
Dianella caerulea
Doodia aspera
Elaeocarpus reticulatus
Entolasia marginata
Eucalyptus scias subsp. scias
Eucalyptus umbra
Gahnia melanocarpa
Glycine clandestina
Myrsine howitiana
Myrsine variabilis
Pteridium esculentum
Rubus parvifolius
Trema tomentosa var. viridis

General reference books

Fairley, A. and Moore, P., 2000. *Native Plants of the Sydney District: An Identification Guide.* Kangaroo Press, East Roseville, NSW: 432 pp.

Greig, D., 1996. *Flowering Natives for Home Gardens.* Angus and Robertson, Sydney, NSW; 344 pp.

Martyn, J., 2018. *Rocks and Trees: A Photographic Journey Through the Rich and Varied Geology, scenery and flora of the Sydney region.* STEP Inc, Turramurra, NSW; 311 pp.

Robinson, L., 2003. *Field Guide to the Native Plants of Sydney.* Simon and Schuster Australia, Cammeray, NSW; 448 pp.

Sankowsky, G., 2020. *A Field Guide to Butterflies of Australia: Their Life Histories and Larval Host Plants.* Reed New Holland, Wahroonga, NSW; 400 pp.

Wrigley, J.W. and Fagg, M., 2003. *Australian Native Plants.* Reed New Holland, Sydney, NSW; 696 pp.

Useful free online resources

PlantNET – New South Wales Flora Online, The Royal Botanic Gardens, Sydney
`https://plantnet.rbgsyd.nsw.gov.au`

The Australasian Virtual Herbarium
`https://avh.chah.org.au`

Australian Plants Society NSW
`https://www.austplants.com.au`

Atlas of Living Australia.
Search by plant scientific name to view photos (Gallery tab) and dozens of interesting details such as how the seeds are dispersed, how long it takes for a seed-grown plant to flower, and how the plant responds to fire (Traits tab).
`https://bie.ala.org.au/`

Australian National Botanic Gardens
`https://www.anbg.gov.au`

Friends of Lane Cove National Park
`https://www.friendsoflanecovenp.org`

Pittwater Gardening Guide
Undated publication by staff of the former Pittwater Council (now known as Northern Beaches Council) and Marita Macrae. Nine detailed maps of localitites of the Northern Beaches identify which of seven vegetation types were formerly found on those sites prior to clearing for residential settlement. For each vegetation type, species are listed with brief description.
`https://files-preprod-d9.northernbeaches.nsw.gov.au/nbc-prod-files/documents/general-information/native-plant-profiles/pittwaternativegardeningbooklet.pdf`
Also reachable by link on bottom of the following page:
`https://www.northernbeaches.nsw.gov.au/environment/native-plants/native-planting-guide/pittwater-ward`

Native Plants of the Northern Beaches, Sydney
Gillian Gutridge's wonderful website of photographic records of native plants of Sydney's Northern Beaches, and bushwalks and sanctuaries indexed by list of plants that can be found in them
https://nbplantareas.com

Yarra Ranges Council (Vic.) Local Plant Directory
https://www.yarraranges.vic.gov.au/PlantDirectory

Australian grass literature references
Now archived and not being actively maintained
https://ausgrass2.myspecies.info

The Blue Mountains Botanic Garden, Mount Tomah
https://www.bluemountainsbotanicgarden.com.au

Seedling database section of website of the Victoria-based revegetation initiative "TreeProject"
https://treeproject.org.au/seedling-database

iNaturalist
Community-driven record of observations of plants and animals around the world, an initiative of California Academy of Sciences and the (US) National Georgraphic Society.
https://www.inaturalist.org

Trees near me NSW
Mobile and web app showing PCTs ("plant community types") and species lists based on user's location, both now and before Europeans cleared the land – an initiative of NSW Department of Planning and Environment. I am not clear on what the source for these PCTs is, and why PWSGF does not seem to be one of them. Using this tool, we can find out that the Pittwater Spotted Gum Forest on Scotland Island falls into the tool's PCT designated *Hunter Coast Lowland Spotted Gum Moist Forest*, which spans an area including the entire Sydney Basin bioregion plus the region from Sydney all the way to the Queensland border (where the scope of the tool ends).
https://treesnearme.app/

Web app from London's Natural History Museum
Allows you to search for what butterflies feed on what plants, in any country. Not terribly thorough, though.
https://www.nhm.ac.uk/our-science/data/hostplants/search/index.dsml

Grasses: Native and Exotic in the Hornsby Shire
Downloadable free 34-page pdf booklet for identifying grasses (native and non-native) in Hornsby Shire, by Ross Rapmund, Hornsby Council, 2013
https://www.hornsby.nsw.gov.au/__data/assets/pdf_file/0006/52377/Grasses-workshop-booklet-2013-July.pdf

PWSGF Declaration as Endangered Ecological Community
Downloadable free 8-page pdf document listing the assemblage of species defining the Pittwater and Wagstaffe Spotted Gum Forest, an endangered ecological community – of which Scotland Island is typical.
https://www.environment.nsw.gov.au/-/media/OEH/Corporate-Site/Documents/Animals-and-plants/Scientific-Committee/Determinations/2013/pittwater-wagstaffe-spotted-gum-forest-nsw-scientific-committee-final-determination.pdf

LibreTexts
Free downloadable series of college-level textbooks in Botany and Geosciences, etc.
https://libretexts.org

Local native plant nurseries

Indigo Native Nursery

https://indigonursery.com.au
EMAIL: info@indigonursery.com.au

CONTACT: Laura Minnebo or David Harris
ADDRESS: Lot 57 Wattle Rd, Ingleside, NSW 2101
PHONE: (02) 9970 8709
David: 0417 626 462
Laura: 0488 528 722

Ku-ring-gai Wildflower Garden Wildflower Nursery

https://www.krg.nsw.gov.au/Things-to-do/Ku-ring-gai-Wildflower-Garden/Wildflower-Nursery
ADDRESS: Visitor Centre, 420 Mona Vale Road, St Ives, NSW
PHONE: 9424 0353

Harvest Seeds & Native Plants

https://www.harvestseeds-nativeplants.com.au/
ADDRESS: 281 Mona Vale Road, Terrey Hills NSW 2084
PHONE: 9450 2699

Cicada Glen Nursery

https://www.cicadaglennursery.com.au/
EMAIL: cicadaglennursery@outlook.com
CONTACT: Michael Dixon
ADDRESS: 1 Chiltern Road, Ingleside NSW 2101
PHONE: 0493 617 744

Stony Range Regional Botanic Garden Nursery

https://www.northernbeaches.nsw.gov.au/things-to-do/recreation-area/stony-range-regional-botanic-garden
ADDRESS: 810 Pittwater Road, Dee Why NSW 2099
Nursery is staffed by volunteers and is open for plant sales and advice
NURSERY OPENING HOURS: Tuesday mornings 9am – 12pm and Saturday afternoons 2 – 4pm.

Sydney Wildflower Nursery

https://www.sydneywildflowernursery.com.au/
ADDRESS: 9 Veno Street, Heathcote NSW 2233
PHONE: 02 9548 2818
EMAIL: info@sydneywildflowernursery.com.au

Comparison tables

Table of ferns

Though there are species of specialised water ferns, the species in this book are generally intolerant of waterlogging. Therefore, if you have clay soil, do one or more of the following:

- amend the soil before planting with well-rotted organic matter

- plant on a slope

- mound soil up

- dig shallow trenches among the planting areas, leading away.

All of these techniques will help clay soil to drain more freely. As most ferns are forest-dwelling, amending the soil so that it more closely resembles humus-rich forest soil should be first on your list.

Species	Usual Max. Height (m)	Drought tolerant?	Sun tolerant?	Shade tolerant?	Likes or tolerates clay?
Adiantum hispidulum (Rough Maidenhair)	.7	A bit	A bit	Yes	Amend with compost
Blechnum cartilagineum (Gristle Fern)	1	No	No	Yes	Amend with compost
Cheilanthes sieberiana (Mulga Fern)	.3	Yes	Yes	Yes	Yes
Davallia solida var. pyxidata (Hare's Foot Fern)	.6	Yes	No	Yes	No; use orchid bark
Lindsaea linearis (Screw Fern)	.3	No	If moist	Yes	Yes
Pellaea falcata (Sickle Fern)	.6	A bit	Yes	Yes	Yes

Table of creeping groundcovers

Many of the groundcover plants are not terribly attractive on their own, but when combined with others that enjoy the same conditions, the result can be a charming tapestry of colours and textures, and the plants will often do better when combined together, as they grow in nature.

A few of the groundcovers I have profiled have invasive or what I call galloping tendencies, which I have noted in those profiles.

When several groundcovers are combined, if there are any ones with galloping tendencies, they are held in check (see photo at right). In the photo, *Hydrocotyle sibthorpioides* (Pennywort), which can be a galloper on its own, is behaving itself because it is combined with several other groundcovers that are good garden citizens, so to speak:

- *Pseuderanthemum variabile* (Pastel Flower)

- *Pullenia gunnii* (Slender Tick-trefoil)

- *Geranium homeanum* (Rainforest Crane's-bill)

I do not recommend *Viola banksii* because not only does it gallup, but it overwhelms smaller plants, and it is difficult to remove; when you try to pull it up, many small nodes break off and remain in the soil. The nodes are semi-succulent and can send up new leaves and shoots. To add insult to injury, *V. banksii* is not drought-tolerant, and if it is allowed to colonise large sunny areas during spring wet weather, it collapses very unattractively when dry weather comes, though unfortunately it does not die. *V. hederacea* is much better behaved, but still, don't let it (or any other) drought-intolerant groundcover colonise large sunny areas.

Commelina cyanea is a galloper, but only while the weather is warm. When cold weather comes, it dies back and growth slows to a standstill, giving other plants a chance to catch up and achieve a balance with no intervention required.

Species	Drought tolerant?	Sun tolerant?	Shade tolerant?	Invasive?
Centella asiatica (Asiatic pennywort)	No	Yes	Yes	Yes, if soil is very moist
Commelina cyanea (Scurvy Weed)	Yes	Yes	Yes	Yes
Coronidium (formerly Helichrysum) scorpiodes (Button Everlasting)	No	No	Yes	No
Dichondra repens (Kidney Weed)	Yes	Only if moist	Yes	No
Hydrocotyle sibthorpioides (formerly H. peduncularis) (Pennywort)	No	Only if moist	Yes	Yes, though it is easy to pull it up. Self-seeds.

Species	Drought tolerant?	Sun tolerant?	Shade tolerant?	Invasive?
Lobelia (formerly Pratia) purpurascens (White Root)	No	No	Yes	No
Oplismenus imbecilis (Slender Basket Grass)	No	No	Yes	No
Pullenia (formerly Desmodium) gunnii (Slender Tick-trefoil)	Yes	No	Yes	Yes, but without causing any problems as it creeps under other plants, not over them. Enriches soil as it is in the legume family.
Veronica plebeia (CreepingSpeedwell)	No	Only if moist	Yes	No, though it can cover a large area and it self-seeds. It is easy to pull it all up, and it is slow growing.
Viola hederacea (Native Violet)	No	No	Yes	No

Table of non-creeping groundcovers and shrubs under 1 m

This size of plant is useful for filling in between larger shrubs, to provide variation in height and visual texture. Another use is in locations where you want to keep all of the plants a smaller size for practical reasons, such as near the house or along paths.

Shorter plants are very useful in an area where you want to create the effect of a wildflower meadow; just select a few grass species (see the Table of grasses) that enjoy the same conditions of light and moisture. There are plenty of sun-loving as well as shade-loving grass species. If you want lots of butterflies and Christmas Beetles, you really need native grasses and similar plants such as gahnias, sedges and lomandras.

Grasses require a high degree of dedication, as there are so many weed species of grass to learn in addition to the native grass species. If your dedication level is not up to native grasses, you can plant ferns in groups amongst your other plants, to provide a similar visual effect. The feel of this look is like a forest glade. There are a few sun-loving as well as the more familiar shade-loving species of fern (see the Table of ferns).

An effect like a rock garden can be created by planting only shorter plants. This is especially effective when there is some other element to add interest to the garden, such as attractive rocks (obviously), winding paths, steps, or a water feature. Shorter plants also work well in a courtyard garden, or alongside a patio.

Some shorter plants may work as mass-planted groundcover along paths and around the base of large showstopper shrubs in a formal style of garden if the location is sunny during the summer. For this use, it may be best to select drought-tolerant, sun-tolerant and shade-tolerant species. This is to avoid the problem where a fast-growing creeping groundcover such as *Viola banksii* colonises large bare areas during the moister, cooler weather of winter and spring. Such plants are "good-time charlies" and though they sure look great in spring, when hot dry weather comes, the above-ground parts wilt and shrivel unattractively.

Species	Usual Max. Height (m)	Drought tolerant?	Sun tolerant?	Shade tolerant?	Likes or tolerates clay?	Flower colour & season
Austromyrtus dulcis (Midgen Berry)	1	A bit	Yes	Yes	A bit	White, summer
Brachyscome graminea (Grass Daisy)	.7	If shaded	Yes	Yes	Yes	Mauve, all year
Brunoniella australis (Blue Trumpet)	.15	Yes	A bit	Yes	Yes	Blue, early summer
Brunoniella pumilio (Dwarf Trumpet)	.1	Yes	A bit	Yes	No	Blue, early summer
Bulbine bulbosa (Bulbine Lily)	.5	Yes	Yes	Light	No	Yellow, all summer
Caesia parviflora (Pale Grass Lily)	.5	Yes	Yes	Some	Yes	Blue, summer
Coronidium scorpioides (Button Everlasting)	.2	No	No	Yes	No	Yellow, spring
Crowea saligna (Willow-leaf Crowea)	1	Yes	No	Yes	Yes	Hot pink, chiefly winter
Cullen tenax (Emu-foot)	.5	Yes	Yes	Yes	Yes	Blue, all summer
Cyanthillium cinerarea (Iron Weed)	.5	Yes	Yes	Light	Yes	Mauve, summer

Species	Usual Max. Height (m)	Drought tolerant?	Sun tolerant?	Shade tolerant?	Likes or tolerates clay?	Flower colour & season
Epacris longiflora (Fuchsia Heath)	1	No	A bit	Dappled	Yes, on slope	Red & white, all year
Geranium homeanum (Rainforest Crane's-bill)	1	Yes	Yes	Yes	Yes	Pink, all summer
Goodenia ovata (Hop Goodenia)	1	Yes	A bit	Yes	Yes	Yellow, all year
Hibbertia aspera (Rough Guinea Flower)	.6	No	Yes	Yes	Yes, on slope	Yellow, spring
Hibbertia empetrifolia (Trailing Guinea-flower)	1	Yes	No	Yes	Yes	Yellow, spring & summer
Hibbertia procumbens (Spreading Guinea Flower)	.2	No	Yes	Yes	No	Yellow, spring & summer
Lagenophora gracilis (Slender Bottle Daisy)	.25	No	Yes	Yes	?	White, summer
Leptospermum macrocarpum (Large-fruit Tea Tree)	1	No	Yes	Yes	Yes	Pink & green, summer
Leucopogon juniperinus (Prickly Beard-heath)	1	Yes	Yes	Yes	Yes (?)	White, winter
Leucopogon lanceolatus (also known as *L. affinis*) (Lance-leaf Beard Heath)	1	Yes	Yes	Yes	Yes (?)	White, winter
Patersonia glabrata (Leafy Purple-flag)	.8	No	Yes	Yes	Yes	Purple, spring
Patersonia sericea (Silky Purple Flag)	.6	Yes	Yes	Yes	No	Purple, spring
Pelargonium australe (Wild Geranium)	.5	Yes	Yes	Yes	No (?)	Pink, summer
Plectranthus parviflorus (Cockspur Flower)	.5	A bit	No	Yes	Yes	Blue, all year
Poranthera microphylla (Small Poranthera)	.1	Yes	No	Yes	Yes	White, summer
Pomaderris mediora (Headland Pomaderris)	1 or 3	Yes (?)	Yes	Yes	Yes (?)	Cream, spring
Prostanthera denticulata (Rough Mint Bush)	1	Yes	No	Yes	Yes	Purple, spring
Pseuderanthemum variabile (Pastel Flower)	.3	Yes	No	Yes	No	Many, summer
Schelhammera undulata (Lilac Lily)	.2	A bit	No	Yes	Yes	Pink, spring
Solanum prinophyllum (Forest Nightshade)	.5	A bit	No	Yes	Yes	Lilac, all year
Viola betonicifolia (Arrowhead Violet)	.15	No	No	Yes	Yes	Purple, spring and autumn
Wahlenbergia gracilis (Sprawling Bluebell)	.2	A bit	A bit	Yes	No	Blue, spring
Xanthorrhoea macronema (Bottlebrush Grass Tree)	1	Yes	A bit	Yes	No	White, spring or summer
Zieria prostrata (Headland Zieria)	.5	A bit	A bit	A bit	Yes	White, spring

Table of wattles (*Acacia*)

The species in the table below are either native to Scotland Island or locally native to the Pittwater area. *A. decurrens* and *A. implexa* are particularly well-suited for planting on hot, dry north-facing slopes to provide fast shade.

Wattles are generally fast growing but also tend to be short lived due to borer beetle attack, so you may need to replant new ones in 10-15 years, or plant slower-growing trees along with your wattles that will gradually replace the wattles as they age.

Wattles have either feather-type leaves (also called pinnate) or the vaguely paddle-shaped "leaves" (called phyllodes) which are technically not leaves. They are derived evolutionarily from the leaf stem, with the leaf blade or surface reduced to nothing. In the seedlings of wattles that have phyllodes, usually the first few leaves will be the normal pinnate type, with the leaf surface getting gradually smaller in subsequent leaves, while the leaf stem gets larger and larger.

Species	Leaf type	Max. height metres	Flower colour	Flower season	Soil pref	Native to Scotland island?
A. decurrens	feather	10	yellow to bright yellow balls	chiefly July-Nov	any; prefers clay; drought tolerant	yes
A. irrorata	feather	12	cream to pale yellow balls	chiefly Nov-Jan	any; may be tolerant of waterlogging	yes
A. paramattensis	feather	15	cream to bright yellow balls	Nov-Feb	any; prefers clay	yes
A. binervia	phyllode	16	pale yellow rods	Aug-Oct	any; drought tolerant	yes
A. falcata	phyllode	5	cream to pale yellow balls	Apr-Aug	well drained; drought tolerant	yes
A. fimbriata	phyllode	6	pale to bright yellow balls	July-Nov	any; drought tolerant	yes
A. floribunda	phyllode	8	white to pale yellow rods	Jun-Sep	well drained moist	no
A. implexa	phyllode	12	white to pale yellow balls	Dec-Apr	any; drought tolerant	yes
A. linifolia	phyllode	4	white to pale yellow balls	chiefly Jan-Aug	well drained; drought tolerant	no
A. longifolia	phyllode	8	pale yellow to bright yellow rods	Jun-Oct	any; drought tolerant; dislikes waterlogging	yes
A. longissima	phyllode	6	white to pale yellow sparse rods	Oct-Mar	any; tolerates drought and waterlogging	yes
A. ulicifolia	phyllode	2	white to pale yellow balls	Apr-Oct	sandy, dry	yes

Table of shrubs and trees up to 3 m

Use this table to find shrubs of the height you want that fit the conditions you have, rather than conditions you might theoretically be able to provide. Full sun for these purposes means four or more continuous hours of direct sun per day. If you have a spot that is full sun (> 4 hours of direct sun per day), and a shrub you want can tolerate sun only if kept moist, and you know that you are too busy to water a garden, then pass that one up.

White flowers go with everything, but for shrubs with flowers of other colours, try this rule of thumb: Don't place flowers of a particular colour (for example, yellow) adjacent to other flowers of the same colour that will be open at the same time. Otherwise, what usually happens is that one outshines the other, which then looks a bit sickly, and the result is not pleasing. Instead, separate them with one or more contrasting (or white) flowers between them. Then the colours don't fight with each other, and the subtleties of each can be appreciated. You can use other shrubs for the contrasting colours, or herbaceous plants, vines, or trees.

Colours that are opposite on the colour wheel make for the most contrast: for example, yellow and purple is an easy combination. Once you have established your two main contrasting colours, other colours can be added onto this backbone in smaller quantities, such as pink, red or blue. An example of some options for a spring-flowering plant palette based on yellow/purple would be one of the species of Prostanthera or *Hardenbergia violacea* (purple); *Pomaderris intermedia*, a species of Hibbertia or Goodenia (yellow); and *Boronia pinnata* or *Indigofera australis* (pink). *Hardenbergia violacea* is not in the table because it is a vine. It can grow as a self-supporting mound or groundcover if you don't have a convenient leggy shrub or small tree for it to climb.

Once you have chosen your colours and plants, don't forget to check that the plants you have chosen have similar requirements. Using the plant palette from the previous example, when you check the table for each plant, you see that prostantheras and boronias don't tolerate drought well. If your site is on the dry side, and you are not likely to be able to provide supplemental water, go with the hardier options for those colours instead, which would be *Hardenbergia violacea* (purple) and *Indigofera australis* (pink). Alternatively, change your plan and possibly choose other moisture-loving plants to go with the water hogs that you have fallen in love with; don't forget to plan how you are going to water them reliably during dry spells.

Species	Usual Max. Height (m)	Drought tolerant?	Sun tolerant?	Shade tolerant?	Likes or tolerates clay?	Flower colour & season
Acacia linifolia (Flax Wattle)	3	Yes	Only if moist	Yes	Yes	White, summer
Acacia longifolia subsp. sophorae (Coastal Wattle)	3	Yes	Yes	Yes	Yes	Yellow, spring
Boronia pinnata (Fern-leaf Boronia)	1.5	No	Only if moist	Yes	No (?)	Pink, spring
Austromyrtus tenuifolia (Narrow-leaf Midgen Berry)	1.5	A bit	Yes	Yes	Yes	White, spring
Breynia oblongifolia (Coffee Bush)	3	Yes	Only if moist	Yes	Yes, on slope	Insignificant green, summer
Commersonia (formerly Rulingia) hermanniifolia (Wrinkled Kerrawang)	1.5	Yes	Yes	A bit	Yes, on slope	Pinky-white, spring

Species	Usual Max. Height (m)	Drought tolerant?	Sun tolerant?	Shade tolerant?	Likes or tolerates clay?	Flower colour & season
Cordyline stricta (Slender Palm Lily)	3	Yes	Yes	Yes	Yes	Lavender, spring
Correa alba (White Correa)	1.5	Yes	Yes	Yes	Yes	White, chiefly winter
Correa reflexa (Common Correa)	1.5	Suffers	No	Yes	Yes	Red & green, chiefly winter
Dodonaea pinnata (Fern-leaf Dodonaea)	1.5	?	No	Yes	Probably not	Red fruits, summer (females only)
Dodonaea triquetra (Hop Bush)	3	Yes	Yes	Yes	Yes	Papery fruits, summer (females only)
Eupomatia laurina (Bolwarra)	5	No	Yes	Yes	Yes	White perfumed, summer
Grevillea arenaria (Sand Grevillea)	2	Yes	A bit	Yes	Yes	Insignificant, spring
Grevillea linearifolia (White Spider Flower)	1.5	Yes	Yes	Yes	Yes	White, all year
Grevillea sericea (Pink Spider Flower)	2	Yes	Yes	Yes	Yes, on slope	Pink, all year
Grevillea speciosa (Red Spider Flower)	2	Yes	A bit	A bit	? Try it on slope	Red, all year
Hakea sericea (Silky Needle Bush)	3	Yes	Yes	Yes	Yes	White perfumed, winter
Hovea longifolia (Long-leaf Hovea)	3	Yes	No	Yes	No	Purple, spring
Indigofera australis (Australian Indigo)	2	Yes	Only if moist	Yes	Yes	Pink, spring
Kunzea ambigua (Tick Bush)	3	Yes	Yes	Yes	Yes	White, spring
Leptospermum polygalifolium (Lemon-scented Tea Tree)	2.5	Yes	Yes	Yes	Yes	White, spring
Logania albiflora (Narrow-leaf Logania)	2	No	No	Yes	No	White perfumed, spring
Logania myricoides (Long-leaf Logania)	5	Yes	No	Yes	Yes	Cream perfumed, summer
Lomatia silaifolia (Crinkle Bush)	1.5	A bit	Part	Yes	Yes	Cream perfumed, summer
Melaleuca nodosa (Prickly-Leaf Paperbark)	3, up to 10	Yes	Yes	Yes	Yes	White honey-scented, spring
Olearia tomentosa (Toothed Daisy-bush)	2	Yes	A bit	Yes	No	White daisies, summer
Ozothamnus diosmifolius (Rice Flower)	2	Yes	Yes	Light	Yes	White, late spring
Phebalium squamulosum (Forest Phebalium)	2	A bit	Part	Yes	Sometimes	White, early spring
Phebalium squamulosum subsp. argenteum (Silvery Phebalium)	1.5	Yes	Part	Yes	Yes	White, early spring
Philotheca myoporoides (Gin and Tonic Plant)	2	Yes	Only if moist	Yes	Yes, on slope	White, spring
Pimelia linifolia (Slender Rice Flower)	1.5	Yes	Yes	Yes	Yes	White, chiefly spring
Platysace lanceolata (Shrubby Platysace)	1.5	Yes	No	Yes	Yes	White, summer
Podolobium ilicifolium (Prickly Shaggy-Pea)	3	Yes	Yes	Yes	Yes, on slope	Yellow, spring

Species	Usual Max. Height (m)	Drought tolerant?	Sun tolerant?	Shade tolerant?	Likes or tolerates clay?	Flower colour & season
Pomaderris intermedia (Lemon Dogwood)	2	Yes	Yes	Yes	Yes, on slope	Yellow, spring
Pomaderris mediora (Headland Pomaderris)	1 or 3	Yes (?)	Yes	Yes	Yes (?)	Cream, spring
Prostanthera incisa (Cut-leaf Mint Bush)	3	No	No	Yes	Yes, on slope	Purple, spring
Prostanthera scutellarioides (Skullcap-leaf Mint Bush)	1.5	No	Yes	Yes	Yes	Purple, chiefly spring
Pultenaea daphnoides (Large-leaf Bush-pea)	3	Yes, if filtered	No	Yes	Yes, on slope	Yellow, spring
Pultenea flexilis (Graceful Bush-pea)	3	Yes, if filtered	No	Yes	Yes, on slope	Yellow, spring
Pultenea villosa (Hairy Bush-pea)	2	Moderately	No	Filtered	Yes	Yellow, spring
Rhododendron viriosum (Native Azalea)	2	No	Morning, if moist	Yes	Yes, on slope	Red, summer
Westringia fruticosa (Coastal Rosemary)	2	Yes	Yes	Yes	Yes	White, all year
Westringia longifolia (Long-leaf Westringia)	3	Yes	Yes	Yes	Yes, on slope	Mauve, all year

Table of small trees (3 – 15 m)

This table will help you select small trees for some problem areas that are frequently found on Scotland Island and other places in the Northern Beaches, such as:

- hot, dry north-facing slopes, to create more shade quickly so as to be able to grow other shade-loving plants. Select **drought-tolerant** trees of the height you want that like or tolerate **full sun or light shade** and **grow quickly**. There are many, but some examples are: *Acacia decurrens, Glochidion ferdinandi.* If you choose a wattle, you may want to also plant a slow-growing tree at the same time, because wattles often deteriorate after ten or fifteen years.

- south-facing slopes where the ground is shaded for much of the winter by the shape of the land, but needs more shade in summer. If you want flowers, select **summer-flowering** trees that prefer or tolerate some degree of **shade**, and there is a good chance that they will flower for you because they have sufficient time after the sun returns to your garden in spring to store the resources that they need in order to flower. Some examples are: *Acmena smithii, Synoum glandulosum.* Spring-flowering trees may work also, with the flowering delayed or decreased compared to trees in gardens that get winter sun.

"SI" in the "Native to" column refers to Scotland Island. Species that are native there and in PWSGF (Pittwater-Wagstaffe Spotted Gum Forest) are generally very adaptable and hardy in many sorts of conditions (not just Scotland Island and Pittwater).

Species	Max. height (m)	Drought tolerant?	Light pref	Fast growing?	Flowering	Native to?
Acacia binervia (Coast Myall)	16	Yes	Full sun	Yes	Yellow, spring	Sydney, SI, Pittwater but not PWSGF
Acacia decurrens (Black Wattle)	12	Yes	Full sun	Yes	Yellow, winter	Sydney, SI
Acacia falcata (Sickle Wattle)	5	Yes	Full sun	Yes	White, winter	Sydney, SI, Pittwater but not PWSGF
Acacia fimbriata (Fringed Wattle)	7	Yes	Light shade	Yes	Yellow, spring	Sydney, SI, Pittwater but not PWSGF
Acacia floribunda (Sally Wattle)	8	No	Light shade	Yes	Yellow, spring	Sydney, SI, Pittwater but not PWSGF
Acacia implexa (Hickory Wattle)	12	Yes	Full sun	Yes	White, summer	Sydney, SI, Dry PWSGF
Acacia longifolia subsp. longifolia (Long-leaf Wattle)	7	Yes	Full sun	Yes	Yellow, spring	Sydney, SI, Pittwater but not PWSGF
Acacia longissima (Narrow-leaf Wattle)	6	Yes	Light shade	Yes	White, summer	Sydney, SI, PWSGF*
Acmena smithii (Common Lilly Pilly)	5	Yes	Light shade	Yes	White, summer	Sydney, SI, Moist PWSGF
Allocasuarina littoralis (Black She-oak)	12	Yes	Full sun	Yes	Brown, winter	Sydney, SI, PWSGF
Allocasuarina distyla (Scrub She-oak)	3	Yes	Full sun	Yes	Brown, spring	Sydney, SI, Pittwater but not PWSGF
Allocasuarina torulosa (Forest Oak)	8	Yes	Light shade	Yes	Insignif.	Sydney, SI, Dry PWSGF
Callicoma serratifolia (Blackwattle)	10	No	Part shade	Yes	White, spring	Sydney but not SI; Pittwater but not PWSGF

Species	Max. height (m)	Drought tolerant?	Light pref	Fast growing?	Flowering	Native to?
Ceratopetalum gummiferum (NSW Christmas Bush)	5	No	Light shade	No	White/red, spring/summer	Sydney, SI, Pittwater but not PWSGF
Elaeocarpus reticulatus (Blueberry Ash)	15	Yes	Light shade	No	White, spring	Sydney, SI, Dry PWSGF
Glochidion ferdinandi (Cheese Tree)	8	Yes	Light shade	Yes	Green, summer	Sydney, SI, Moist PWSGF, Dry PWSGF
Homalanthus populifolius (Bleeding Heart)	6	Yes	Full sun	Yes	Green, spring	Sydney but not SI or Pittwater
Jacksonia scoparia (Native Broom)	4	Yes	Full sun	No	Yellow, late spring	Sydney, but not SI; PWSGF*
Lomatia myricoides (River Lomatia)	5	Yes	Semi-shade	No	White, summer	Sydney but not SI; Pittwater
Persoonia levis (Broad-leaf Geebung)	5	Yes	Full sun	No	Yellow, summer	Sydney, SI, Dry PWSGF
Persoonia linearis (Narrow-leaf Geebung)	5	No	Dappled	No	Yellow, summer	Sydney, SI, Dry PWSGF
Synoum glandulosum (Scentless Rosewood)	8	No	Dappled	Yes	White, summer	Sydney, SI, Moist PWSGF
Syzigium paniculatum (Magenta Lilly Pilly)	10	Yes	Light shade	Yes	White, spring	Sydney, SI, but not Pittwater
Trochocarpa laurina (Tree Heath)	10	No	Dappled	No	White, summer	Sydney, SI, Pittwater

* Studies differ as to whether the species is a component of PSGF

Table of grasses

Grasses can be classified as either "warm season" or "cool season" according to which season is best for planting seed, and when they have their most active growth. Warm season grasses function best in warm weather, and their seeds should be planted in spring. That way, you give them the longest growing season in their preferred range. Cool season grasses don't function as well in hot, dry weather, and their seeds should be planted in autumn. Some grasses can grow just fine all year long; unfortunately, the widely hated non-native *Ehrharta erecta* (Ehrharta) is one of these.

Many grass species have a seed dormancy mechanism, which means that few seeds will sprout if sown fresh. They generally need at least two (up to twelve) months' storage time for the dormancy period to end. For these species, wait until the next preferred season to plant them (autumn or spring according to its preference). For example, Kangaroo Grass is a warm season grass, so plant it in the spring after you collect the seed, and it will grow strongly through spring and summer.

If the species doesn't have seed dormancy, seed can be planted any time as long as there are still a couple months remaining to go in its seasonal preference, so that the seedlings have time to grow.

Some grasses are difficult to grow from seed, and should be propagated from divisions instead.

A "?" for the "Seed dormancy" column means I don't have data for that species. As a general rule, assume all native grasses have seed dormancy. Wait at least two months to plant the seeds, as long as there is time for the seedlings to develop in the preferred season; otherwise wait until the next occurrence of the preferred season.

Species	Common name	Max. height (m)	Drought tolerant?	Light pref	Warm (C4) or cool season (C3)?	Seed dormancy?	Native to?
Cymbopogon refractus	Barb Wire Grass	1	Yes	Full sun	Warm	No	Sydney, SI, Dry PWSGF
Dichelachne crinita	Longhair Plume Grass	1.5	Yes	Full sun	Cool	?	Sydney
Echinopogon ovatus	Forest Hedgehog-grass	.7	No	Dappled	Cool	Yes	Sydney, SI
Entolasia marginata	Right-angle Grass	.3	No	Dappled	Both	difficult	Sydney, SI, Dry PWSGF
Microlaena stipoides	Weeping Grass	.7	Yes	Dappled	Cool	No	Sydney, SI, Dry PWSGF, Moist PWSGF
Oplismenus aemulus	Slender Basket Grass	.3	Yes	Dappled	Cool	?	Sydney, SI, Dry PWSGF
Oplismenus imbecilis	Basket Grass	.3	Yes	Dappled	Cool	?	Sydney, SI, Dry PWSGF, Moist PWSGF
Panicum simile	Two Colour Panic Grass	.7	Yes	Full sun	Warm	?	Sydney, SI, Dry PWSGF
Poa affinis	Forest Grass	1.2	Yes	Dappled	Cool	Yes	Sydney, SI, Dry PWSGF
Themeda triandra	Kangaroo Grass	1.5	Yes	Full sun to light shade	Warm	Yes	Sydney, SI, Dry PWSGF

www.ingramcontent.com/pod-product-compliance
Lightning Source LLC
Chambersburg PA
CBHW060957030426
42334CB00032B/3268